SHARK ATTACK

SHARK ATTACK

Jerry Tarkanian and His Battle with the NCAA and UNLV

Don Yaeger

With the Cooperation of Jerry Tarkanian

HarperCollins*Publishers*

HarperCollins books may be purchased for educational, business, or sales promotional use. For information, please call or write: Special Markets Department, HarperCollins Publishers, Inc., 10 East 53rd Street, New York, NY 10022. Telephone: (212) 207-7528; Fax: (212) 207-7222. ·

FIRST EDITION

Designed by George J. McKeon

Library of Congress Cataloging-in-Publication Data
Yaeger, Don.
　　Shark attack: Jerry Tarkanian and his battle with the NCAA and UNLV / Don Yaegar.　1st ed.
　　　　p.　cm.
　　ISBN 0-06-017980-5
　　1.Tarkanian, Jerry, 1930– 2. Basketball—United States—Coaches—Biography. 3. University of Nevada, Las Vegas—Basketball—History. 4. National Collegiate Athletic Association—History. I. Title.
GV884.T37Y34　1992
796.323 ' 092—dc20
[B]　　　　　　　　　　　　　　　　　　　　　　　　　　　　　91-58362

92　93　94　95　96　RRD 10　9　8　7　6　5　4　3　2　1

To Allison, whose willingness to love and support
me through all this—again—keeps me going.

Contents

Photographs follow page 180.

Acknowledgments

First and foremost, I'd like to thank Jerry Tarkanian and the many other people in Las Vegas who cooperated in the reporting done for this book. Sources from all sides of the dispute agreed to be open and honest in an effort to chronicle this ever changing story. None of those who cooperated—including Tarkanian—received a penny for their help. And none of them—including Tarkanian—had any editorial control over the writing of this book. The extent of Tarkanian's cooperation was his willingness to answer all questions, some of which he grew tired of hearing, during many hours of interviews.

That said, this book couldn't have gone from concept to completion in four months, as it did, without a great deal of help from the many reporters, attorneys, administrators, athletes, and coaches who lived this tale. Under such a tight deadline, 120 of those people found time to squeeze one or more interviews with me into their schedules.

My thanks to attorney Jan Brown, who helped me fight the maze of Nevada law to pull public records from UNLV. Reporters Greg Bortolin and Bruce Pascoe of the *Las Vegas Review-Journal*, Steve Carp and Jeff German of the *Las Vegas Sun*, Dan Burns of KVBC, Ron Futrell of KTNV, Scott Higgins of KLAS and Rich Martin from KNEWS Radio spent hours sharing stories and theories with me.

Also, stories written by former *National Sports Daily* reporter Ian O'Connor, *Los Angeles Times* reporter Danny Robbins, *New York Times* reporter Bill Rhoden, *USA Today*'s Steve Wieberg, Tim Dwyer of the *Philadelphia Inquirer*, Kristina Rebelo and Doug Looney of *Sports Illustrated*, Pete Prisco of the *Florida Times-Union*, and former

Las Vegas Review-Journal staffers Bob Sands and Joe Hawk all proved helpful.

Some of the information for this book was gathered in my reporting for *Undue Process: The NCAA's Injustice for All*, published by Sagamore Publishing of Champaign, Illinois. Other books were important as well, including: *Swee' Pea and Other Playground Legends* by *Newsday*'s John Valenti; *The Boardwalk Jungle* by Ovid Demaris; *Tark* by Jerry Tarkanian and Terry Pluto; *Tarkanian: Countdown of a Rebel* by Richard Harp, Ph.D., and Joseph McCullough, Ph.D.; *Interference* by Dan E. Moldea; and *Wise Guy* by Nicholas Pileggi and Henry Hill.

I also must thank friends Lester Abberger and Pete Dunbar, who helped me keep the manuscript focused, and the editors and legal staff at HarperCollins. Thanks, finally, to Basil Kane, who has been the soul of patience with me.

SHARK ATTACK

1

The Resignation

"This is tough for me," Jerry Tarkanian said, interrupting himself as he choked backed the tears. "After eighteen years ..." His voice faded off as his right hand, holding a Styrofoam cup, started to quiver. He looked to his right at the university president, Robert Maxson. Then, for just a moment, Tarkanian dropped his head.

Except for the power winders of the dozen or so news photographers snapping away, the room fell silent. It really was over. The winningest coach in college basketball history—both on the court (where he was 599–120 at the time) and in court (where he was 5–1)—was resigning.

All the speculation was laid to rest.

It had been a tortuous two weeks since the *Las Vegas Review-Journal* had published front-page pictures of three UNLV basketball players—Anderson Hunt, David Butler, and Moses Scurry—in a hot tub with convicted sports gambler Richard "The Fixer" Perry. Although Tarkanian wasn't in the photos, they put him in hot water, too.

Those two weeks, although more intense, were representative of the previous two years, during which his team had played through unbelievable adversity, including countless visits from National Collegiate Athletic Association (NCAA) investigators, on-

and off-court scuffles, injuries, and a constant barrage of negative news stories.

Despite all those distractions, that team had won one national championship and forty-five games in a row before losing a two-point heartbreaker to Duke at the 1991 Final Four. Just two months before he was forced to resign, Tarkanian was coaching a group of players that was being hailed as the greatest collection of talent ever to lace up sneakers.

That Tarkanian had arrived at this point was no accident. He had been beaten down in what can be shown to have been a calculated effort aimed at undermining his support in the community and the university. Employees at the same university that he put on the map of higher education had worked quietly toward this end. For months, they stabbed him in the back until he bled to death. One by one, stories—many of which, time would show, were exaggerated—had been leaked to the media. University officials had met with the community's business elite in an effort to convince them Tarkanian and his team "no longer projected the image Las Vegas desired." They had help from the NCAA, whose constant scrutiny of Tarkanian and his team had made the letters UNLV synonymous with the dark side of college sports. But they had help, too, from Tarkanian, whose narrowly focused basketball mind and penchant for signing hard-luck players others wouldn't touch had provided fodder for those who were firing cannons at him. "Jerry lost this game," one of his many lawyers said. "But he committed enough turnovers that he shouldn't have been surprised."

Some have called what happened to Tarkanian a "conspiracy." Others scoff at the term, claiming everything was done "for the good of the university." But almost all will admit that Jerry Tarkanian didn't go from national championship coach to the unemployment line in fifteen months without a lot of behind-the-scenes maneuvering.

Asked after the press conference about the "conspiracy" by one reporter, interim athletic director Dennis Finfrock, an active player in this game, asked for anonymity before saying, "If that's what it takes to restore law and order, that's what it is."

"Dennis Finfrock's definition of law and order might not match with that of the rest of society," Lois Tarkanian, Jerry's wife, said.

"Call it whatever you want, it was evil. It was an agreement among individuals to perform together an evil act, and that's an exact definition of conspiracy that can be found in the dictionary."

One UNLV coach whose program benefited greatly from the money and profile that Tarkanian's basketball team gave the athletic department described it this way to sportscaster Ron Futrell: "Dennis Finfrock was sent out to start fires so that Maxson could complain when the smoke got thick. They were definitely working together."

"The president and Finfrock, they did what they had to do to get Tarkanian out," said former *Review-Journal* sports editor Bob Sands, himself a recipient of leaks from the two. "I would never call it a conspiracy. But was this their goal? No doubt about it. Would they have stopped if the hot tub pictures hadn't caused him to resign? I doubt it. This was something they'd wanted for a long time, and how best to get the community on your side than to dirty Tarkanian up? You know, this is a public relations situation in reverse. It was a tough sell. They did what they had to because Tarkanian is so powerful. Maxson would not have moved unless he felt as if he had everything in place to get his job. And I think he, at that point, did have it. I think after all the stories, he had the community on his side. He [Maxson] had my backing."

Conspiracy or not, this effort had left Tarkanian the fighter—the man who battled the most powerful organization in amateur sports for most of his adult life—without the energy to fight any longer.

It seemed, Tarkanian said, as if the bad publicity that had swirled around him and his program for years had now become a tornado. Finally, on this dry, hot summer morning, it was sweeping him away.

The night before, Tarkanian and Lois had struggled through the writing of an "appropriate" letter of resignation. They wanted every word to be right, projecting a tone that was upbeat—at least as upbeat as one can be when he's giving up his life's work and love:

Dear President Maxson,
Many people have asked me over the past several years how long I intend to continue as a college coach. I always replied that I would contin-

ue as long as I was having fun and enjoying it. It is obvious I am not having much fun at the present time. The emotional strain of recent weeks has left an empty cup.

As you know, I have been a vocal opponent of what I perceived to be the improper and unethical investigative practices on the part of the NCAA's enforcement division, as well as the absence of such fundamental protections as due process rights. My willingness to stand and fight has made me the target of virtually non-stop investigation and attack by the NCAA, which has cast a perception of me that will never change. Unfortunately, this long-running dispute has also harmed those around me, including my players, coaches, family and friends, as well as the University and the community.

The latest round of inaccurate, but damaging, rumors has proven to be the final straw. I love this university and I do not want to cause it any harm. In addition, although I have been toughened over the years by the pressures of these battles, the pain I now see in my children's eyes makes me realize none of this is fun for anyone.

I thus have decided to leave college coaching. After 18 years as UNLV's head basketball coach, I am hereby announcing my intention to step down as head basketball coach and as a senior assistant athletic director at the end of the 1991–92 basketball season and to formally retire my employment with UNLV at the end of the 1991–92 academic year. Please allow this letter to serve as notice of my resignation of employment and tenure effective at 12:01 on July 1, 1992.

I hope my teams and staff will be remembered as being hard working and dedicated, having great love for each other and great loyalty to the university and the Las Vegas community.

Thank you for the support you have shown the program. I wish you and the University the best of progress in the future. I certainly will always be a Runnin' Rebel in my heart.

There it was. In black and white. Tarkanian, his hand shaking, had trouble signing his name. But early on that Friday morning, precisely 431 days and 12 hours after he reached the pinnacle of college coaching and won UNLV's only national championship, Tarkanian slid that letter into an envelope and handed it to Maxson.

As Tarkanian slipped on a suit and tie—the outfit he felt least comfortable in—and headed out the door that morning, he asked Lois to stay behind. "Don't come, Lois. Please don't come," he pleaded.

"His lawyer had just told me two hours earlier to be sure to be there," Lois said. "So I asked Jerry, 'Why? Why shouldn't I go?' 'Because it will be too sad,' he told me as he went out the door. I think maybe he thought he would cry, which he almost did. But I wanted to be there to show that we weren't taking this as a defeat, but rather a challenge to move on and do more and different things."

When Tarkanian walked into the posh new Alumni Center, site of the news conference, to announce his resignation, his son Danny threw his arm around him. The room had the atmosphere of a wake. All eyes focused on Tarkanian. Even normally irreverent reporters approached Tarkanian cautiously, not sure what to say. Along the back wall stood dozens of faculty and friends, some with tears in their eyes. Others, including Finfrock, showed no hint of emotion.

Maxson climbed behind the microphone-laden head table and asked Tarkanian to join him. "Coach Tarkanian came here eighteen years ago and what he did, he brought a national spotlight to Maryland Parkway," the wiry president said, referring to the main street near campus. "He brought a spotlight to a little campus that was not mature enough to have a spotlight on it. But he put a spotlight on a basketball program that almost overnight, he took to national prominence. In an almost unprecedented way, for eighteen years he kept that program at the national level, he kept it with national recognition. He did it with certainly the most exciting brand of basketball I've ever seen and thrilled millions of Americans with that exciting brand of basketball. I don't know that much about basketball but I know that the run-and-shoot offense that he had and that sort of in-your-face defense that he practiced, changed in my judgment ... his coaching changed the tempo of college basketball all over the nation.

"This is the passing of an era at UNLV. There is no question that Jerry Tarkanian is a legend."

It was as close as Maxson had come in two years to endorsing Tarkanian. And it came on the day Tarkanian was resigning. The president, a master wordsmith, had been careful not to embrace the embattled coach or his players. Maybe, many of Tarkanian's closest friends believe, it was because he knew this press conference was coming. He probably didn't know the date or the time, but, like everyone except Tarkanian, he sensed the end was near.

One onlooker described Maxson's faint praise of Tarkanian by using a story about fishing, one of the many hobbies Tarkanian has tried but never enjoyed: "When you reel a fish in, you can scoop it up with a net or use a gaff, which is like a baseball bat with a spike through it, to pull the fish into the boat. You gaff the fish to make sure he doesn't get away. When you use a gaff, it's bloody. I couldn't help but sit there and think that Maxson finally had gaffed Tarkanian. He finally had him where he couldn't get away. And it was bloody. Then Maxson stood there and praised the fish for getting in the boat."

Several others who came to watch the resignation were so bothered by Maxson's long-winded introduction of Tarkanian that they turned and left. Many were disgusted by his drawn-out obvious apology to the *Las Vegas Review-Journal* for having a morning rather than an afternoon press conference. The timing of the announcement allowed the rival afternoon *Las Vegas Sun* to break the official word of the resignation. As Maxson's words dragged on, Tarkanian said he "remembers just feeling sick. We had built one of the best programs in the country. I kept thinking, 'How did this happen?'"

He had plenty of time to ponder the thought as Maxson kept talking: "We've had some rather long meetings this week, as you well know because most of you were waiting for us outside the door when we came out of those meetings," Maxson rambled on in the press conference. "We met on Wednesday and we met again on Thursday and I guess we talked, maybe nine or ten times during the week by telephone. But I want you to know that when Coach was weighing the options that he was going to take, and that's what he wanted to discuss with me—he wanted to discuss with me the things he was thinking about—and when he told me that it was his intention to announce his retirement today, he told me that he was not going to ask to be paid for the final two years on his contract. In fact, he did not ask the university for one dollar. He told me that he was going to resign as basketball coach, he was going to give up his tenured professorship, that he was going to retire."

Finally, eleven minutes after they sat down, Maxson introduced Tarkanian.

"I remember eighteen years ago when I came to the university, we had a press conference," the coach reminisced. "I think it was in the building right next door. We had about one or two TV stations and about two sportswriters covering the event and maybe three or four other people. There were about ten people in the room in 1973 when the announcement was made that I was coming here. I've had eighteen great years here and I hope that the next year's going to be the best. I know a lot of people think that we're going to really be down. We probably, we're not going to be like we've been. But we're going to circle the wagons and we're going to play harder than we've ever played and we're going to be very successful.

"I've enjoyed everything about the university. I really feel fortunate that I've been able to coach this long. I told a couple of writers yesterday when I was in college I had a job working for a national biscuit company and I used to count the hours until it was lunch break and count the hours until the day ended and count the days until Friday came along. And I've really been fortunate because I really feel my whole coaching career's been fun. Going to work has been fun. The most difficult time's been the summers. I want to wish UNLV the best. I'm really happy to be here for this next season for several reasons. First of all, I did want to appear in front of the NCAA as the basketball coach. Secondly, I was very concerned about my assistant coaches. Thirdly, I wanted very much to be here when we start a whole new starting five. And you know, I've had a whole lot of people speculate that once Anderson Hunt decided to go pro that the coach would be leaving also because all five starters were gone. And I didn't want that to be the case. I'm really going to try to get our team, our coaches together and make it the best year we've ever had."

Tarkanian reminded reporters that he had never left a job with the talent cupboard bare and he wasn't going to start now. In fact, when Tarkanian came to UNLV from Long Beach State nearly two decades earlier, he refused to allow his talented Long Beach players to follow him into the desert. The sole person Tarkanian took with him to UNLV was team manager Gil Castillo, the only one who knew exactly how to fold Tarkanian's famed towel.

As he wrote in his letter to Maxson, Tarkanian said the barrage of negative stories about the players and their involvement with Perry finally had taken its toll:

"I've been in a constant battle with the NCAA and that's been pretty hard on me and my family and people closely associated with me. And then this recent thing, it's just been so hard on my family. I'm used to this and I can handle this pretty well. I can just block myself out of that. But I go home and see it hurting my family and that bothers me. It was on the front page every day for about nine days. It was absolutely incredible. My wife would get up and say, 'Guess what's in the paper today?' I'd say, 'Don't even show me.' And when you live that way for nine days, I mean, it was just absolutely incredible, especially after what we had been through the past several months."

Tarkanian, known for his dry wit and great storytelling, even attempted to joke about his plight during the press conference. Maxson suggested, as Tarkanian had said, that many believed the coach would accept an NBA offer once Anderson Hunt decided to enter the professional basketball draft.

"I think Coach thought Anderson was going to take him with him, but Anderson didn't take him," Maxson said with a smile.

"Yes he did," Tarkanian quipped, referring to the ultimate result of the hot tub photos. "He and two other guys."

In an awkward way, the crowd joined Tarkanian for a laugh. Here was one of the greatest coaches of all time in one of the most difficult of circumstances, and he was taking time to laugh, to crack jokes about himself.

To those who know him, the exchange spoke volumes about Tarkanian's outlook on life. He takes his basketball very seriously. Everything else ... well, there generally hasn't been much else, so it couldn't be that serious.

"You know, that's been on my mind for a long time really," Tarkanian told a reporter inquiring what he would do for enjoyment once he retired. "I have to figure out something that I can do of interest because I don't have a lot of interests. I've got to figure out something. I think this year I'm going to try to hit a golf ball a few times and see how that feels. And I'm going to try to read a few books and see how I enjoy that."

Psychological profiles show people who achieve greatness or distinction in their chosen field often do so only after pushing all other interests aside. They become obsessive, focused, consumed, almost blind to the outside world. The definition fit Tarkanian to a

T. These people are fascinating to observe. Most of the rest of us cannot identify with them, but can watch in awe and a little bit of envy. The tales of Tarkanian and his single-mindedness border on folklore in Las Vegas. There was the day the space shuttle *Columbia* exploded. Former athletic director Brad Rothermel shared the gloomy news that "the shuttle blew up" with Tarkanian, who thought Rothermel was talking about the minivan that traveled from campus to Las Vegas's Strip. When it was explained to him, Tarkanian sheepishly admitted he didn't know America had such a spaceship. There was the family dinner when one of his children asked what he thought of Gary Hart. "Who's he play for," Tarkanian asked, totally serious. And the time his wife took him to a ballet. After dozing off, he was awakened by applause. "Who scored," he asked his wife. His friends say he can regurgitate career statistics about obscure centers from no-name schools, yet not know there was a war going on in Vietnam. Those who have invited him on fishing trips and golf outings tell similar stories. Tarkanian refused to hire assistant coaches who owned golf clubs or a camper. Nothing interests him like basketball, and he wanted to be surrounded with like-minded people.

On the court, that one-dimensional nature has served as Tarkanian's strength. Distractions that could derail other programs served only to motivate Tarkanian and his basketball-minded Rebels. Off the court, it was among his greatest weaknesses. As his critics correctly pointed out, Tarkanian was known as an administrator who delegated freely, but didn't follow up to make sure the work was done. He figured the university hired people to deal with other problems, his challenge was to remain focused on Xs and Os. And when members of his staff failed to deliver, he seldom dealt with the problem sternly. His loose and forgiving style created a bond with his players, but was, in the mind of university administrators, intolerable when it came to operation of a big-money, high-profile Top 20 basketball program.

"One of the things that has caused Jerry some PR problems has been the fact that he let others handle an awful lot of things," Maxson said later. "He coached, he focused, but he let other people be responsible for things and I think at times you can get in trouble there. That was a weakness. You have to be the boss. You have to run it, it doesn't matter if you're the president of the university or the basketball coach. You are responsible, even if someone below you was to do the job. That means you have to be careful in giving out those assignments. That could have been a problem for Jerry, no doubt about it."

Tarkanian's style also left him vulnerable politically in a business that has become increasingly political. He would rather talk basketball with a doorman at a casino than have a polite dinner conversation with the casino's owner. Tarkanian's relationship with the working stiff helped him build the support base that fills the 19,000-seat Thomas & Mack Arena. But that support base couldn't save him as long as his opponents had played politics with the city's movers, shakers, and opinion leaders.

"I've never felt good doing that [playing politics]," Tarkanian said two months after he resigned. "I guess I should have been better at it. They outpoliticked me. I felt more comfortable talking to the average sports nut."

The inability to play politics or to develop a life outside of basketball were two of the many characteristics that have made Jerry Tarkanian what he is. Some have said that if he had been more judgmental of others, done a better job of picking his friends, and worked harder at succeeding on the social scene, he would still be coaching at UNLV today. But the truth is that if Tarkanian had done any of those things, he likely wouldn't have engendered the walk-on-coals respect from his players, wouldn't have become such a great student of the game, and wouldn't have been among the best coaches ever to pace the sidelines. His strengths were his weaknesses; his weaknesses, his strengths.

"There was a day that coaches had to win to keep their job," Lois Tarkanian said. "Jerry did that. Then they said you had to graduate your kids. Jerry was doing that. It wasn't because someone said you have to graduate more and it wasn't because it had become a national issue. Way back in 1977, Jerry requested the university hire an academic adviser for athletics and use money earned from the basketball team's Final Four appearance to pay for the position. I sat down one day and discussed the matter with him, how it wasn't enough just to get college experience, even though some is better than none. I told him if he truly cared about his players, he owed it to them to structure a program that would help them attain those degrees. Those were the key words for him, 'if he truly cared.' From then on, he made sure there was money and help put toward academics. Heck, most people wouldn't believe it, but nearly half of all the kids that have played one single minute for Jerry since he came here eighteen years ago have got their degrees. That matches up very favorably with national statistics for all students attending college.

"Now, when they said you have to start playing politics to be a coach, that's where they got Jerry. We told him he needed to start calling people and asking them to go to lunch. He just didn't feel comfortable doing it. All he wanted to do was coach basketball. They never really knew Jerry. They thought he was tough and demanding. If they knew him, they would have known that all it would have taken was for the administration to direct him to change. He used to always say, 'Coaches don't fire presidents, presidents fire coaches.' He'd have done anything he was directed to. I told Jerry a long time ago that I was sickened by what was happening. He told me that basketball had been very good to us. I told him, that's great, so if you want to stay, start playing the game. He never could.

"I remember that day during the resignation, our youngest granddaughter, Dannielle, started to cry during the announcement. It wasn't real loud, but I saw [Regent chairwoman] Carolyn Sparks turn her head real quick and look at her. She wasn't scowling or anything, but I recall looking at her [Sparks] and remembering when we had asked the university to spend a little money getting good PR for the good things the basktetball team was doing. We wanted to brag about the graduation rate, the fact that fifty-five percent of the players off of our teams that had been ranked number one in the country [1983, '87, '89, '90, and '91] had graduated, that we had the first Rhodes scholar candidate athlete in the state, that so many of our players were coming back to graduate after their eligibility was up. We had twice the graduation rate of the general student body. Nobody ever hears those things. But she [Sparks] and Maxson killed that idea for a public relations campaign. She never helped us get the positive word out. Then we ended up there in the same room and my husband was resigning. I almost got sick. But after the press conference, I felt exhilarated. We'd finally be able to leave this mess. There were so many vicious people around us. Each time I had contact with them, I felt as if I needed to bathe."

While some writers pointed to the hot tub pictures as the beginning of Jerry Tarkanian's end and others point to Tarkanian's recruiting of risky prospects, Tarkanian now believes his downfall began in 1984, the day Maxson arrived in Las Vegas. What was happening that day in the Alumni Center wasn't just about hot tub pictures. It wasn't just about graduation rates, and it wasn't about recruiting. It was about image—Tarkanian didn't fit the image that Maxson wanted to project. And it was about ego—in Las Vegas, Tarkanian was the main event, Maxson the undercard.

Things obviously were very different in college basketball, in Las Vegas, and at UNLV in 1991 than they had been when Tarkanian waged what has become one of the greatest duels in college sports, his battle with the NCAA. When the NCAA ordered UNLV to suspend Tarkanian in 1977 for ten alleged rule violations, the university president complied, but was visibly pleased when Tarkanian sought a court injunction setting the penalty aside. The university let it be known that if the fantastically successful coach won an injunction, the university wouldn't complain.

That, Tarkanian said, was loyalty. The university stuck with him and by him. He returned that loyalty by rejecting at least two offers to coach the Los Angeles Lakers when UNLV wasn't much more than a dot on the collegiate basketball map. Several other calls from the NBA simply went unanswered.

Loyalty. It's a big issue to Tarkanian. He used the word once in his letter of resignation and seven times during the press conference. It is one of his defining characteristics. He looks for it in others and swears you can count on it from him.

"I believe the key to a relationship between a coach and players is loyalty," Tarkanian once wrote. "I know that kids will mess up at times. I know that on occasion they will do stupid things. When I was a kid, I messed up sometimes and I didn't always make the wisest decisions. But if a kid is loyal to me and to his teammates and to the program and the school, he'll always get a second chance and a third and a fourth. I'd rather take a kid who was a thief than a kid who is disloyal. You can teach a kid not to steal, show him why he was wrong, but it's difficult to develop loyalty in someone who has never shown it before. I always feel that if he is a loyal person, he will eventually straighten out. I never run off a kid who is play-ing poorly or who is injured. If I gave him a four-year scholarship commitment, I'll stick by him even if he can't help us on the court. Loyalty is really a two-way street. Lots of people demand loyalty but are not willing to give it back."

As he wrote that in 1988, Tarkanian had no clue how significant those last two sentences would one day become. Although he didn't see it then, Tarkanian sees it now. He was standing by the university, its president, and its athletic director long after they had left him. His "loyalty," he said, wasn't being returned. Instead, those who worked for the university were masterminding, as Bob Sands had put it, "a public relations campaign in reverse."

On a smaller scale, what happened at UNLV might appear to be a struggle between academics and athletics or a power play between an image-conscious president and a popular coach. That's what some at UNLV would like you to think. But those things hap-pen on campuses all over America without this type of ending. What happened at UNLV was all that and more, much more. It is a study of hypocrisy, jealousy, ego, power, betrayal, and naiveté. It was simply disguised as a battle for academics because, in the end, who can be against academics? And with academics as the flag, UNLV officials could justify any act in the name of the cause. Was this done to benefit the university's academic standing, or did it happen because, to use the basketball analogy, there weren't enough basketballs out there for both Maxson and Tarkanian to play on the same team?

"The pain this brought to Jerry, I could handle," said Lois Tarkanian. "It hurt, but after all, he's over sixty years old and he was warned repeatedly about the character of the individuals involved. The pain it brought to our children was harder, but I knew this was going to happen and for years actually had been preparing them. It hurt, but they were ready. We had been able to develop the acceptance of the hurt because it was balanced by far more years Jerry had in coaching than we ever thought he would have, considering the power of the NCAA enforcement staff and the jealousy and insatiable need for power exhibited by several within the university. The pain that was unforgivable, however, was what the UNLV administration did to the players. Understand that the young men playing for UNLV came because they believed in us. They believed Jerry when he said what a fine university it was. They believed the coaches when they talked about loyalty to the school and how we were all part of a university community. Then they faced this. Maxson told Jerry, Danny, and myself numerous times how much he wanted Jerry to stay at UNLV, how we had to stick together against those 'outsiders wanting to cause trouble.' We were puzzled when he wouldn't come out publicly with strong statements supporting Jerry. When we asked him and [university general counsel] Brad Booke about it, they indicated it was important for the president to not be too supportive publicly in order to maintain a posture of neutrality during the NCAA investigation. Chuck Thompson, our lawyer, would tell us over and over again that Maxson wouldn't come out publicly because while he was telling Jerry he supported him, he already had told certain movers and shakers in our city that he wanted Jerry out. How could he continue to keep their support in helping with his master plan if he came out too publicly for Jerry? We didn't believe Chuck, but it turned out he was right. It was a brilliant Machiavellian move on Maxson's part. For anyone in the know that morning of the resignation, the stench of insincerity and hypocrisy filled the room as Maxson spoke."

"As I sat there at the press conference," Tarkanian's youngest daughter, Jodie, said, "I said to myself, this doesn't seem like real life. It's more like something you see on television or read in a Danielle Steel novel. It was all about getting someone out of your way."

The Tarkanians' youngest son, George, saw this day coming years earlier. For that reason, he took every win as a gift and felt he had to stop asking God for more once Tarkanian won the 1990 championship. His father, though, didn't have the same foresight.

"The day I resigned, I felt relieved," Tarkanian said several months later. "That whole morning just didn't seem real. I felt relieved and yet at the same time I kept asking myself what happened? I kept thinking about how frustrated I had been that all the positives about our players never got out. I knew that never again would UNLV have as great a group of kids athletically, academically, and as human beings. Why hadn't anyone been willing to find out the truth about these kids? That's when I was thinking it just seemed my battles with the NCAA continued to stir up controversy which was spilling over onto our players. But I didn't feel any animosity toward Maxson for that. I actually felt good when I walked in there [to the press conference]. I felt like I was doing the right thing for my family and the university. I was tired of all the negative stuff. Finally, all this negative stuff would end. I wanted no more shots taken at what I'd worked eighteen years to build.

"I don't feel good about it anymore. Not now that I'm sure this wasn't a coincidence. I believe there were people here who wanted me out. But they didn't have the guts to tell me. Instead, they worked at undermining me. And they were successful. People had warned me for years that something like this was going to happen. I never believed any of them. When my friends would tell me not to trust Maxson and Finfrock, I'd just tune the friends out. Loyalty to the university was most important, and I just couldn't believe they would be saying, as Maxson did, that he wanted me to coach as long as he was at the university while he was really feeling something so totally opposite. You wouldn't believe the number of times the president told me we had to stick together or we had no chance. Even up to that day I resigned, I felt good toward him. I suspected that Dennis [Finfrock] and Sheila [Strike-Bolla, Finfrock's assistant] had probably leaked stuff to try and hurt us. But Maxson kept saying great things to me about what I had done for the university. He told me over and over how he wanted me to be his coach as long as he was at UNLV. But to others, he was saying something else. And when everybody warned me, I told them I believed the president. The irony of it all is that I always felt I had good relations with the president. At the Thomas and Mack Arena, many times he would come down and sit on the bench before the game. Chuck [Thompson] and my other friends hated that. They told me over and over that that was his way of showing that he and I were friends when really he was knifing me. He introduced me to his mother one time and told me I was her hero and how much she liked the program. He'd tell me how much Sylvia [Maxson's wife] liked me and the program. He told me I was such a good coach I could probably take five kids from the West Side and be competitive. Every time he'd say something positive and I'd share it with Brad Rothermel, Brad would say, 'I bet you'll get a great night's sleep tonight knowing that the president's behind you,' then he'd laugh at me like I was a fool. But I believed Maxson. I was stupid."

At the very least, Tarkanian was blind. He couldn't believe that the president or others within the university wouldn't want *him*. And if the president didn't want him, he couldn't believe the president wouldn't just say it. The university would not have become what it is without him. Now, its leadership quietly was saying, it could not become what they wanted with him. He couldn't believe the university he'd fought to continue working for might one day feel it had outgrown him. And he never thought that the egos of those around him would not rest until he was gone.

"I guess there was a lot I didn't see," Tarkanian said.

Until, that is, long after he'd been blinded by all those television lights on that Friday, June 7, 1991.

2

The Thrill of Victory

It was unbelievable, really. There was forward Larry Johnson, arguably the best player in college basketball, diving along the sideline for a loose ball, tossing it behind his back with his right hand as he crashed to the floor. The ball whipped quickly to point guard Greg Anthony, who held it just long enough to freeze the defense before lobbing it into Stacey Augmon for a lay-up.

Who would have thought it would be this pretty? Or this easy? Never in the history of college basketball had there been a championship game quite like this. Not during the undefeated championship seasons of Indiana, North Carolina, or San Francisco. Not even during that fabulous run UCLA took through history.

Here they were, two teams battling for the national title. And by halftime, there wasn't much of a battle left. Nor were there really two teams.

UNLV 103. Duke 73. It was the most one-sided game in fifty-two years of NCAA basketball championship history. And all the NCAA staff that had tried to run Tark from coaching could do—all the players from Duke could do—was watch in wonderment.

Despite the many records his teams had set for offensive prowess, it was UNLV's stifling defense that buried Duke. By forcing fourteen turnovers in the first half, UNLV took a 47–35 lead into the locker room. There, Tarkanian stuck with his pregame prediction that this contest would be won or lost on the last shot. "I told 'em Duke can come back; they never give up," Tarkanian said, recalling his halftime speech. "We have a saying on this team, 'Tighten the vise, Tighten the vise.' Even the guys on the bench picked it up in the second half."

His team came out and so thoroughly overwhelmed Duke in the opening minutes of the second half that Tark was forced to swallow those words. "At least they tasted good," he quipped later. The game was such a blowout that the all-important last shot was taken by little-used guard David Rice, the eleventh man on Tarkanian's thirteen-man squad.

Duke was so off its game that when forward Brian Davis was fouled and center Christian Laettner walked over for the traditional high five, Davis missed and accidentally hit Laettner in the face.

Afterward, Tark was nearly as overwhelmed as was Duke. His eyes teared up and he became short of breath as he embraced each of his sweating players in a full-body hug. As a tear trickled down his right cheek, he fought to maintain his composure. The man who always had something to say about the NCAA suddenly was speechless when that organization was forced to hand him its most coveted trophy.

"Not in my wildest dreams, not in my wildest dreams," Tarkanian repeated over and over as reporters asked if he ever believed his team would win the one game that had escaped him in twenty-one years of Division I coaching.

His own players, caught up in winning the game as much for Tarkanian as for themselves, barely were aware of how devastatingly awesome they had been. "You're in the middle of it, and you're rolling, and you don't even know you're playing so well," Larry Johnson, UNLV's first consensus first team all-American, told *The National Sports Daily.* "All of a sudden, you're up by 30, and it's like 'Whoa. How'd we get *here?*'"

The fact they were there at all was a minor miracle. Many talented teams don't make it to the Final Four. Only one a year gets to take home the trophy in the winner-take-all tournament. But none has ever battled through so much on the way to putting an exclamation point on its season. Theirs was a bumpy ride down a path full of potholes, detours, and diversions. It was a season that would have caused lesser teams to fall.

"These kids have been through so much adversity," Tarkanian said after the championship game. "There were a lot of times when I thought our season was going down the drain. But we kept coming back. And when we had to play our best, we played our best. A lot of teams would have folded their tents and gone home a long time ago. Not our guys, though. They've become closer. If you think about it, it's amazing what they've played through."

That was putting it mildly. This team experienced more peaks and valleys than the Rocky Mountains, site of the national championship game it so desperately wanted to win.

Everything was looking up for the Rebels when Johnson, the 1989 junior college player of the year, decided to take his talents and join Augmon, his longtime friend and former Olympian, in Vegas. Together, they would anchor the best front line in college basketball.

UNLV was so sure this was the real thing that it commissioned a preseason poster showing the team's two stars standing shoulder to muscular shoulder atop a mountain with the neon lights of Las Vegas in the background. Johnson, just a shade over 6'5", gathered a small mound of gravel to stand on, allowing him to look as tall as the 6'8" Augmon. "This is going to be an equal partnership," Johnson said with a healthy grin. Across the poster ran the words "The Big Year Is Here!"

Others believed in the Rebels as well. In a nearly unanimous choice, the nation's basketball writers and coaches had declared during the preseason that UNLV was the team to beat.

It didn't take long for somebody to beat them. Only this loss was self-imposed. Before the season began, starting center David Butler and power forward Moses Scurry were suspended for six games apiece for academic failures.

Then, on the opening day of practice, Scurry, redshirt freshman Barry Young, and UNLV recruit Bobby Joyce were arrested on charges of obstructing police officers who were responding to a fight at a party off campus. Scurry and Young spent the night at the Clark County Detention Center and were released on their own recognizance. Joyce posted bail. Police said the three players and more than 100 others who attended the party were told to leave the area immediately. But the three reportedly stayed behind and argued with police, and Scurry used profanity in berating the officers. Scurry told Tarkanian that he refused to leave until police unclogged the parking lot at the apartment complex and let him take his car. "We've told the players many times that they can't go around getting involved in things that reflect poorly on themselves and the program," Tarkanian said. "They can do so many positive things in the community and one negative thing can ruin it all. They have to accept the responsibility that goes along with being a Rebel."

When the Clark County district attorney's office opted not to file charges against Scurry and Young, Tarkanian decided against any sanctions. Joyce, who was not on the team, was charged with resisting arrest, a misdemeanor.

A week later, the *Las Vegas Review-Journal* published a lengthy story about the cars that Rebel players were driving. While researching the story, photographers from the newspaper had followed several Rebel players around the city, taking pictures of the stars and their cars at home, at the arena, and while they were out with friends. The newspaper reported that Greg Anthony, owner of a small business, was purchasing a six-year-old BMW, but had been seen driving a 1986 Nissan 300ZX owned by the half brother of a former UNLV player. It also pointed out that Anthony's backcourt running mate, Anderson Hunt, was driving his girlfriend's 1988 BMW convertible, that Augmon was purchasing a 1988 Ford GT coupe, and that Johnson was driving a new Nissan 300ZX, which was purchased by a friend in Texas, where he grew up.

"To even ask a question of that magnitude, that really offends me," Anthony, who spent his summers working as a congressional aide in Washington, D.C., told the *Review-Journal*. "If I was a white guy driving this car, this wouldn't be happening."

Even Tarkanian, who had learned long ago not to wage war with those who buy ink by the barrel, expressed outrage about the press secretly following players. "This is incredible," he said when the newspaper asked him for a comment. "Really incredible. If I was a player, I'd be really upset."

From that point on, Las Vegas reporters covering the team and its troubles became lightning rods for Tarkanian and his players. And vice versa. The friction became so intense, several players went the entire season without talking to the press. The press took every opportunity—and there were many—to return fire.

"A lot of stuff happened with the '87 team, too," said television sportscaster Jerry Olenyn. "But I think a lot of it, people just turned their heads. People were so in love with the '87 team. Those guys were a pleasure. I'm ashamed to admit it, but I was rooting for them to win. I never felt that way this year. It wasn't a pleasure to cover them like it was in previous years. Tark said this was a great group of kids. This was not a great group of kids."

As the season progressed, the not-so-merry-go-round with the media began spinning faster and faster. This was a contest that the Rebels couldn't win.

"It was like the media had it in for us," Anthony said after he was selected by the New York Knicks in the first round of the 1991 NBA draft. "It was the start of our believing that the only people we could trust was ourselves. It became us versus them. And there were a lot of them."

That tension with the media proved to be both a blessing and a curse. While it helped the team turn inward and work as one, it also resulted in increasingly negative publicity, something Tarkanian's detractors could use while making their sales pitch that his days surely needed to be numbered.

All this, and the team hadn't even played its first game. Without Butler and Scurry, the Rebels dropped two of their first five contests and fell quickly from the perch of college basketball. A fourteen-point drubbing by Kansas in the Preseason NIT and an eighteen-point loss at Oklahoma left UNLV ranked fourteenth. Confusion reigned as the team struggled to live up to predictions.

The outcome of the Oklahoma game actually could have been much worse. A university audit done in conjunction with an ongoing NCAA investigation had discovered that nine players had failed to repay incidental charges incurred while on road trips the previous year. Just two days before the Oklahoma game, Tarkanian was informed by the NCAA that the seven must serve a one-game suspension. "I couldn't believe it," Tarkanian said. "It was incredible."

Even more incredible was the NCAA's demand that all seven players should serve their time immediately, a decision that would have left Tarkanian with only five scholarship players and two walk-ons for the nationally televised game with the twelfth-ranked Sooners. "We were scheduled to fly to Oklahoma on Friday morning," Tarkanian remembers. "Then I got the news. I figured we might as well just take our seven players, fly in the day of the game, and get out of there. Who needed to go early with seven players?"

Because UNLV couldn't determine which player in each room had incurred the expenses, officials quickly arranged a deal to delay the penalties until January, when they would agree to bench two of the suspended players per game.

The NCAA declared the unpaid hotel bills—which included room service charges, pay-per-view movies, and long-distance calls—were an "extra benefit" that had been conferred on the UNLV players. It argued that the university should have forced repayment of the bills, even though the university produced letters written to each of the host hotels asking that player phones be turned off and that players not be allowed to bill meals or movies to their room. The hotels involved confirmed to the NCAA that they had received the letter and acknowledged that they had ignored the request. But the NCAA said the letter didn't show enough effort on the university's part. "I don't believe anything like this has ever happened," Athletic Director Brad Rothermel said at the time. "If we are responsible for the players' hotel bills, even after we have a contract stating that no long-distance or incidental charges are allowed, then are we responsible for their power and water bills, too?"

A week later, the same investigation that turned up the unpaid hotel bills revealed that three players—Jones, Scurry, and Butler—had used university phones to make long-distance calls. All three had their eligibility suspended until they repaid the university or signed notes setting up a repayment schedule. Butler was suspended for one game, Tarkanian said. The others were able to resolve their differences more quickly.

Once Scurry and Butler found their way out of the newspapers and onto the court, the Rebels ripped off six wins in a row—including impressive victories over sixteenth-ranked Iowa and Number

11 Arkansas—before being upset at New Mexico State, 83–82. UNLV was starting to prove it was worthy of its preseason clippings. Until, that is, they were sidetracked again.

The players' anger at losing to the Aggies paled in comparison to their reaction to the next of what seemed like a never-ending string of crises for these Rebels. At 1:00 A.M., just twelve hours before his team was to suit up against Temple in Philadelphia for another nationally televised game, Tarkanian received word that the NCAA had ordered Hunt to sit out the game. As the players listened intently while riding the team bus to the Spectrum, Tarkanian told the team about the call he'd gotten. Hunt, who came to UNLV as a part-time student his first year while he worked to increase his ACT score, had opted to pay for that first semester by arranging for a student loan. In so doing, he didn't lose any eligibility. When Hunt's board score rose above the NCAA minimum, he accepted an athletic scholarship for the second semester of that year. At that time, arrangements were made to deduct his loan repayment from his scholarship check each month. In December 1989, the athletic department shifted the responsibility of handling scholarship checks to a different staff member, who did not deduct the loan portion from the check, Tarkanian said. By the time it was discovered, Hunt had missed two loan payments—totaling $359—and the NCAA declared him ineligible. Two days later, Hunt's older brother overnighted the university a check and his eligibility was restored.

"In the huddle before the game, Greg [Anthony], being the captain, said, 'Hey, we're going to show them [the NCAA] that we can do it, no matter what,'" David Rice remembers. "He looked at everyone and said, 'ABC,' which was our little slogan—Adversity Builds Character. That was the saying for the year. We had had a great day of practice with Anderson the day before. Now we didn't know what to expect. We went out and played pretty inspired basketball."

Although UNLV won the Temple game, 82–76, Tarkanian was steamed. "These distractions are getting out of hand," he said. "I've never heard of anything like what happened to Anderson. I sometimes wondered what else could go wrong that season. I got to the point where I was afraid to pick up the phone because I didn't know what was going to happen next. The Hunt suspension is probably the one that made me the maddest. They could have checked on that and let us know earlier in the week. They definitely should have known before one in the morning."

Frustrated, several players told reporters that all of the distractions had put the team on the verge of collapse. "I don't think we've united as a team," reserve point guard Stacey Cvijanovich said. "The chemistry isn't there."

And the distractions would only get worse. UNLV's effort to delay the one-game suspensions for his players on the hotel incidentals allegation had kept the NCAA at bay. Now it was time to pay up. The NCAA, not knowing which player charged the incidentals, suspended both athletes in each hotel room. The NCAA's decision to ban the players had resulted in coast-to-coast criticism about the apparently vindictive manner in which the organization was coming after UNLV. There were no shortage of columnists who pointed to the suspension of Travis Bice, a bench-riding shooting guard, as evidence of the NCAA's pettiness. Bice, according to the NCAA, had skipped out on paying $7.51—$5.36 for an unitemized expense at a hotel in Denver and $2.15 for a jar of peanuts taken from the minibar of a hotel in Long Beach, California. That's precisely what this had become—an investigation of peanuts. Bice denied having eaten the peanuts and toyed with the idea of suing the NCAA. Tarkanian talked him out of it because "we didn't need any more distractions."

Despite all the bad publicity, the NCAA didn't back down. Two hours before tip-off, Anthony and Butler were ordered suspended for the game against UC Santa Barbara, one the Rebels squeaked out, 69–67. "We were on our way into the locker room to get dressed when they told us," said Rice, Anthony's roommate.

On the way to the airport three days later for the trip to Louisiana State, Augmon, the team's defensive stopper, and forward Chris Jeter were told they would have to sit out. The two already had checked their luggage with the team trainer and had to pull the bags off the plane. UNLV lost, 107–105, as LSU's Chris Jackson blew by other Rebel defenders and scored thirty-five points. When Utah State came to Las Vegas for a conference game three days after the LSU trip, Bice and Scurry were benched by the

NCAA. The team didn't need them, though, in a 124–90 blowout. Barry Young and James Jones did their time as UNLV rolled over North Carolina State two days later. The ninth "guilty" Rebel, back-up center George Ackles, had been given a medical redshirt. So the NCAA ordered him to miss the first game of next year.

Only Cvijanovich, Johnson, and Rice survived the NCAA's wrath.

"We all felt as coaches that the NCAA was coming down with these suspensions in an effort to break our concentration and get our team to lose our focus," Tarkanian said. "We felt we were totally in the right on the NCAA charges. We had contracts with the hotels that stipulated the kids would not to be allowed to charge incidental expenses. If the hotels made the mistake, the university's position is that the hotel should collect from the athlete himself. We provided the hotels with the name and address of the athlete. We thought the university fulfilled its obligation."

The national sympathy the Rebels received for the suspensions was lost, though, when a bloody brawl erupted during the waning moments of the game against Utah State. Writers who had jumped on the NCAA for overstepping the bounds of fairness suddenly dropped that story and began referring to the Rebel players as "thugs."

The melee's origin actually dated back twelve months, when Utah State coach Kohn Smith openly questioned UNLV's recruiting tactics, encouraging reporters to check out the expensive cars and expensive clothes owned by Rebel players. UNLV coaches and players bristled at the accusation, but said little—until the teams met on the court. The five-minute fracas began with seven seconds left in a game that long ago had been decided. Chris Jeter apparently head-butted Aggie forward Gary Patterson, whom Jeter claims had hit him in the mouth several times throughout the game. Patterson required fifteen stitches to close the gash in his forehead. After the game, television replays show, Utah State sophomore Kendall Youngblood challenged Jeter, yelling, "Hit me, motherfucker. Hit me." Jeter responded with a punch to Youngblood's face. Youngblood was left with two cuts under his eyes, each of which required two stitches to close. As players from both sides began throwing punches, Scurry threw two wild punches which hit

Smith, the Aggie coach. Scurry would later say he didn't recognize Smith as a coach because he was wearing a sweater and not a coat and tie.

"This might go back to what I said last year, and that was a mistake," Smith said after the game. "It was just a dumb thing for a rookie coach to say. I have tried over and over again to apologize for what I said."

Tarkanian issued a strong apology, as did Brad Rothermel and Moses Scurry. Jeter sent a handwritten letter to Youngblood asking for his forgiveness. But apparently, that wasn't enough for Maxson, who seized on the national attention and drafted a letter to Utah State president Stanford Cazier.

"The behavior of all of our players involved in the disturbance at the Utah State–UNLV game was inexcusable," Maxson wrote. "I am ashamed and embarrassed. On behalf of all of us here at UNLV, I apologize to you and to the entire Utah State University community for that behavior. Such acts do not represent the more than 16,000 law-abiding, decent students here who are appalled, as I am."

The Faculty Senate then jumped on the bandwagon, debating a proposed reprimand that read, in part: "The Faculty Senate of the University of Nevada–Las Vegas is angered by the long history of negative incidents and bad publicity generated by certain athletic programs and the athletic department. Such incidents have degraded the university and the Las Vegas community." After debate, the resolution was tempered to endorse Maxson's apology and the suspension of Scurry and Jeter and said the Senate "was keenly aware of recent activity which has brought discredit and nationally unwelcome publicity to our university."

The players—only three of whom were white—and coaches were incensed. Assistant Coach Cle Edwards sent Maxson a letter questioning the president's motives. "You have never addressed the problem of the continual harassment the UNLV basketball team undergoes each and every game they play [at Utah State] in Logan, Utah," Edwards wrote. "You fail to mention that our athletes have been called, and I quote, 'Niggers, Ghetto Blasters' and other sordid and prejudicial/racial names. The hostility from their fans is so thick you can feel the tension in the arena. All you do is condemn our team for its bad behavior without really examining the causes behind the incident. The statement of 'I told him that behavior didn't reflect the behavior of over 16,000 students that go to school here' makes the public believe that everyone who attends UNLV is beyond reproach except for the UNLV basketball team. This statement has a subliminal message of racism."

Anthony, who often spoke for the team, said, "No one is proud of what happened, but that's life and that's reality. There are fights in corporate America, those things happen. This is a competitive society we live in. Like I said, while we were not proud of what happened, we apologized, we suffered a lot of ridicule for that. He really didn't need to add to the critics. To say that we're not law abiding students or something like that, I really think that is a racist statement. But we just basically, we expected it from him, to be totally honest.

"Fortunately, we had enough support from within our own family, to you say hey, screw them if that's the way they want to treat us. Because we're going to keep being good people, working hard, and trying to be successful in life. You know, a couple of years from now, a lot of those same people will be calling us, asking us to do this and do that, you know, and we remember all those little things. I keep a little diary of what people said exactly. I don't say anything to anybody, I just remember. When they call, that name will ring a bell, and I'll go back and look it up and see what was said, and I'll be ready."

"When we played Utah State in their gym, we made every effort to express our apology and regret for the fighting incident," said Lois Tarkanian. "We presented a bouquet of roses to the head coach and said a few words. Then just as the second half started, green water spurted all over the UNLV bench. It came from under the court behind the bench and was almost like a sprinkling system. Jerry got soaked, as did some of the players. The game was delayed as dry clothes were found and water mopped. Jerry laughed it off, and no one from UNLV made a big thing of it."

Maxson paid no attention to the criticism from the players and coaches, instead demanding that he be given the opportunity to talk to the team before its next home game against North Carolina State.

"A lot of guys didn't want to have anything to do with him," Rice said. "But the coaches told us to just sit there and listen to what he had to say. He came in and said he was very proud of our accomplishments, but he thought of us as his children and any time that his own children misbehaved that he had to get on them, so that's what he was doing in terms of the Utah State game. I don't think the guys much appreciated being called children."

As the team prepared to play, the crowd at Thomas & Mack, like President Maxson, voiced its disapproval. During the N.C. State game, Scurry's appearance on the playing floor was roundly booed by the usually rabid fans. Tarkanian suspended Jeter for the next two games and the rematch scheduled for later in the season at Utah State. Scurry, who seemed to find trouble around every corner, also was told he would sit out the next contest with the Aggies.

Then, just as the furor over the Utah State incident started to die down, Anthony, the team's vocal chord, suffered a bone-jarring spill during a game against Fresno State. The flashy guard drove the lane during the first half, scored a lay-up, then fell headfirst, hitting the ground with a sickening thud and snapping his neck backwards. Doctors initially thought Anthony's incredible fall may have broken his neck. He hit the court so hard his face bounced up and came crashing down a second time. The wildly cheering crowd suddenly fell silent as Anthony lay motionless. A few minutes later, he was carried from the court. X rays indicated he had fractured his jaw in two places. He would be out at least six weeks. Doctor's orders.

"I was scared," Tarkanian said, remembering the moment. "It really looked like this was going to be a really serious injury. He was so tough."

But in what would prove to be the most significant event of the season, Anthony showed up for practice the next day, his jaw wired shut. Trainers special-ordered a three-pound hockey helmet fitted with a football face guard from a factory in California. After two days of practice, the gutsy Anthony asked to start the next game—without the helmet. In that game, a rematch with the New Mexico State team that handed UNLV a one-point loss earlier in the year, Anthony scored ten points, dished out six assists, had two steals, and two rebounds in thirty-two minutes of play. His presence, though, meant more than his numbers. "We all said that if he can play, we better play hard," said Johnson, who stepped in to support Anthony when one Aggie player brushed an elbow against Anthony's face. The team responded with its most dominating game of the regular season, a 109–86 victory. UNLV went 15–1 from that point on, losing only in an upset to UC Santa Barbara.

"Greg's injury actually worked to our advantage," said Rice. "He was so fast that at times it almost looked like he was out of control. With the broken jaw, he slowed down and played more in control."

Anthony wasn't the only Rebel who spent more time with doctors than with trainers. Cvijanovich separated a shoulder just minutes after Anthony broke his jaw. Butler sprained his knee during the same game, and Bice didn't even dress for the game because he had contracted chicken pox. Additionally, Jeter missed three games with mononucleosis, Scurry and Hunt both suffered sprained wrists, and Ackles broke his wrist, causing him to miss the entire season. At times, Rebel practices found more players on the sidelines than on the court.

Just in case injuries, fights, suspensions, and a grueling schedule weren't enough to derail this team, NCAA investigators were making biweekly trips to Las Vegas during the season, checking on allegations stemming from the now three-year-old investigation into the recruitment of Lloyd Daniels. (Daniels, the troubled high school phenom from New York City, had been adopted by one of Tarkanian's assistants, sending a stream of investigative reporters and NCAA staffers to Las Vegas sniffing for wrongdoing.)

Players became so tired of the NCAA's harassment that they occasionally played games with the investigators. During one interview with the NCAA, Larry Johnson was asked about every visit he had made to Las Vegas dating back several years. Who paid for the airline ticket? Did anyone pick you up at the airport? Where did you stay? The questions went on and on. None of Johnson's answers proved to be of value to the NCAA. Finally, the flustered investigators asked Johnson if they'd missed any of his trips.

"Yeah," Johnson said. "You missed one from earlier this year when I came from home."

"Who paid for that ticket?" investigator Dan Calandro asked.

"Tarkanian. Coach Tark did," Johnson said. Suddenly, the investigators lit up like The Strip and Johnson's lawyer, Steve Stein, started choking.

"Coach Tarkanian paid for the ticket?" Calandro asked.

"I got you, I got you," Johnson said in jest while he flashed his now famous grin at the NCAA duo. "Truth is, you paid for that trip. The NCAA paid for it 'cause they asked me to go to Chicago and do an antidrug commercial. I was just foolin'."

Neither Calandro nor his partner, Robert Stroup, found much humor in the moment. Stein and Johnson, though, laughed about it for weeks.

"No doubt about it, they were trying to throw us off our game," Johnson said of the NCAA. "Even the way they handled the suspensions, by waiting until the last minute to do it, was their way of trying to throw us off."

NCAA Enforcement Director David Berst, in an interview with Las Vegas television reporter Dan Burns, denied the charge. But he did so in an unusually evasive way. "If what we were trying to do was adversely affect the team … we'd be better at disrupting the team than we certainly have been over the years if that was what we were setting out to do," Berst said.

"It sounded to me like he said they were trying but weren't doing a very good job," Burns said after listening to the interview several times. Whether it was their intent or not, the NCAA was, in fact, disrupting the Rebels.

"We probably didn't have ten practices all year with the entire team present," Tarkanian said. "Several times, kids missed practice because the NCAA had come in and pulled them off the court to interview them. We never knew who was going to show up for practice."

Nor, as Hunt's suspension at Temple showed, did they know who would be available at game time. Only one player, Johnson, played in all thirty-one regular season games. Only two players, Johnson and Rice, were available for all of those games. All told, ten different players were forced to miss at least one game due to injury or suspension for a total of thirty-seven man-games lost. The thirteen scholarship athletes played only seven games during the regular season as a complete unit.

Through all these trials, Tarkanian kept trying to sell his players on the advantages of the unfolding events. It worked. Not only did the team begin to believe it was on a mission to defeat the world, it believed that the loss of so many players for so many key games actually *was making them better.*

"It made us gel together," Augmon said. "There was always someone missing in one of our games. It just made someone else rise to the occasion. Once we had everyone strong, by that time everyone really had their confidence. Everyone accepted each other and accepted their roles. It just tied us all together. It helped us strengthen our bench."

The diversions allowed Tarkanian to mold his starters—each of whom likely could have starred at any Division 1 school in America—into a single-minded unit. "To experience turmoil to the point that we have, you either regress or progress," the always articulate Anthony said before the championship game. "It's pretty obvious which way we've gone."

Maxson wanted to make one more visit to the team, this time right after the last home game, a battle with Louisville. "The players didn't want him to come in after the comments he'd made about the Utah State game," Tarkanian said. "I had a meeting with the team and told them that he was president of the university and he wanted to talk to them and it was their responsibility to respect him. See, they figured Georgetown and other schools had fights just as bad and their school president didn't write letters demeaning the individuals. They were truly sorry for what they'd done, but they felt he made them look worse than they were. After the game, I had to go to the coach's television room. The other coaches told me that when Maxson went in to talk, some of the kids went back into the shower and others just had their heads down. They all were just bitter."

Ironically, the team that had struggled to keep itself together during the regular season showed no signs of falling apart once postseason play began. Blessed with the unusual situation of having all thirteen players in uniform and available, UNLV blew through the Big West Tournament, winning three games by an average of twenty-two points. Named the top seed in the NCAA's West Region, the team won three of its six tournament games by thirty points. Arkansas–Little Rock was the first to fall, 102–72. Then came Ohio State, 76–65.

And in the game that proved to be the surprise of the entire tournament, the Rebels literally slipped by unheralded Ball State, 69–67. The Cardinals' Paris McCurdy, with the ball and a chance to tie the game, slipped on his drive to the basket, turning the ball over. After the game, several Cardinal players exchanged words and a few shoves with some of the Rebels. "Coach Tark yelled at all the guys involved," Rice said. "He said, 'I never want to see you participate in something like that again. We're one game from the Final Four. That behavior is not only unnecessary, it reflects poorly on all of us. Let's enjoy the fact we're one game from the Final Four. Let's show class.'"

In the West Regional final, Loyola Marymount, which had dedicated its tournament to its late star forward Hank Gathers, became the next bump on the Rebels' road to Denver and the Final Four. Golden Nugget Corporation chairman and Mirage Hotel and casino owner Steve Wynn asked Tarkanian for the opportunity to address the team before the game. Concerned about the scuffle after the Ball State game, Wynn told the players they were "ambassadors" for Las Vegas and needed to "be good sports. Try this on. What would happen if you go out there and shake hands and say good luck, and in doing so, they could look in your eyes and know you've already won the battle."

"I always considered Steve and Elaine Wynn to be friends," Tarkanian said of his decision to give Wynn, who was also one of Maxson's biggest supporters, a prized speaking spot before the team. "They helped our program in many ways and were great supporters. A great many of our former players are working for Steve and have made a home in Las Vegas because of their support. It was the first time I had ever let anyone other than our coaches talk to the team. I thought he gave one of the most inspirational talks I have ever heard."

The players said they were baffled by Wynn's message. They weren't baffled, though, by their mission. UNLV won convincingly, 131–101. On the night before the Loyola game, Augmon's father, who had not seen his son since childhood, showed up at the hotel. The two stood in Augmon's room and cried. Augmon found his father a ticket, then went out and put on a show for him, scoring thirty-three points on his way to being named the West Regional's Most Valuable Player.

Finally, there were only four teams left. Georgia Tech threw a scare at the Rebels, leading at the half, before UNLV's defense shut down the Yellow Jackets, 90–81. The only team that stood between this team and history was Duke. This was good versus evil. The Choir Boys versus The Bad Boys. Isaac Newton versus Wayne Newton.

By the time they got to Denver, there was no doubt in the players' minds that they were being betrayed by their own university. When President Maxson asked for the opportunity to speak to the team before the game, the players told Tarkanian they'd walk out. Tarkanian gracefully asked the president to share his thoughts at the team's game-day breakfast. When the coaches finally allowed Maxson in the meal room, only a couple of players remained.

"I tried to smooth things over and asked if he could come in and speak while they were having breakfast," Tarkanian said. "The players felt very strong about this. It was like he would knock them while he could, never coming out and publicly supporting them, but once the national championship came, he tried to be friendly. They didn't want any part of it."

"We had no use for whatever he wanted to say," Anthony said. "We had to keep positive. There was nothing he could do that was positive."

Us against Them started to take on new proportions. No longer did these Rebels see themselves simply fighting the media. Or the NCAA. Now the war was at home.

Maxson was replaced on the pregame speaking circuit by Chicago Bears great Walter Payton.

"It was so great to have a guy that had already made it, a guy that we all want to be like, come in and tell us he was a fan of *ours*," Rice said. "Then he told us he'd admire us whether we won or lost. He enjoyed us for being us. His was unconditional support. It was so different than what we'd been feeling about the administration and the NCAA and everything else that it really fired us up."

After the championship game, Rothermel scrambled to put together a welcome-home celebration for the team at the Thomas & Mack Arena. "I had planned to have the players take the stage while the arena was dark, then have the lights come up on them," Rothermel said. "But he [Maxson] threw that plan away. He decided he wanted to lead the team onto the stage, which he did. He held his hands high, flashing victory signs. Wasn't this the same man that just two months earlier had written a letter to Utah State saying these players didn't represent the rest of the university?"

A day after the parade, the Faculty Senate—the same Faculty Senate that voted to censure the players after the Utah State game—passed a resolution praising the team. "The win is a tribute to the talent, dedication and hard work of our players and coaches," the resolution said.

These ironies weren't lost on the players.

"He [Maxson] walked out ahead of all of us and I guess he thought he was the star," Augmon said "I wasn't happy with him standing up there saying 'I'm so proud of these children.' It just reminded me of what he said after the Utah State game. But I know how he is, so I just do the same thing to him. I just shake his hand and smile, knowing deep down inside I don't trust him. I just gave him a fake smile and a fake handshake and went on about my business. We were the champions and he couldn't take it away."

"I was so proud of those guys for being able to put all of that aside," Tarkanian mused after the championship game. "Just think how many games we would have won without all this adversity."

"I think if you look at all we endured, it really dispels the myth that the media tried to paint about that team," said Rice, who became UNLV basketball's second Rhodes scholar candidate. "They tried to say we had no character, that this wasn't a group of great guys. This team's talent was exceeded by its character. But any group of guys without character would have folded two seasons ago. Instead, we received pressure from the NCAA, the media, the administration and because of the kind of people we are, we were able to draw closer and be even more successful. We probably ought to send thank-you notes to the NCAA and all those people who said negative things. They helped us win the national championship."

NCAA suspensions. Fisticuffs. Injuries. Media scrutiny. Criticism from their own university. For one Monday night in Denver, none of it seemed to matter.

3

The Agony of Defeat

July 20. Jerry Tarkanian uses the date as a moment in history much as others use December 7. For three months and eighteen days, his UNLV team had basked in the glory. National champions. As more than one of his players had said, no one could take that away from them. Better still, Rebel stars Larry Johnson and Stacey Augmon had passed up lucrative contracts to play in the NBA and an offer to play together for $1 million apiece in Italy. All for the opportunity to make history. They wanted to go undefeated, repeat as national champions, do all the things you're not supposed to do in this day of college basketball parity.

"That was one of my proudest moments in coaching," said Tarkanian, who also turned down two deals that summer which would have landed him in the NBA. "For years, people have talked sarcastically about how UNLV players are getting paid too much to leave school. Larry and Stacey's decision shows how untrue that is. Those guys would have made millions in the NBA. But they wanted to come back to be part of the team. That showed so much loyalty."

It seemed the only team with a chance at beating them would have to start the NCAA's David Berst at shooting guard. On July 20, that team showed up. The dream of back-to-back championships—a feat that had not been accomplished since UCLA captured the last of its seven consecutive titles in 1973—was taken away before the first fast-break basket of the year.

In a decision resolving his thirteen-year legal tug-of-war with Berst and the NCAA, the organization Tarkanian once compared to the Third Reich, had blitzkrieged Las Vegas. The NCAA's Committee on Infractions announced Tarkanian's squad would have to sit out the 1991 tournament. Their shot at history was now a blank.

Tarkanian's lawsuit stemmed from the NCAA's 1977 order that he be suspended as UNLV's basketball coach for alleged rules violations. The university complied with the NCAA's demand and fired its coach. Tarkanian sued the university, claiming it could not dump him based on the NCAA's investigation because the organization had violated his due process rights. As a state employee, Tarkanian argued that the NCAA—if it ordered his suspension—was a "state actor" and had to treat him as the state would. A Nevada state court agreed that the NCAA was a state actor and had violated Tarkanian's rights. It granted a restraining order to Tarkanian, keeping the university from taking his job. The NCAA appealed the decision all the way to the U.S. Supreme Court, which agreed that Tarkanian's rights had been violated, but ruled in the NCAA's favor on the question of its role as a state actor. But the Supreme Court also let stand Tarkanian's restraining order against the university, keeping it from carrying out the NCAA's ordered suspension of the coach. So, in 1990, thirteen years after the NCAA demanded that UNLV suspend its coach, the NCAA decided UNLV's team should face additional penalties because Tarkanian's court order had kept the university from meting out his portion of the penalty. To get at Tarkanian, the NCAA decided that his fabulously talented team should be denied the opportunity to play for a second national championship.

It was July 20.

The decision brought national criticism the NCAA's way. It also sent shock waves through Las Vegas. Tarkanian's son, Danny, a one time Rebel point guard who now was a Las Vegas lawyer, had gone with his father to discuss the final outcome of the court case with the NCAA. Just before noon on July 20, Danny called his mother at home for a little advance notice on the NCAA's decision, which was to be announced at a press conference minutes later. When Lois Tarkanian told her son the team was being banned from the 1991 tournament, he almost blacked out.

"I had been there when the Infractions Committee had debated what penalty to give us," Danny Tarkanian said. "I thought we might lose some scholarships, maybe have some limits on recruiting. But I never thought there was a chance they'd do something like that. I thought my mom was joking. I said, 'C'mon. What are they really going to do.' She said the same thing. I couldn't believe it. When we met with the Infractions Committee, [SEC Commissioner Roy] Kramer put his arm around my dad and said, 'Don't worry, you'll be all right.'"

Almost immediately, Tarkanian's world began crumbling around him. First, the Las Vegas community, which had served as Tarkanian's power base during his long-running feud with the NCAA, showed signs it had grown tired of his crusade. In the past, the community had stood firmly behind Tarkanian. But this time, a television poll showed an overwhelming number of Las Vegans believed Tarkanian should step down for the year, separating his talented squad's future from his personal battle. "That was something I had volunteered to do anyway," he said. "So I agreed with them." Then, a poorly planned rally—not sponsored by Tarkanian—to show community support for the persecuted coach drew only twelve people. The *Review-Journal* questioned whether Tarkanian's support was waning.

"I never felt like the community wasn't behind me," Tarkanian said. "I was willing to sit out the tournament and told everyone that."

Tarkanian was offended that some in Las Vegas were using the NCAA's decision against him. How could they not see that this was further proof of what Tarkanian had fought so long and hard to prove—that the NCAA was vindictive, unfair, and had it in for UNLV and him? The question roared through his mind over and over.

Tarkanian immediately called President Maxson and counsel Brad Booke with an offer. "Let's face it," Tarkanian said. "The NCAA isn't after Stacey Augmon and Larry Johnson. The NCAA is after me. I'll step aside. I won't coach in the tournament. They've got to let the team back in." The coach even offered to give up his contractually guaranteed share—10 percent—of any postseason moneys earned by the basketball team.

Maxson and Booke agreed the offer might satisfy the NCAA's hunger. They told Tarkanian, though, that the offer shouldn't become public knowledge until after it had been made to the NCAA. It made sense, so Tarkanian agreed to keep quiet.

But Booke betrayed the agreement a few weeks later, Tarkanian said, twisting the story by telling reporters that the university was contemplating asking Tarkanian to step aside. "He made it sound like the university was making the offer and it would punish me," Tarkanian said. "That wasn't the deal at all." At his son's insistence, Tarkanian called a press conference to set the record straight. This was his offer, not the university's.

Within an hour, Tarkanian's longtime assistant, Tim Grgurich, announced that if Tarkanian didn't coach in the tournament, he wouldn't either. Later that day, team members huddled. They decided that UNLV basketball had become a family affair and they weren't going anywhere without their "father."

"We met with Coach Tark yesterday," the team wrote in a letter signed by each player. "We appreciate what the coach said, but we don't feel what's happening is fair or justified. After talking to our lawyer, Steve Stein, we would like to say the following:

"We are a team. We are a close team, but more so, we are a family. Coach Tark is not only part of our family, he is the head of our family. He is like a father to all of us. We do respect Coach Tark's feelings and his decision. However, we urge the NCAA to allow our family to remain whole and compete for the National Championship. Our family went through a lengthy and difficult time together by the NCAA last year. Each of us was interviewed several times by investigators from the NCAA. We know of no wrongdoing by us, the coaches or the university. Our family came to play. We want to play. Let us play together!"

Greg Anthony told his mates during a private meeting that the team's goal now would have to be to go 30–0, stay undefeated through the regular season, making that year's national championship a farce. "They can never take being undefeated away from us," Anthony told the team.

"Coach was showing his loyalty to us by offering to sit out,"

Anthony said later. "We wanted to show him the same respect. We came here to play for him. It wouldn't be right if it were any other way."

Loyalty. There's that word again.

The fallout continued when the two greatest high school recruits ever to commit to UNLV—California stars Ed O'Bannon and Shon Tarver—decided to back out of their oral commitment. Worse, they didn't just decide *not* to play for UNLV. They decided to play *for* Tarkanian's most hated rival—UCLA coach Jim Harrick. Tarkanian, aware that the pending NCAA investigation had made life in Las Vegas a little precarious, had encouraged the two men not to sign a letter of intent, allowing them to transfer without sitting out a year.

UCLA was the school Tarkanian long ago had claimed was cheating while the NCAA looked the other way. And Harrick, the Bruin coach who inherited this windfall of talent, had, as a high school coach in 1973, complained to David Berst that Tarkanian had broken rules to sign forward Jackie Robinson. Harrick had coached Robinson at Morningside [California] High and had hoped to take him to Utah State, where Harrick would be an assistant coach the next year. "He [Robinson] and I were going to make a decision about his college choice for three years," Harrick told Berst in a telephone conversation Berst secretly tape-recorded. "All of a sudden, I'm out of it. I hope you don't think I'm bitter. I'm really not."

Later that same year, Robinson signed an affidavit claiming that Harrick suggested to Robinson that he concoct allegations against Tarkanian, thereby nullifying his commitment to UNLV. "He [Harrick] said I could still go to Utah State," Robinson swore in his statement. "[He said] 'Just tell that man from the NCAA that Tarkanian gave you $5 or something like that.' He shows me a letter of intent filled out for Utah State and he said, 'Sign this and we can have [NCAA investigator Lester Burks] take care of the rest.'" Robinson refused Harrick's request and went on to star at UNLV. Although Harrick lost that recruiting battle and his allegations never stuck, his attempts to help the NCAA take down Tarkanian finally paid off in 1990. The addition of UNLV's lost recruits, O'Bannon and Tarver, allowed Harrick, a notoriously average recruiter, to claim one of the nation's best recruiting classes.

Although O'Bannon and Tarver abandoned UNLV, none of the

school's stars of the moment did. Because the NCAA ban would keep the team from competing in the tournament for one year, all of the team's seniors were given the option by the NCAA of transferring to another school and playing immediately. Both Johnson and Augmon received calls from more than a dozen schools.

"I was back here at home," Augmon remembers of the moment he heard the news his Rebels couldn't repeat. "I called Larry and asked him what are we going to do. When the draft question came up, we said we were going to stick it out with Coach. Now other coaches, they were like vultures, they said we could transfer. I knew what I was going to do. But I wanted to know what he was going to do. When I asked him, he'd say, 'What are you going to do?' We kept going back and forth. We started laughing at one point. Then I said I'm going to stay with Coach. It was a while before we contacted Coach because we knew he didn't want to influence us about going or staying. You know Coach would never make a decision for a player. He feels it's our life and he didn't want us to stay and regret it."

Johnson and Augmon, like their teammates, decided to set their sights a little higher. Rather than playing for the national championship, they would play this season for themselves.

While news of the NCAA's decision was dominating the headlines, a move of equal significance was taking place down the hall from the UNLV basketball office. Athletic Director Brad Rothermel, a longtime Tarkanian ally, decided Maxson's subtle attacks on the athletic program weren't worth dealing with anymore. The pressure finally forced him to announce his resignation as athletic director. As his replacement, Maxson tabbed Dennis Finfrock, a former UNLV wrestling coach who had been director of the Thomas & Mack Arena since its opening in 1983. Finfrock's relationship with and opinion of Tarkanian were 180 degrees opposite those held by Rothermel. Several people who worked with Finfrock through the years said he made little attempt to conceal his contempt for Tarkanian, regularly suggesting the university would be better off without him.

Suddenly, the darts being hurled at Tarkanian weren't just coming from the NCAA. Or the president's office. They were coming from his own athletic director. The foxhole suddenly got smaller.

Within a week of his selection, Finfrock called Tarkanian into his office and, in a request that the coach will never forget, suggested he resign. "You can be a hero," Finfrock told him. "If you step down, we'll get back in the tournament and everyone will believe you did it for the kids."

Stunned, Tarkanian responded by letter. "I was very disappointed that you would even entertain any thoughts of my stepping aside to be a hero," he wrote on September 6, 1990. "After our discussion, it became quite obvious that you had thoughts in that direction and have completely missed what all the action has been about. I was under the impression that you were totally behind our program and I would have your full support as you earlier had personally indicated to me. I want to make this very clear. In 1977, there was not one single scrap of documented evidence against me during the NCAA hearings. I went to court and exercised my rights as any other American citizen would have done. I fought a 13-year legal battle at great expense with the heavy emotional pressures upon my family. I have never wanted to fight the NCAA, but feel I became involved in what is now far more than a job; it is a moral responsibility to all coaches and athletes who will follow. It would have been so easy to leave for the Lakers and have far more money and what many consider more prestige. It would have been so easy many times, including this year, to accept offers made to me. I stayed because I felt it was the morally right thing to do. It was very disturbing to have anyone suggest I give up now."

"I felt like we were good enough friends I could do that," Finfrock said later when he was asked about the meeting. "I told him there were problems and more problems that were going to be coming, you know, every time we turned around. I was trying to warn him, basically, that there were a lot of problems. Every time we turned around, there was some other impropriety or some other irregularity."

"Friends?" Tarkanian asked rhetorically when he heard Finfrock's quote. "I've never liked him. I've never trusted him."

"Dennis does not describe that incident accurately," said Lois Tarkanian. "He asked me to come into his office before Jerry entered. In fact, Jerry went to his office looking for me.

"The first thing Dennis said after I sat down was 'I know you didn't want me to be athletic director.' We said a few words and then I told him the thing that concerned me was that he was not humanistic and I felt that quality was necessary in interacting and leading others.

"He then suggested to me that Jerry should step down as coach. 'He could be a hero,' Dennis said. 'You don't understand,' I told him. 'I don't think Jerry should do that at a time when the players have showed such commitment to stay.'

"'Do you really think,' he said, 'that the NCAA will ever leave UNLV alone as long as Jerry is here? I know they haven't been right in many of the things they've done, but we have to live with them.' And so it went. I remember at one point when I protested, he stated, 'And I've got lots of powerful friends too.' If that didn't sound like a threat, what would?

"Then Jerry came into the office. I told him that Dennis thought it would be best if he stepped down and he could be a hero. Jerry at first seemed surprised and then angry. Dennis then backed off the point.

"I think Dennis brought up the subject to me because he knew I wanted Jerry to leave college coaching. He obviously knew I wasn't his friend, since he knew I didn't feel he was the best selection for athletic director. I later conveyed Dennis's comments to Brad Booke. His answer was interesting: 'I've never heard him say that.' Nothing about not hearing Maxson say it, or even anything about it not being the thing to say. It was obvious to me that Maxson, Dennis's and Booke's direct superior, had begun his final moves to have Jerry gone.

"Fortunately, I conveyed Dennis's comments to others besides Booke, or the two of them might now claim they never said them. It was the beginning of the big trade, the Tark for NCAA respectability. What was morally right didn't seem to enter Dennis's mind."

The flame of optimism that had allowed Tarkanian to maintain his combative spirit flickered on July 20. Finfrock's words nearly snuffed it out. Tarkanian turned his back on Finfrock and walked out. He kept going until he arrived at the family's condo in San Diego. It was time to put all of this aside and relax. It was time to put together one more of those I'll-show-you kind of seasons. But, hard as he tried, Tarkanian couldn't get his mind into the upcoming year. He couldn't force himself to sit down and think basketball. For years, he had spent summers at the beach, drawing Xs and Os in the sand, diagraming play after play as the tide washed each one away. This summer, there was no such energy.

"I've got to get my head into the season," Tarkanian told a reporter just days before practice was to begin. "This is the first time I've come into a season without having everything pretty well formulated in my mind. I just can't get into it yet. This has all taken so much out of me."

The summer's dizzying events made the opening of school— normally one of the craziest periods around the basketball office—a welcome respite. Each fall, the entire basketball team enrolls in a conditioning class that allows coaches to begin working them into shape. On the first day of class, Las Vegas attorneys Steve Stein and Alan Jones met the players in the practice gym for a short pep talk.

"We're going to work things out," Stein told the players. "You leave the legal winning to us. You go out and win on the court. We'll get you in the tournament."

"These guys are being ridiculously optimistic," David Rice wrote in his journal. "I wonder if they'd try to put a line like that on the players at Duke, and if so, I wonder if the Duke players would believe it? One of the guys said the meeting was 'a white man's dream.' A bunch of guys who couldn't play basketball coming in and deluding us into believing that we'd be in the tournament."

Already, Stein, his partner David Chesnoff, and several other lawyers had developed a legal strategy that they believed would force the NCAA to allow UNLV to defend its title. Chesnoff said that Johnson and Augmon had rejected the cash being thrown at their feet by the NBA because they had been told there was no way the NCAA would keep the team out of the tournament. The lawyers pointed to words spoken by former Committee on Infractions chairman Charles Alan Wright in testimony before a U.S. House of Representatives subcommittee in 1977.

When asked by Representative Bob Eckert of Texas whether additional penalties should be imposed on UNLV because a court order precluded suspension of the coach, Wright told the committee: "I would think it would be utterly outrageous if in that circumstance the council were to say, 'Well, inasmuch as the penalty against Coach Tarkanian has fallen, we have to do something else against the University of Nevada at Las Vegas.'"

"I remember sharing those words with Stacey and Larry," Chesnoff said. "I think they've got a great lawsuit against the NCAA here. It looks to me like they made a business decision on the good faith that the NCAA wouldn't lie." The lawyers presented UNLV with a case on behalf of Johnson and Augmon that a number of legal theorists said the players could not lose. Because they had been counseled that the NCAA would not make a decision contrary to its own former Infractions Committee chairman, Augmon and Johnson spurned the NBA. To ban them now could leave the university and the NCAA open for a lawsuit claiming millions in lost wages. Or so the theory went.

In fact, the opposite was true. Both Augmon and Johnson had repeatedly been warned that there was a chance they wouldn't be able to play in the 1991 tournament because of the Lloyd Daniels investigation. They returned to UNLV, both players agreed, "because we're having fun and it was the right thing to do."

Still, it sounded like a good case and the lawyers believed it would work.

Though some of the team members had little faith in the strategy, they played along. And they did their part. From the day practice began, Tarkanian could see this was a group that was even better than the championship team of the year before. Gone were starting center David Butler and sixth man Moses Scurry. But in their place, Tarkanian would have 6'9" George Ackles at center with 7' Elmore Spencer and 6'10" Melvin Love as backups. As talented as Butler and Scurry were, their replacements showed even more potential. The Rebels were number one, and, as the commercial says, they were built to stay that way.

It appeared UNLV would pick up right where it left off—both on the court and off it—from the championship year. Spencer and Love were declared academically ineligible for the first semester and couldn't join the team until December. And Ackles still had to serve his one-game suspension from the hotel bill investigation of the year before.

Then Augmon's onetime girlfriend pressed assault charges against the star, claiming he struck her at a UNLV football game. Augmon told coaches the former girlfriend had tried to kiss him in front of his girlfriend of the moment and he simply pushed her away. A week later, the *Los Angeles Times* reported that Augmon had tested positive for steroid use while he was a member of the 1988 U.S. Olympic team. The story, it was later proved, was wildly off base. Chris Jeter was injured in a car accident. The university announced it was investigating how Jeter got tickets to the heavyweight championship fight between Buster Douglas and Evander Holyfield. To cap it all off, Big West Conference commissioner Jim Haney called the NCAA after *Sports Illustrated* ran a cover photo of Augmon and Johnson wearing designer clothes lent to them by the magazine. Because the suppliers of the clothes were credited in the magazine, Haney asked the NCAA if the two players had not violated rules prohibiting commercial endorsements by college athletes. The NCAA originally decided the two men were in violation and suspended them. A day later the suspension was overruled.

After two months of negative publicity—and much thought to the validity of a lawsuit filed by the players—the NCAA agreed to consider other penalty options in exchange for allowing UNLV to defend its title. The legal threat had worked. Tarkanian, Maxson, Booke, and Danny Tarkanian were summoned to Chicago for another meeting with the Infractions Committee. There, the UNLV contingent made four alternative penalty offers, each of which was to be considered exclusive of the others:

• The team would sit out the 1992 tournament.
• Tarkanian would not coach in either the 1991 or 1992 tournaments.
• Tarkanian would sit out the 1991 tournament, forfeit his part of the team's revenues, and be suspended from recruiting for one year, and the basketball program would accept a reduced number of official visits by recruits.
• Loss of network television for 1991–92, loss of scholarships in 1991–92, reduction in official visits in 1991–92, and no off-campus recruiting by the basketball staff for one year.

Again, UNLV's representatives left optimistic. The committee promised to give them an answer in the next few weeks.

On November 19, the eve of the team's season opener, the word came out of Kansas City—UNLV could defend its title, but would be banned from the 1992 tournament and would be kept off live television in 1991–92. The elation was muffled only by the fact the committee had done precisely as UNLV had asked it not to and had combined two of the offered alternatives. "I felt like they put a bullet to our head and told us we could choose which chamber would fire," Tarkanian said. "We took the lesser of two evils and neither one of them was right."

Still, it was the closest thing to good news that Tarkanian had received since ... July 20.

"We had a great practice that day," David Rice remembered. "LJ [Johnson] came into the locker room singing. Augmon was in a great mood. Everyone was dancing in the locker room like shackles had been broken."

With a sigh of relief, the season began. Quickly, UNLV refreshed the memories of those who might have forgotten how awesome this team could be, blowing out the University of Alabama-Birmingham, 109–68.

Just as quickly, the schism between the basketball program and Finfrock, the new athletic director, began to widen. Finfrock had made it plain that there was a new sheriff in town and that he would be watching Tarkanian and his program with an eagle eye. It didn't take long for Tarkanian to realize how serious Finfrock was.

After UNLV's second game, a fifty-point drubbing of the University of Nevada-Reno, Tarkanian was quoted in the local newspaper as saying, "They [UNR] were saying they were as good as we were; it was the damnedest thing. So we went and bought a bunch of papers and passed them out. We didn't have to get them fired up after that." Finfrock's staff clipped the quote and sent it to the NCAA. Shortly thereafter, Tarkanian received a memo from Jaina Preston, UNLV's compliance officer, informing him that "with regard to a quote attributed to you in the local newspaper, please be aware of a recent NCAA related interpretation which considers the purchase and distribution of newspapers to student-athletes by the coaching staff an 'extra benefit' under NCAA bylaws."

The pettiness of the NCAA now had taken hold within his own athletic department.

The Rebels' third game, a road trip to Michigan State for a nationally televised game, was UNLV's first chance to test its talent against Top 20 competition. There were a lot of questions the nation's sportswriters and basketball fans wanted answered. Had all the emotion of the team's troubles taken any toll on the players? Could the Duke game have been a fluke? Was UNLV so dominant that everyone else would be left playing for second place? By game's end, the answers were clear. UNLV 95, Michigan State 75. And the Spartans were lucky it was that close.

UNLV was so good that most opponents found themselves playing for a notch in that third column—"moral victories." Even then, most weren't successful. The Rebels beat Princeton by 34. Florida State by 32. Fullerton by 31 and 21. San Jose State by 32 and 22. Utah State by 31 and 43. Irvine by 41 and 28. Long Beach by 51 and 47. Rutgers by 42. Fresno State by 49. Santa Barbara by 27 and 28. UNLV was beating its opponents by an average of 35 points per game, well over UCLA's record of 30.3 set in 1973.

"I tell you what," Tarkanian said early in the year. "I've liked the way the games are going. I've hardly even used my towel all season. My brother even said to me, 'I've never seen you talk to friends and smile before the games like that. You used to be a basket case.'"

During a ceremony before the Princeton game, UNLV's first at home, a large red banner was unfurled and lowered from the rafters at the Thomas & Mack: "UNLV National Champions 1990." Out of respect for Tarkanian's hatred for the organization, the NCAA's initials appeared nowhere on the banner. Tarkanian said he was not pleased the initials had been left off. He wanted the world to know he had won the NCAA tournament. UNLV officials were so confident this was just the first of back-to-back championships that the banner was hung slightly off center in the arena. No sense having to move it when the second one was strung up.

"It was a great night for UNLV basketball," Tarkanian said.

It was followed by one of UNLV's worst days. A package from the NCAA arrived that next day spelling out the particulars of the organization's four-year investigation into the recruitment of schoolboy star Lloyd Daniels. Twenty-nine allegations of NCAA rules violations were included in the official letter of inquiry, or OI. Two of those allegations named Tarkanian directly. Once again, the NCAA managed to rain on Tarkanian's parade.

For Lois Tarkanian, the combination of another NCAA battle and a series of internal attacks that already had begun seemed too much to handle. "After the OI came from the NCAA, I started to see it all clearly," Lois said. "As early as October, I told Jerry, 'I understand you stayed this year because the kids came back. I don't care what you do with this program next year, but I will have nothing to do with it because you have people here at this university who are not good human beings.' I said, 'Jerry, they're going to slice you up, piece by piece. And I can't stand watching it.'"

The news went from bad to worse. Two weeks later, the *Los Angeles Times* reported that NCAA's sources said the fresh set of charges, if proven, could cost UNLV its 1990 title. Among the allegations was an accusation that Barry Young, a seldom used reserve on the championship team, had been provided tutoring during the summer before he enrolled at UNLV. If true, that would be a violation and Young would have been ineligible to compete. Because Young had played late in the blowout of Duke, scoring five points, his presence on the floor could allow the NCAA to ask for its trophy back.

Incredibly, the team managed to deal with all these goings-on without missing a beat. The winning streak kept getting longer, the point spread wider. The starting five often found themselves on the bench early in the second half, posing a problem most coaches would willingly deal with. Midway through the year, Grgurich told Tarkanian he was concerned that the starters weren't getting enough playing time. "We ask them to go all out in practice, then sit them down early in the game," the assistant said. But Tarkanian had no desire to beat teams by margins greater than those already being put up. Despite the huge disparity in scores, most coaches had thanked Tarkanian for "not running it up."

UNLV was 19–0 and riding a thirty-game winning streak that dated back nearly twelve months. Some sportswriters, while acknowledging UNLV's talent, had, however, discounted many of those wins as victories over patsies from the Big West. As good as they were, it seemed the Rebels still had more to prove.

Bring on Arkansas. The once beaten Razorbacks, with three surefire NBA players, a stifling defense, and a deep bench, were ranked second in the nation. UNLV was first. If anyone had the talent, team speed, and conditioning to run with the Rebels, this was the group. The game would be played in Fayetteville's Barnhill Arena, giving the Hogs a little extra advantage. It was called the biggest regular season college basketball game since Lew Alcindor faced Elvin Hayes in that memorable Houston-UCLA game two decades earlier, and students had camped outside the arena for a week to insure themselves the best seats. The game received more hype than the Super Bowl, drawing more than 270 reporters from as far away as Japan.

Not only was the 9,640-seat arena sold out, Arkansas had decided to provide UNLV with only 59 seats for the game rather than the 200 seats that had been promised. And even those weren't very good. This became the toughest ticket in Arkansas history. The snub left many Rebel boosters without tickets.

Embroiled in another controversy, this time over how he doled out the 223 home season tickets that were part of his employment contract with the university, Tarkanian told several of his close friends—including Lorimar Productions founder Irwin Molasky, restaurateur Freddie Glusman, and casino host Mike Toney—that he couldn't come through with good seats for the game. The few tickets given to UNLV were being handled by Finfrock, and he had made it clear he wasn't going to provide them to Molasky, Glusman, and Toney, whom he had collectively referred to as "Tark's cronies." So the three went through CBS, which was televising the game, and had an extra row of seats installed behind the team bench. Their ingenuity, though funny at the time, proved to be another nail in Tarkanian's coffin. Even though Tarkanian had nothing to do with securing the seats, it helped further the image that Tarkanian's program was too influenced by and directly tied to outsiders. That was precisely the image Finfrock and Maxson had been using against the coach.

Adding fuel to the fire, Glusman approached Finfrock the night before the game in the hotel bar and promised the athletic director, "No matter where you're sitting, I guarantee you we'll have better seats." Infuriated, Finfrock stormed from the bar.

As the two teams took the court the next day for pregame warm-ups, a nervous Tarkanian stood, palms sweating, at courtside watching his players. He already was playing the game out in his mind and was deep in thought when he heard a familiar voice screaming his name behind him. As he turned, a red-faced Finfrock was racing toward him.

"Where in the hell did they get those tickets," Finfrock yelled, pointing to Molasky and Glusman. "I don't know, why don't you ask them," Tarkanian responded.

"What am I going to tell Cashman and Smith who are sitting with me way up there?" Finfrock said, referring to car dealer Jim Cashman and *Review-Journal* executive Fred Smith, whose company plane Finfrock had ridden to the Arkansas game.

"Tell them to get to be closer friends with Irwin," Tarkanian responded.

"Here we were getting ready to play the biggest game of our lives and he was yelling at me about tickets," Tarkanian said later. "I couldn't believe it."

Glusman and Toney also had gotten to know several officials in the Arkansas athletic department and, through that relationship, had been able to get locker room passes for UNLV's side of the arena. "Freddie handed me a pass and gave one to Walter Payton, who had come to the game with us, too," Danny Tarkanian said. "And we all went down to the locker room. I go in and the door closes behind me and I guess it closed right on Finfrock. He was trying to get in and the security guard grabbed him and asked him if he had a pass. Finfrock said, 'I don't have a pass, but I'm athletic director.' Right then, Freddie goes, 'Excuse me, excuse me,' and he shows his pass and walks right past Finfrock. Finfrock was livid. He went absolutely nuts."

The timing of Finfrock's pregame tirade confirmed for Tarkanian that the interim athletic director had little regard for the pressure Tarkanian and his team were under. "We were trying so hard to prove that we were above all the bickering," Tarkanian said. "We were trying to prove we were better than that."

They also proved to be better than Arkansas. A lot better. The game lived up to its hype for a while as the Razorbacks used a 10–0 run to lead by six midway through the first half. The Arkansas advantage was cut to four, 50–46, by halftime, and the Razorbacks' rabid fans—some of whom had awakened Augmon and Johnson the night before by calling their room to squeal "soooooweee" over the telephone—were in Hog heaven.

UNLV silenced the home crowd, though, by coming out of the locker room and taking off on a 16–2 scoring spree, putting the Rebels up by ten. The lead eventually mushroomed to twenty-three before Tarkanian slowed the high-octane offense down, allowing Arkansas to close the final gap to 112–105.

The debate now became not whether the Rebels were the best team that season but whether they were the best of all seasons. Was this team—with great balance, undeniable self-knowledge, unselfish ball movement, and ferocious defense—better than San Francisco in '56? UCLA in '68? Indiana in '76? "You'll never hear me talk about that," Tarkanian said, giving the obligatory response to the inevitable question.

Once Arkansas had fallen, the biggest challenge facing these Rebels was not off-court distractions, as it was in the 1989–90 season, it was focus. During the championship year, no one expected them to win. In 1990–91, no one expected them to lose.

"A lot of our senior year, Coach didn't do a lot of coaching during practice," Augmon said. "We were already there. We knew the program. We knew the system. We knew what Tark wanted and expected from us. Each and every one of us had accepted our role by then. Coach's biggest worry was keeping us focused, coming out and playing hard every night. This last year with us, his greatest job was trying to inspire us to go out and play hard every night. We were losing intensity, but we were still winning by twenty or twenty-five points. I guess we started getting kind of bored out there. It's kind of hard to say, but the level of competition wasn't at our level. We didn't have to play our hardest with some teams and still beat them by twenty-five points. Coach wasn't happy at all. But we would say in our minds, 'Look, Coach, we beat them by twenty-five points.' That wasn't right. To make up for it, Coach would try and hype the teams we were playing. After a while we just turned that off. We've been around. We've watched a lot of TV. We know the teams just as much as Coach knows the teams. So he would hype a player up, and we would know the player. We would have already played with him in the summer leagues or somewhere at the World Games. And he would pump this player so high that me and Larry would say, 'Come on, Coach.' Then he'd start laughing. All the coaching was done 'cause he had us clicking well. He had us running the right things at the right times. We were making the right decisions during the games. So his hardest part was keeping us motivated."

Only one real challenge—a date at November 25 New Mexico State—remained during the regular season. Before the game, Tarkanian worried that his team might be taking the game too lightly. He watched in a pregame shoot-around and saw that none of the players were talking. "On the bus on the way to the game, I asked Larry [Johnson] if we were ready," Tarkanian said. "He said, 'Yep, Coach. We're ready." Enough said. UNLV led by as many as twenty-nine before settling in for an 86–74 win, matching the score of the teams' earlier meeting that season.

ESPN commentator Dick Vitale announced during the telecast of the game in Las Cruces, New Mexico, that sources inside the NCAA had informed him that four Rebels—including two starters—would soon be suspended as a result of "extra benefits" given them during their recruiting trips to UNLV. Sure enough, the NCAA announced two days later that Johnson, Ackles, and reserves Bobby Joyce and Everic Gray were declared ineligible because they had charged in-room movies, phone calls, and room service to their hotel rooms while on their official recruiting visits to Las Vegas. The total value of all these "excessive" benefits: $129. "It says in the rules you can entertain a recruit," Tarkanian said. "It also says you can feed a recruit. I don't see where ordering room service or watching a movie in his room is excessive or gives you a recruiting advantage."

An appeal by UNLV led to their immediate reinstatement. Tarkanian later discovered that it was UNLV, not the NCAA, that had initiated the call that led to the suspensions. University counsel Brad Booke admitted he had been responsible for the call, but said he was attempting to make sure none of the Rebel players had any NCAA problems before they began play in the NCAA tournament.

The constant harassment had Tarkanian talking about throwing in his now famous towel and heading to the NBA. On the same day as the NCAA suspensions, the *New York Times* reported that Tarkanian "was looking into coaching an unnamed NBA team."

"This is just one more form of harassment from the NCAA against our program," Tarkanian told the *Times*. "These are nice kids. They don't deserve it. I've had enough."

In pregame ceremonies at UNLV's final home game—the last

time the team's seniors would run baseline to baseline in the Thomas & Mack—Lois Tarkanian echoed her husband's sentiments. "No matter what happens, we'll always love you for making our time here special," Lois told the hushed fans in what sounded more like a farewell speech for her husband than for the seniors. Throughout the darkened arena, fans looked at each other trying to figure out what it was she meant by those rather omimous-sounding words. "It was my way of saying good-bye, because I did not intend to come back," Lois said.

Difficult as it is to imagine, Tarkanian had a problem as he began penciling in his starting lineup for this game against the University of California-Irvine Anteaters. Years ago, he had begun a tradition of starting all of his seniors in their last home game. But this year he had six seniors and didn't know which of them should open the game sitting on the bench. Finally, he approached Irvine coach Bill Mulligan with an idea. UNLV would start all six seniors and immediately take the technical foul for having too many players on the floor.

"As long as he wanted to give us the free throws," Mulligan said with a chuckle, "I was willing. Actually, I didn't even want to give the technical, but the refs said I had to. I thought it was kind of clever. But it proves how wary he was of us."

Tarkanian thought it was a clever idea, too. For a few minutes, he wondered if maybe he had been too clever. Irvine hit the free throws to lead 2–0 and before long the scoreboard read 6–1 and then 12–7, advantage Anteaters. "We were down 6–1, and I started thinking maybe I wasn't so smart," Tarkanian confessed. "What if we lose by two?"

It didn't take long for Tarkanian's worries to fade. Final score: UNLV 114, UC-Irvine 86.

Senior Greg Anthony almost didn't get the chance to join his teammates for their farewell blowout. Although he had begun the season by asking, and being granted, permission from the NCAA to renounce his scholarship so he could further his private business interests, the NCAA announced a change—make that a lack—of heart. Anthony, a Young Republican with political aspirations, had passed the exam for a realtor's license that summer and also had joined with three friends to form a fledgling sportswear and silkscreening company. His decision to turn down the $12,000-plus scholarship was featured in newspaper articles across the country as the epitome of entrepreneurship. But when CBS analyst Billy Packer told Anthony's story to a nationwide television audience, the NCAA stepped in and reversed its decision. It suspended Anthony and required him to sell his portion of the sportswear company and accept his scholarship before he could continue playing. "He [Anthony] cannot use his name, reputation or athletic skill to endorse a commercial product," the NCAA's Rick Evrard said. On the day before the UC-Irvine game, Anthony complied and was reinstated without missing any games.

What did the two most recent scrapes with the NCAA teach Tarkanian: "That the NCAA wants to make a billion dollars selling the television rights for people to watch these kids play, but they won't let these kids watch a $7 movie on Spectravision. And the NCAA doesn't want our players to get anything off of what they've achieved. At least not while the NCAA is getting rich off them."

UNLV ripped through its final three games and downed three opponents in the Big West Tournament by a combined seventy-two points. For the year, the Rebels were 30–0, having won by an average of 28.9 points. They had won thirty-three consecutive games at home, twenty-eight straight on the road. They had won each of that season's thirty games by at least twelve points and had led wire-to-wire in twelve games. In short, they dominated.

Undefeated, unchallenged, and unbelievably good, the Rebels had only to wait for the NCAA's pairings to figure out what road they would have to travel before landing in Indianapolis for their shot at a second national championship. Tarkanian, ever the pessimist, predicted that the NCAA would send his team to Rikers Island and Alcatraz for first and second round games. When the pairings were released, Tarkanian looked through the West bracket and saw potential games against Georgetown, underrated Utah, and an always tough Arizona team standing between UNLV and the Final Four. He quipped that his team was being sent on the Bataan Death March. It didn't turn out to be *that* bad, at least in the first round.

As part of a public service campaign, the Rebels agreed to wear "Buckle Up for Safety" T-shirts while warming up for their first tournament game, against Montana. The shirt may have been more of a warning to the other sixty-three teams than it was a plea for highway safety. Montana obviously wasn't strapped in tight enough as the Rebels sped by, through and around the over-matched Grizzlies, 99–65.

UNLV then faced Georgetown, the team Tarkanian said he feared most. With its Twin Towers of Dikembe Mutombo and Alon-zo Mourning, Georgetown had the potential to pound the ball down low. And UNLV had no one to stop them. Fortunately, the Hoyas were unsuccessful, losing 62–54. The Rebels, though, didn't play well, leaving many to wonder if the team was on cruise control and whether that was good enough to take it to the Promised Land.

In the third round game, with Utah, questions about the Rebels' intensity intensified. Even Tarkanian worried aloud that his team was not hitting on all cylinders. "We didn't have the degree of intensity for our man-to-man [defense]," Tarkanian said. "But we won by 17. Who's beaten Utah by 17? Who's beaten Utah at all?"

Anthony said afterward that the team's falloff could be traced to the last two weeks of the regular season. As the team entered the NCAA Tournament and began to sense the change, Anthony said he began feeling pressure that he hadn't felt in the past.

If anything had, in fact, fallen apart, it all seemed to come back together in the Regional final game with Seton Hall. In the second half of what was a close game, the Rebels ran away. Better still, they looked as dominating as ever in beating the Big East champion Pirates, 77–65. "We're back," Anthony proclaimed after the game.

On to Indianapolis and a rematch with Duke. "They have all the advantages," Tarkanian said to a skeptical media. "We have matchup problems with their big guy [Christian Laettner]. They have the motivation to make up for last year's game. [Duke guard Bobby] Hurley has something to prove. It's going to be tough. Really."

Like Augmon and his teammates, the media had grown tired of hearing Tarkanian's constant predictions of doom. After all, which team was riding a forty-five-game winning streak? Which team was being compared to the greatest of all time? Which team won last year's final by thirty? No one was taking Tarkanian seriously. Maybe that was the problem.

Before the game, UNLV practiced at North Central High School, not far from the team's hotel. "I don't know how to tell you to be ready," Tarkanian told the team. "I already have talked to you about the psychological advantage that Duke has. They know they can't lose worse than last year. They're going to play harder than anybody you've ever played."

From the opening tip, the evidence mounted that Tarkanian might be right. Grant Hill took off and hit a breakaway lay-up. Two-nothing Duke. At the four-minute mark, Duke led, 15–6. Duke coach Mike Krzyzewski had spent the previous week trying to convince his team that it really was capable of winning, despite the fact forty-five teams before them had failed miserably. At the end of the first four minutes, it seemed Duke's players believed Krzyzewski was right.

Duke's lead didn't last long. UNLV went on a 12–3 run to tie the score. But the tone was set, and it was very different from that of a year ago. UNLV took a 43–41 halftime lead. There was a silent confidence among the Rebel faithful. Other teams had kept it close for a half, only to be overwhelmed by one of those patented 18–0 scoring runs early in the second half. The only question at halftime was when the run would come.

It didn't. Laettner opened the second half with a basket and free throw to put Duke up. Then the two teams started trading baskets and leads. The longer the game went on, the more confident Duke became. And the more frazzled UNLV looked. Midway through the second half, Duke's Bill McCaffrey tackled Hunt on a breakaway lay-up. On the next possession, Augmon threw a retaliatory elbow and was hit with an intentional foul. A few minutes later, Hurley hit Hunt even harder as the UNLV guard drove for a lay-up. The two teams began arguing. Johnson got caught shoving a Duke player and was slapped with a technical. These were mistakes UNLV hadn't made all year. But worse mistakes were still to come.

With 3:51 left, Anthony drove the lane and scored a basket that appeared to put the Rebels up, 76–71. But Anthony was whistled for a charge, his fifth foul of the game. And the basket was waived off. For the first time all year, the guy with the keys to the Ferrari was sent to the bench and this high-performance machine was going to have to do it without him. Anthony gathered his teammates at center court, apologized, and told them he loved them. For the first time in thirteen months, that wasn't enough. Without Anthony, the Rebels scored only three points in the last four minutes.

At 2:14, Hurley hit a huge three-pointer, cutting the lead to 76–74. A confused UNLV team then pulled another first when Augmon casually dribbled the ball as the forty-five-second clock expired. In thirty-four games, the Rebels had never committed a shot clock violation. This was not the time to start. Duke came back and, with 1:02 remaining, Brian Davis hit a lay-up and was fouled. He hit the free throw, and, unbelievably, Duke led, 77–76.

Johnson was fouled while grabbing a rebound thirteen seconds later and stepped to the line where—after shooting 82 percent for the season—he missed both shots. Duke's Thomas Hill stepped in the lane on the second shot, giving Johnson another chance. He converted and the game was tied.

Duke decided to play for the last shot, running a modified four corners offense that sent every player looking for a backdoor lay-up. It looked as if Hill had found the shot, with fifteen seconds left. But he missed the short jump shot. Laettner rebounded and was fouled.

With 12.7 seconds remaining, he calmly stepped to the line and knocked them both down. Krzyzewski told his players not to allow Hunt the inbounds pass, forcing Johnson to bring the ball up. As bad as it looked, it still didn't look bad. The best player ever to wear a UNLV jersey had the ball and a handful of options. Johnson took the ball to the right side and, for a moment, was open for a three-pointer. Laettner came charging at him, so Johnson kicked the ball over to Hunt, who rushed a twenty-five-foot prayer that clanged off the back of the rim and into Hurley's hands.

Tarkanian often had bragged about Johnson's unselfishness, how he shared the limelight and the ball with his teammates. On this occasion, though, the coach wished Johnson had been a little more selfish.

For the game, UNLV's bench scored only three points. Augmon scored only six, on 3 for 10 shooting. Duke hit 52 percent of its field goals against a defense that had not allowed anyone to shoot better than 47 percent all year. And the team that had played and won so often suddenly appeared tentative, as if it were playing not to lose.

"A lot of our shots were not falling," Augmon said in an understatement. "Duke played well. Once we got behind, each one of us was trying to bring us back by ourself. Instead of the team concept of passing it around until we got the open shot we were coming down the court and we'd have one pass, then one of us would try to take it to the hole. Even myself, I caught myself trying to bring us back. Instead of trying to keep it as a team and pass it around. We had very few tight games like that. We choked."

As if they were in a daze, UNLV's players began stumbling into the locker room. Lois Tarkanian had talked to them all year about handling any loss with grace. It's just that no one believed that loss would come—especially at the Final Four. "I told them that if they didn't win the national championship, that didn't at all diminish all they had accomplished," Lois said. "I tried to prepare them for it because it was almost too good to be true. In the end, I think it helped."

While other coaches—Purdue's Gene Keady, Lou Henson of Illinois, and the membership of the Black Coaches Association—complained about the officiating, Tarkanian and his players did not. When pressed by the media to explain the loss, Anthony said, "We can sit here and make excuses all day, but the fact is we got outplayed. They deserved to win. No one can say they didn't earn it." And on their way to the locker room after the game, Augmon grabbed Hurley and wished him luck in the championship game. The Rebel response led Duke's Mike Krzyzewski to praise UNLV for the second year in a row. "Last year they won big, and did it without taunting, did it with class," Krzyzewski said. "This year, they lost a tough one, and showed just as much class."

Back in the Hoosier Dome, Rebel fans stood in disbelief. Danny Tarkanian sobbed in his mother's arms for ten minutes. "You don't get more than one chance to make history," Danny said over and over again. "This was our chance."

"It hurt when, after the game, I saw my dad crying," Danny Tarkanian said. "I had never seen him cry before in my life."

The media started playing the "What if" game. What if Larry Johnson hadn't passed up the last shot? What if Bobby Hurley had been called for an intentional foul when he hammered Hunt? What if Greg Anthony hadn't been called for the charge and sent to the bench? What if ...

Others, including Athletic Director Dennis Finfrock, began sharing theories with the media that were much more serious. Finfrock served as an off-the-record source for several writers, telling them the Rebels were arguing in the locker room before the game over what T-shirt they would wear once they won the championship. Several players have confirmed that Johnson told Anthony before the game that he had no intention of wearing a shirt Anthony had printed up and was prepared to market. But all have agreed it was not the shouting match Finfrock had leaked to the media.

Another rumor had Stacey Augmon—who played one of the worst games of his collegiate career—crying in the locker room *before* the game because he knew he had agreed to throw the contest. Still another had Augmon meeting Richard "The Fixer" Perry in Atlantic City the day after the game.

"One thing we heard from one source was that Augmon was crying before the game, alleging or hinting that maybe he was involved in some kind of point-shaving scheme," *Review-Journal* writer Bruce Pascoe said. Asked if the rumors that Finfrock was spreading the story were true, Pascoe said: "I can't tell you my sources. But I think you could probably … Let me put it this way, if it wasn't him, it would be somebody related."

"Everybody was looking for an excuse," Pascoe said. "Not only the administration, but the fans. The team just doesn't go through killing everybody like that all season and then just look so strange. It wasn't that they got beat, it's just the way it happened was so odd, you know, with Augmon like he's never looked all year, Johnson not taking the final shot, and Anthony fouling out. These things hadn't happened so there was a lot of speculation that there was some weird chemistry. That's when I think a lot of the rumors started about possibly something happening in the locker room. We heard a lot of things from sources within the team and, you know, within the administration."

"It was sick," Tarkanian said. "We couldn't just lose a basketball game. We couldn't just have an off night against a very good team. If we lost, it had to be because something was fixed. When I heard that, I went through the roof. To say the game was thrown is financially ludicrous. You know how much someone would have to bet to make enough to pay the players for their lost NBA salaries? Do you know how much that game probably cost Augmon in his negotiations?"

"I heard it," Augmon said of the game-throwing rumor. "It all hurt because I would never let down my teammates for some money. That was part of the scam, trying to bring us down. It was our turn to excel in the next level, but when things like that come out, the NBA guys could have stayed away from me. Anybody who thinks I'd risk that is just plain stupid. He's plain stupid."

ESPN reported that when Anderson Hunt's shot bounded off the back of the rim and the horn sounded, David Berst thrust his hand in the air and announced, "The drinks are on me." Berst denied the story, although ESPN announced that several reporters heard him make the comment. When Rebels fans Bob and Toby Goldberg wrote Berst to express their outrage over the comment, Berst again declared the story unfounded. "I did not make the comments referred to in the article and I did not buy anyone a drink," Berst wrote in his letter. "I did enjoy the game immensely, however."

Even before the game, rumors began floating through the crowd that Tarkanian was on his deathbed. Some predicted that the only way Maxson, Finfrock, and others would leave him alone was if he won a second championship. Imagine, the winningest coach of all time having to win a second national championship to save his job.

The *National Sports Daily* quoted sources saying Golden Nugget chairman Steve Wynn—one of Maxson's biggest supporters— threatened to pull his casino's $2-million-a-year gift to the university if Tarkanian were not fired. Wynn and Maxson denied the report. But all the rumors seemed confirmed when Maxson made an appearance on "This Week with David Brinkley" the morning after the upset.

Asked repeatedly by host Sam Donaldson if he supported Tarkanian, Maxson declined to answer. "Frankly, it's not my intention to discuss the merits or demerits of a university employee on national television," Maxson said when pressed. Donaldson said Maxson's answer was "no vote of confidence." The president didn't respond.

"His silence was deafening," one Las Vegas columnist wrote after the show. "At least now we know exactly where he stands."

Once they had returned to Las Vegas, Maxson attempted to quell the uproar over his television appearance by calling Tarkanian to his office for a visit. "He wanted me to promise that I would stay four more years," Tarkanian recalls. "He said I was the only one who could take the team through the coming NCAA probation. He assured me the *National* article that said he wanted me out was not true. That's when he said he wanted me to coach at the university as long as he was president."

Just hours after the game, several Rebels decided they didn't want to spend the next two days in Indianapolis with nothing to do. It was Easter weekend and Tarkanian agreed that anyone who wished to leave early could do so. Augmon, Hunt, and Anthony took him up on the offer, heading to Pasadena, Detroit, and Washington, D.C., respectively.

The next morning, several players, coaches, and their wives went to Easter mass. On their way out, Tim Grgurich looked over at Lois Tarkanian. "Nobody in the country could have accomplished what these kids did the last two years under these circumstances," Grgurich mused. "Not even Duke."

Despite the Tarkanians' request against it, confident planners in the UNLV athletic department had spent the previous week putting together a parade and rally honoring the team for a second national championship.

"I told them, please don't do that," said Lois Tarkanian. "We feel it's almost like a jinx to count so surely on winning, but nobody listened to me.

"After the game, Laura Clontz asked me about the parade and I said please delay it a couple of days. The players are so hurt, give them time to recover. Right now they feel they've let the city down. You see, the members of the athletic department in charge of such things were different from the people with whom we had dealt for years. They didn't understand and we were so worn down and sad that we didn't realize how they were thinking."

Despite the loss, Finfrock declared the parade should go on. But when it appeared several of the players might not attend because they had left town, Finfrock canceled the ceremony and blamed the players for his decision.

It was a minor thing, really. Yet it set the tone for the remainder of the spring and summer as this mixed bag of players who had gelled so perfectly into a team would be discredited by those they should most have counted on.

In their final, silent protest over the treatment they and the coaches had received, the six seniors, four of whom were graduating on time, voted not to walk through graduation ceremonies.

"It should have been the greatest day of my college career, better than winning the national championship," said Augmon, who came to UNLV as a Proposition 48 player given little hope of graduating. "No one in my family has ever graduated from college. It was hard not to walk. We'd waited all these years and our parents were waiting for us to walk. I had to tell my mom that I wasn't going to do it. My mom's very easygoing. She was kind of sad. But I promised her that I would make it up to her in some other way. It was sad that I didn't get to experience that.

"But we could just see President Maxson putting all six guys who graduated up there, line us up and talk about how fine we were and how proud he was of us," Augmon said, trying his best to imitate Maxson's Southern drawl. "We didn't want that. We didn't want to get used. The lowest point in my whole time there was watching how they treated Coach. He brought that university so far and they trashed him. We did it [protested] for him, too."

"It really is sad that those kids had feelings that strong against the administration," Tarkanian said. "They accomplished more for the university than most kids ever will accomplish for a university. But they felt so let down they didn't walk through graduation. That's terrible. I wonder if anyone in the administration feels bad about that?"

4

The Courting of Jerry Tarkanian

When the Rebels of UNLV took the court for their final home game of 1973, not much was at stake. The team was 14–12 and had no chance of competing for the championship of the West Coast Athletic Conference. All that coach John Bayer was hoping for was a little respect. And it would be wonderful, he thought, to get it during this regionally televised game against Santa Clara. As he sent his team to the floor, one of his players recalled, Bayer's message was simple: "Play your hardest and remember that people will be watching."

What the people saw was embarrassing. Not only did the team get drubbed on the court, losing by sixteen, but a dispute over a referee's call led some fans of the not-yet-Runnin' Rebels to throw popcorn, ice, and crushed cups onto the playing floor. Remember, people were watching—even if there were only 450 or so in the stands.

Scattered that afternoon throughout the Rotunda, the team's 6,200-seat home court, was a group of Las Vegas businessmen who had decided several years earlier to adopt the fledgling university's athletic program. Although none of them had graduated from

UNLV, the group formed the University Rebels Club, a booster organization that had no official link to the university. Their desires weren't born simply out of philanthropy. They realized that if the university's athletic program could one day bring big-time competition to town, the fans of those visiting teams would fill their hotels, play their slots, and eat at their restaurants. It was a matter of enlightened self-interest.

Their first desire, really, was a respectable college football program. Football, they believed, was the sport that would draw the most fans—and, thus, the most money—to Las Vegas. If a football team from the Midwest scheduled a game against UNLV, their logic ran, then fans of that team might schedule a vacation around the game, spending three days to a week in the city that never sleeps.

"In football, there is a tremendous opportunity to have five or six big-money weeks during the season," said "Wildcat" Bill Morris, owner of the Landmark Hotel and one of several members of the Rebels Club who had played college football. "You get sixteen to eighteen thousand people in town. They are all sports fans. They aren't all here to go to a convention and sit around and watch exhibits and all that. They are here to play. And when I say play, I mean at the tables. So a football crowd of eighteen thousand is worth a convention center crowd of one hundred thousand. They spend that much more money gambling."

The Rebels Club had decided several years earlier to start a football program at UNLV. When the administration and the University's Board of Regents wouldn't hear of it, the boosters decided to go to the Legislature and do it their own way. But their request for $150,000 from the Legislature came back one zero short. The $15,000 kicked in by the state hardly covered the cost of buying lockers for the locker room that they couldn't afford to build. So those in the Rebels Club dug into their own pockets and came up with another $100,000 to begin the college football program they so desired.

"The first $27,000 went to build a dressing room," said Morris, the club's president at the time. "We didn't even have a place in the old gymnasium for the football team to suit up. Then we bought blocking sleds and pads, equipment, balls, the whole thing. We had some money left over for scholarships, but not an awful lot, but again, someone from [coach] Bill Ireland's hometown of Ely, Nevada, a high school friend named Jerry Collis, was the head football coach at Bakersfield J.C. We took the entire Bakersfield team—twenty-seven players—over here and it became the Rebels team the next year. So we started off with a pretty good club, we had an eight-game schedule that first year. We won seven and lost in the last game to Cal-Lutheran, a close game. The university didn't have a football field; we played that season in the Elks Stadium. This is no exaggeration, at one end of the field they used it for the Elks annual rodeo. When they kicked the point after a touchdown or a field goal they kicked it into the buck and shoot, so they had to climb over a couple of fences to get the ball out. And then you could imagine the condition of the field. It was rough because of cows and horses and everything and a lot of sprained ankles, and so Ireland said he just couldn't play here anymore, it's too dangerous for my boys to play out there, where the cows and the horses have kicked up the turf. The next couple of seasons, the Rebels played at Las Vegas High School, and it was pretty difficult to recruit kids and demonstrate you had a strong program when you were playing at a high school. We realized we were a long way from where we wanted to be."

They also realized that getting there could be expensive. "Wouldn't it be better if the university had a money-making athletic program, like basketball, that could carry the football team through its infancy?" Morris remembers someone asking.

The answer was obvious. It was just as obvious during that last home game against Santa Clara that this basketball team was not going to fit the bill. It was time, everyone concluded, for a change.

The Flame restaurant, just off the strip near the Desert Inn casino, was a hangout for leaders of this loosely aligned group—guys like Morris, a football star during his day at the University of Nevada at Reno, Sig Rogich, now an adviser to President George Bush, Brad Welch, a local investor, Wayne Pearson, a close associate of then governor Paul Laxalt, and Davey Pearl, a boxing referee who raised money for the Rebels Club. After several games during that 1972–73 season, the group gathered informally to hash out ideas.

They already had agreed that to make money in basketball, they needed an on-campus arena that, if filled, could be both an imposing recruiting advantage and rake in loads of cash. So, again with limited support from the university, the Rebels Club funded a $38,000 demographic study defending the need for the 19,000-seat arena. It took the Rebels Club ten years of lobbying the Legislature and Congress before the members' dream of an arena finally became reality. The boosters worked through Laxalt to help fund the project by arranging for a $50-per-slot-machine rebate on the federal slot tax.

Obviously, these were big-time dreamers with big-time connections.

Over on the campus of the school known affectionately as Tumbleweed Tech, the vice president for academic affairs had another vision. He, too, loved athletics. But he was tired of going to academic seminars around the country and realizing no one had heard of UNLV. "They kept asking, 'You *really* have a university in Las Vegas," Donald Baepler recalled. "How come we've never heard of it?"

Baepler saw athletics as a way to give his tiny school an identity. It doesn't matter how they hear of you first, as long as they remember, he said. And chances were slim that this three-building university with only a gravel road for an entrance would become a beacon in higher education by waiting for its academic programs to gain notice. It might take years for it to be seen even as a flashlight.

"There have been many, many studies done around the country in terms of what a prominent, let's not talk about national champions, but what a prominent football program or basketball program means to admissions, the number of people that apply and particularly the number of out-of-state-type admissions," Baepler said. "And when you take a look at state universities like Michigan, UCLA, North Carolina, it's no accident that they have outstanding football and basketball programs. To be outstanding academically and outstanding athletically, I think the two go together. This was part of a plan. This was thought out.

"The decision also was that we wanted to have an athletic program that was good enough to pull the public closer to the university. Early on, there was a conscious effort to get the community involved with the university because we needed to get that public support in order to get things off and running and reach a measure of academic credibility. Although Las Vegas was growing, the Legislature was still controlled by the North and it was very difficult to get the Legislature to take us seriously. And we wanted academic communities outside of Nevada to take us seriously, too. Did we want to use athletics to establish UNLV as a university? You bet. But did we expect hiring Jerry Tarkanian would bring us a national championship? No way. We figured we'd keep him six, maybe eight years and during that time he'd make us respectable. We figured it would be the coach after Tarkanian that would have the greatest impact."

Rogich, an advertising executive at the time, knew that the basketball program also could do for Las Vegas what others hoped football would do—remind tourists that there was a warm friendly town out west waiting to bleed them dry. "For a town who's main industry is tourism, you can't do it any better than this," Rogich said. "For us to appear in every newspaper in America every day with the University of Nevada at Las Vegas, it might just prompt someone in a windstorm or a rain storm in Buffalo to visit the town. For a town that's always selling its name, and spending millions of dollars to do it, the University of Nevada Las Vegas on the front of jerseys and in box scores was the right kind of name for us to be successful."

Baepler joined forces with Morris, Rogich, Welch, Pearson, Dr. Ted Jacobs, and Pearl in the search for a new coach. Their list of requirements was simple: win games, fill the soon-to-be-built arena, win games, make money for other athletic programs, win games, increase the university's name recognition, win games, and give the community a team it could rally around. And do it all quick.

Their short list of candidates was very short. Jerry Tarkanian, they all agreed, was their man. His track record in junior colleges and at Long Beach State proved he met their criteria.

"We zeroed in on him because he had already demonstrated what he could do," Morris said. "He had a tremendous record. I think he had one losing season when he was at Antelope Valley High, and nobody can remember that. But when he was at Riverside, he won the state JC champinship. When he was at Pasadena, he won the state JC championship, and then moved over to Long

Beach and won that league and went to the NCAA play-offs. He just had a fantastic record, instant success. We had our eye on him for some time. We knew he could do it here."

Tarkanian's coaching record read like a fairy tale. He spent five years at Riverside City College, where he compiled a staggering 147–23 record, including three consecutive state championships and four league titles. He moved on to Pasadena City College where, in two years, his record was 67–4, winning another state championship one year and finishing second the next. At Long Beach State, Tarkanian became one of the first Division I coaches in America to reach regularly into the junior college ranks for talent. His recruiting classes included only four freshmen in five years. Still, he produced five first round NBA draft choices. Using those junior college players with whom he felt so comfortable, Tarkanian's five-year record at Long Beach was 122–20, with four trips to the NCAA Tournament. Better yet, he won all of the sixty-five games he played at home while at Long Beach, including three wins over teams in the Top 10. He did all this with a recruiting budget that never was more than $3,000 and while laboring in the long shadow of America's premiere basketball program—UCLA. Adding polish to those records was the fact that he accomplished each at schools previously unaccustomed to basketball success. Riverside was last in its conference the year before he arrived, Pasadena had eight consecutive losing seasons before he began coaching there, and Long Beach was a Division II school the year before Tarkanian arrived and had never competed for a conference crown.

"We knew the numbers and there wasn't anybody else in the picture," Baepler said. "These were somewhat before the times of affirmative action."

Twice in years past, different members of the group had approached Tarkanian about taking the UNLV job when it had come open. But the timing never worked out.

"There was a group of guys from Vegas led by Brad Welch who used to come to the Junior College Tournament when I coached junior college and we won the Junior College Tournament four years in a row," Tarkanian said. "No one's ever won that tournament more than twice in a row. We won it four years in a row. If it weren't for two overtime games, it would have been six times in a row. And anyway, those guys wanted me in the Vegas job when I was in junior college. The first time was in 1963, ten years before we worked it out. Things didn't work out the first time and my college roommate, Rolland Todd, got the job. He was going to go up as my assistant but I had a hassle over, we had a hassle over what rank I was going to come in at, and so forth, and anyway, they gave the job to the guy who I was bringing in as the assistant. Rolland and I were good friends so I came up to see some of his games and I got to know some of the people through him."

On their third try, the boosters from Las Vegas caught Tarkanian at the right moment. His Long Beach 49ers, ranked seventh nationally and featuring all-American Eddie Ratleff, were drawing miserably at the Long Beach Arena. "On his way down the steps out of the arena after a game with Fresno near the end of that 72–73 season," Lois Tarkanian remembers, "Jerry turned to me, Lute Olson [his eventual successor at Long Beach State, now coach at Arizona], and his wife, Bobbie, and, with a big sigh, said, 'It's embarrassing, thirty-five hundred people and you've got an all-American here like Ed Ratleff and a team that's ranked third in the country. Its embarrassing.' Then he just talked about how he couldn't get the people in town interested."

Only once during his five years as coach did the arena sell out. That was for a game against nationally ranked Marquette University and coach Al McGuire. Tarkanian thought the fan support shown at the Marquette game, which Long Beach won in an upset, 76–66, might create the rabid following he so desired. It didn't.

In the stands at that game were several UNLV boosters, including Pearl, Rogich, and Baepler. "I was inwardly rooting for Marquette because I knew that if Long Beach won, it would probably cost us another $20,000 of Jerry's contract," Baepler recalled later. "Right behind me was this lady, screaming and yelling and cheering like no one you've ever seen while I was making polite little remarks for Marquette. That, of course, was Lois, I later discovered."

"Long Beach was always really a Trojan town," Tarkanian said. "The big boosters were all USC graduates who donated big amounts of money to USC. But their businesses were in Long Beach so, you know, they supported Long Beach. But only in a minor way. I also was frustrated because Long Beach was a very poor school. We were in the Top Ten in the country four years in a row and I didn't even have a secretary, I didn't have my own office, my assistants had to teach classes, I mean we were different from any other major college, anybody else who was in the Top Ten. And we couldn't find jobs for our kids. I had one player who was six-foot-eight and the only job we could find for him was cleaning the inside of subcompact cars. It didn't work too well."

The lack of fan support coupled with the university's meager commitment to basketball cemented Tarkanian's desire to move on. About that time, three of the Las Vegas businessmen showed up to ask the big question again: What will it take to get you to UNLV?

"It seems to me that over three or four months I traveled down I think on two or three occasions just to ask him that question," Rogich said. "And I talked to him on the phone probably every day for an average of an hour a day. I probably spent hundreds of hours on this. I made it my special project. No one thought we were going to get him. No one believed me when I told them I thought we were. I had other coaches call me about the job and I said, 'I think we're going to get Tarkanian.' They said, 'When you don't get him, would you consider me?' They didn't think he would ever come there, but we just made the job too attractive to turn down. We were too enthusiastic. We gave him what he wanted, it wasn't so much a matter of money, we didn't have much money frankly."

Tarkanian hadn't been recruited this hard when he was a high school athlete. He was starting to enjoy all the attention, and his heart began to leave Long Beach.

"My last year at Long Beach I kind of felt it was going to be my last year, but I kind of thought I was going to go to Arizona State," Tarkanian said. "The athletic director who hired me at Long Beach [Fred Miller] was at Arizona State, so I kind of thought that's where I would be going. We kind of talked about it, but UNLV just started calling and calling and calling and Arizona State wound up having a great year that year. By the middle of December, UNLV had just gotten in there so strong, they were calling all the time."

Tarkanian answered with a list of his own.

"I told them that the only way I would consider the job was if they made it really a big-time job," he said. "I didn't want my assistants to have to teach, I wanted to have a full staff, the full amount of coaches you could have. Everything I asked for, they gave me, everything. Everything I asked for. I wanted my own office. I wanted my own secretary. They gave me my own secretary."

Like a kid just before Christmas, he asked for a little more than he thought he could get. Santa delivered.

A car, he said. Take two, they said. In fact, we'll even get someone to buy your gas.

A salary increase. We'll double the $27,000 you're making now.

A paid newspaper column and a radio show. No problem. We'll even get a clothing store to provide your duds.

We'll even arrange to have your house built at cost. Speaking of building, we're also working to build one of the finest college basketball arenas in the country.

As a means of boosting his salary even further, the group agreed to give Tarkanian handfuls of season tickets to Rebel home games. He could sell the tickets or give them to family or friends.

"At that time we were playing in the Rotunda," Morris said. "It would seat sixty-two hundred people. When we hired Tark, I don't think we ever filled the place, and even when Tark first started out, he wasn't filling it. So they gave him tickets when tickets were not worth anything. It was just one of those things. He didn't put any monetary value on it. Believe me. And, believe me, neither did we."

Despite all the attention, Tarkanian wasn't sure he should gamble on Vegas. The boosters from Long Beach decided to make the decision even more difficult. They promised him an office, a secretary, and a little more money. And they arranged for a part-time job as public relations director of the *Queen Mary*, a luxury liner docked nearby.

Lois, not a fan at the time of Las Vegas, added her two cents: "I said to him, are you crazy, why would you want to go out in the middle of the desert for a job like that. Jerry said, 'Lois, Las Vegas is a college town.' You know, that sounded very stupid to me at the time. But he was right because in Las Vegas everything centers around the university. He saw a town ready to explode for a winner. At Long Beach you had competition from the Dodgers, from UCLA, from USC, from everywhere. We had come to Vegas pretty regularly before that. His mother came with us. She loved to play keno and Jerry loved going out with his friends in town. I never liked the place. I used to sit in my hotel room and read books all day."

The UNLV boosters sent Pearl to stay in a hotel a few blocks from Tarkanian's home in Huntington Beach. He was to be there to talk and to listen, answer questions, and relay messages. Rogich estimates that he and Pearl spent "several hours each day" on the phone trying to work out the deal that would bring the Rebels a new coach. Minor among the many issues Tarkanian and Pearl discussed was the fact that both schools were then under investigation by the NCAA. During the fall of 1972, NCAA investigators had interviewed Long Beach football and basketball players looking for rules violations. The investigators reportedly told Athletic Director Lew Comer that if allegations were forthcoming, the university would hear about it within thirty days. Six months later, when the conversations with UNLV got serious, Tarkanian asked, and was assured by Comer, that nothing would come of the NCAA. "We looked at it as one of those things, wait your turn in the barrel," Morris said of Tarkanian's NCAA trouble. "It was recognized that USC and UCLA were extremely jealous of his accomplishments and people felt that jealousy was the root of some of his NCAA problems." In Las Vegas, Bayer's program also had been under scrutiny. But that investigation was made "inactive" by the NCAA several months before talks of hiring a new coach came up.

Tired of being held in limbo, Long Beach president Stephen Horn demanded that the coach make up his mind. Horn told Tarkanian he could understand if the coach wanted to leave for an established program, but going to UNLV was "a slap in the face for Long Beach and a lateral move at best." Even though he didn't know what he planned to do, Tarkanian agreed to hold a press conference the next day to announce his decision. Horn's response helped Tarkanian—and UNLV—immensely. The president sent word that Tarkanian's press conference only could be held on campus if the coach was staying at Long Beach. "I was insulted that suddenly Horn was trying to pressure me," Tarkanian said. He decided to leave.

When Tarkanian finally said yes, Pearl rushed the coach and his wife to the airport for a flight to Vegas. "I had the flight schedule memorized," Pearl said. "We weren't going to let this slip away. I even sat next to them on the airplane so no one else would talk to them."

They landed in Las Vegas and were greeted by a handful of reporters. This was big news in the town that loves winners. The Tarkanians were whisked over to the office of university president Roman Zorn. But Zorn, upset over the way the University Rebels Club had, in his opinion, usurped the university's hiring process, said he was unavailable to meet Tarkanian. He said he was busy.

"That group was not chartered by the university," Zorn said years later. "It had no official standing with the university. I did not think the university should relinquish total control of the athletic program to boosters. I wasn't terribly enthused about the way they went about it. I wanted them to be sure to look at other people as well as Tarkanian."

While Pearl and several others tried to convince Tarkanian that Zorn's rejection was just "a scheduling problem," other boosters got Zorn on the phone and "shared their thoughts." Two hours later, Zorn found time on his schedule to meet the coach.

"I've hired a lot of people," Zorn said. "But this was the only time in my life a person brought their spouse along for the final interview. She didn't say anything. I'm sure she was making a judgment. She's a very strong influence. I'm sure she was trying to decide if it would be good for her family to come to Tumbleweed Tech. In the end, I did acquiesce in the hiring of Jerry Tarkanian and recommended him to the Board of Regents."

"That's funny," Pearson said when he heard Zorn's explanation. "I don't think he really had much of a choice. It was like a rump convention. You couldn't hire anyone like that today."

The day after the Regents meeting, Zorn introduced Tarkanian as the school's new coach. Amid all the hoopla, Tarkanian was careful not to build expectations. "We're going to work real hard and hope we can do the best that we can," he told the press. "We're not promising anything. All we can do is go out and do the best that we can."

Seven months later, during Tarkanian's first game as Rebel coach, anticipation was in the air. He hadn't promised anything, but the crowd was expecting a lot. By halftime, things were looking great. The Rebels led Texas Tech by fifteen points. Then it all fell apart. Missed free throws. Bad passes. And UNLV lost by four. All that buildup, and he promptly registered an "L" after his first game.

"I went home and vomited," said Rogich.

"That was a long night, it was a tough night," Tarkanian said. "It was my first home loss in eleven years. I never lost a home game my last six years in junior college and five years at Long Beach. I remember, I had never had a radio show in five years at Long Beach State and I thought this was really great. My first year at UNLV I got a radio show, and I was really excited about it. But we got beat. After the game, the guy came by and canceled the radio show. He said to tell Tark to shove that radio show up his ass."

5

Here Comes the NCAA: Round One

The good news for Sig Rogich, Don Baepler, and the others who vigorously worked to lure Jerry Tarkanian to Las Vegas: there weren't many games like that season opener against Texas Tech. After the heartbreaker, UNLV won nine in a row and ended that first year 20–6. With all that winning, Tarkanian even got his radio show back.

When they hired Tarkanian, they asked him to win. That he did. He won more games than anyone could believe. Even in a city where things happen fast—you can get rich in a hurry, about as fast as you can go broke—Tarkanian wowed Rebel fans by turning a program around so quickly. And he coached a brand of basketball that fans couldn't wait to watch and recruits couldn't wait to play.

His second year at UNLV, he abandoned his half-court, walk-the-ball-across-the-time-line offense in favor of a trapping defense that pushed the ball back down the court at breakneck speed. The Rebels made the NCAA play-offs that year for the first time ever. The next year, same result.

By 1977, the offense was so well oiled that UNLV led the nation in scoring, breaking every offensive record kept by the NCAA. The defense was so tough that the Rebels led the nation in margin of victory. And the team that just four years earlier was lucky to draw 1,000 fans to a home game had four times that many buying tickets for road games in the NCAA play-offs. The University Rebels Club recruiters appeared to be geniuses.

UNLV tuned up for the NCAA Tournament by playing Louisville's third-ranked "Doctors of Dunk" just three weeks before the play-offs. The Rebels pulled out a 99–96 win in a contest that convinced the nation this team was no fluke. As the tournament pairings were released, Tarkanian saw that his team of Davids had to look Goliath in the eye. The University of San Francisco Dons, with only one loss, a number two ranking, and center Bill Cartwright to their credit, were first up for the Rebels. For the first time ever, a national television audience was introduced to the little university that could. UNLV gave them a show longtime Rebel fans still talk about. In the first ninety seconds, UNLV scored twelve points on the way to a 63–44 halftime lead. The defense forced thirty-two USF turnovers, and the offense, led by Reggie Theus's twenty-seven points, lit up the scoreboard so often the official scorer sprained his wrist. When it was over, UNLV's 121 points was an NCAA Tournament record. San Francisco's giants had been beaten by twenty-five. It was a game that still must rank among the top five contests for a program that has had its share of games that were declared "big."

The next week, UNLV avenged an earlier season loss to Utah to advance to the Western Region Finals, where everyone—including UCLA—expected them to meet UCLA. But Idaho State caught the Bruins looking ahead and dumped Tarkanian's archrivals, 76–75. Only the Idaho State Bengals now stood between UNLV and the Final Four. The game was great for a half, then the Rebels coasted to a twenty-seven point win, 117–90.

In Atlanta, UNLV faced the nationally known and respected North Carolina Tar Heels, a team with more high school all-Americans on its bench than Tarkanian had ever talked to. The Rebels showed none of the big-game jitters that some pundits predicted, leading by six at the half. That lead quickly jumped to ten points, with 17:15 left, when the game's most crucial play occurred. Coming down with a rebound, Glen Gondrezick hit teammate Larry

Moffett in the nose, sending Moffett, the Rebels' big center, to the bench. When he returned two minutes later, the Tar Heels had scored nine unanswered points. North Carolina took the lead a few minutes later and went to its four-corner offense. UNLV, though, kept clawing back. Trailing by two with under a minute to play, UNLV's Tony Smith stole North Carolina's inbounds pass and flicked it ahead to Theus. Theus dribbled twice, then threw the ball away, and, at the same time, charged into North Carolina's John Keuster. Keuster hit one of the free throws and the game was over. North Carolina won, 84–83.

Lost in the Rebels' misery was the astonishment of their feat. Just four years after he arrived in Las Vegas—and just ten years after UNLV became its own university—Tarkanian had taken the Runnin' Rebels to the Final Four of the NCAA Tournament. UNLV became the youngest university ever to reach the mountaintop of college sports. It also became a university with a national name. Tumbleweed Tech was officially dead.

"I was getting letters from all over the country asking for one of our T-shirts or a ball cap," said Baepler, who by then had become university president. "Our applications for admissions went up drastically. I never had to answer the question of 'What is UNLV?' again."

He did, though, have to answer a new batch of questions from cynics and competitors. How did your program turn around so fast? How did that coach that looks like a bad night's sleep recruit all that unbelievable talent? What did it take to get *those* kids into school? Can you really win all those games without cheating?

The questions weren't new for Tarkanian. They had dogged him at every stop in his career. But they were getting louder and more frequent as his teams played for higher and higher stakes. The national media started picking up on the questions when he was at Long Beach. They questioned why he had left the California school with the NCAA in his rearview mirror. Now, at UNLV, the NCAA was on the horizon, too.

In an article published shortly before he left for UNLV, *Newsweek* wrote that "envious rivals grumble that Tarkanian fields a piebald collection of dropouts, gymnasium gypsies and friendless problem children from all over the country. No other coach, they say, could have tried to sneak such a crew studded with academic misfits past the admissions office."

Image. The buzzword of the eighties began haunting Tarkanian a few years early. One writer referred to him as a "hoodlum priest." *Sports Illustrated* called him the "Pied Piper of Negro youngsters." He was often tabbed as the "Father Flanagan of college basketball."

He didn't look the part of a great coach—those deep-set eyes, sloped shoulders, a nose that was broken three times by errant elbows on a basketball court, and a pate shaved so close it appeared he was bald. The look, like the coach, was simple and unaffected. Said Tarkanian of his hairdo, which looks more like the fuzz on a tennis ball than any picture you'd find on the wall at the beauty parlor: "What happened was, I was letting it grow. But the wind is always blowing and it blows my hair all over and I'd have to come inside and pat it and brush it down. I had a hairdresser, he kept telling me how I gotta comb it this way or that way to cover certain spots. I just got tired of all that. Instead of being phony, I figured I'd just get it cut."

"I've never claimed to be a saint," Tarkanian said in 1991. "I've helped my players at times. You can't make a kid work as hard for you on the court as we do and then turn your backs on them off the court. Coaches who say you can are either lying or don't want to admit that they're doing it, too. But I've never broken a major rule, never bought a player or given one a car. There are some places where you hear they're still doing that. People don't realize that even the NCAA, which has looked for every little thing in our program, has never accused us of cars. But because the NCAA has worked so hard to damage my reputation, no one will ever believe that."

"I realize I've got an image problem," said Tarkanian, who hired a Los Angeles public relations firm in 1990 to help him get endorsements and speaking engagements. "I could go on a picnic and there'd be a controversy."

The beating put on Tarkanian's image grew in direct proportion to the beatings his teams were putting on opponents on the court. As he was building his program in Long Beach, Tarkanian began to realize that the whisper campaign that was damaging him was, in part, the work of cross-town rival UCLA. So Long Beach faculty athletic representative Frank Bowman went to visit UCLA's venerable athletic director, J. D. Morgan, a mover and shaker in NCAA circles. "I asked J. D., 'What do you think our problem is at Long Beach?'" Bowman recalls. "He told me personally, 'Frank, Long Beach has grown too big, too fast,' and he said, 'You haven't built up any credits along the way. You're always going to have investigations going on, as we do here, but you are being overly criticized and scrutinized because you've grown too big, too fast, and you've stepped on a lot of toes doing it. In athletics, as in many other things, you need to build up credits along the way. Your people need to become part of the official group, and you haven't had people serve on committees and do things and pay their dues.'"

If winning too often, too quickly wasn't enough to draw the attention of the NCAA, Tarkanian decided to make sure the short hairs in Mission, Kansas, knew who he was and how he felt about them.

During Tarkanian's fourth year at Long Beach, the school's swimming and football programs fell under the scrutiny of NCAA investigators. Having watched wholesale cheating at UCLA go unchecked, Tarkanian, who wrote a column for the local *Long Beach Independent Press-Telegram*, decided to devote two of his weekly columns to what he perceived as the NCAA's selective enforcement of its rules. He began by questioning the investigations of "such powerhouses as Western Kentucky and Centenary College." "The University of Kentucky basketball program breaks more rules in a day than Western Kentucky does in a year," Tarkanian wrote in the first column. "The NCAA just doesn't want to take on the big boys."

Then, in January 1973, he wrote: "The NCAA could take another major step in the right direction by revamping its investigative policies. The NCAA investigated and then placed on probation the New Mexico States, Western Kentuckys, Centenarys and Florida States, while the big money-makers go free. If the NCAA is genuinely concerned about recruiting and other athletic irregularities, it should be willing to take a look at all schools. It seems totally unfair that the NCAA doesn't look at the schools that are making money for the NCAA through television appearances. It's a crime that Western Kentucky is placed on probation but the famous University of Kentucky isn't even investigated, even though Tom Payne's story has come to light."

Payne was a 7' Wildcat star, the first black basketball player ever recruited to the school. After his playing days at Kentucky had ended, Payne admitted to reporters that Wildcat boosters "supported" him while in college because he had no money. The NCAA never investigated the apparent violations of the rules in Lexington, even though Payne's statements had appeared in print. Rather than following up on the stories out of Lexington, NCAA investigators chose to spend their time chasing a series of minor violations across the state in Bowling Green, home of Western Kentucky.

The second column reached the desk of Warren Brown, then the NCAA's assistant executive director. He fired off letters to Jesse Hill, the commissioner of the Pacific Coast Athletic Association, of which Long Beach was a member, and to Tarkanian's boss, Long Beach athletic director Lew Comer.

"Enclosed for your leisure-time reading is a copy of a newspaper article which I presume was written by Jerry Tarkanian," Brown wrote in a letter to Hill dated January 26, 1973. "It always amazes me when successful coaches become instant authorities. As in the case of this article, such instant authorities reflect an obvious unfamiliarity with facts. Tarkanian is no exception in this regard. I wonder whether he considers California State University, Long Beach, in the 'big money-maker' category."

Brown made little effort to conceal his threat. In late March 1973, four days after Tarkanian accepted the UNLV job and nearly three months after that second column, NCAA investigators expanded the Long Beach swimming and football investigation to an official inquiry and added Tarkanian's basketball program to the list of teams under scrutiny. A year later, the NCAA placed the 49ers' basketball and football teams on three years' probation—including the loss of television appearances for both programs and a two-year banishment of the basketball team from the NCAA Tournament—for twenty-three rules violations.

Although Tarkanian had left for UNLV before the Long Beach investigation was complete, it didn't take the NCAA long to get his forwarding address. NCAA records that later were made public show that the NCAA investigation of UNLV that had been made "inactive" before Tarkanian became the school's coach was reactivated March 29, 1973—six days after he accepted the job. And the first entry into the reopened file was a newspaper clip detailing the career move.

While at Long Beach, Tarkanian received help in writing his newspaper column from Sports Information Director Gary Wright, now with the Seattle Seahawks. When the coach walked into Wright's office with the idea for his first shot at the NCAA, Wright suggested he think about it again. "I remember asking him if he was sure he wanted to take this on and advising him that I thought it was a bad idea," Wright said. "But he had it in his head that this was what he wanted to do."

Tarkanian, as he so often does, ignored the advice and dictated the first volley in his war with the NCAA. "Sure, I wish I'd not gotten into it," Tarkanian said nearly twenty years later. "I wish I'd have listened. People kept telling me not to mess with those guys, that they would destroy me. I just couldn't believe that could happen. I believe it now."

While he acknowledges that he would have been better off not writing the columns, Tarkanian has since declared every day open season on the NCAA. "They're already upset with me," he said. "There isn't anything I could say that's going to get them any madder." That's why he's kept up his criticism of NCAA enforcement, repeatedly saying the same things he wrote in 1973 that started all his troubles. For example, of a 1986 investigation at UCLA, he said: "I'll guarantee you they won't do anything to UCLA. They'll throw them a banquet." And of a 1985 NCAA decision placing Idaho State on two years' probation, Tarkanian said sarcastically: "When you look at it, thirty to forty percent of high school all-Americans go to Idaho State, don't they? Every year, Idaho State gets all those guys. They don't even have enough money in all of Pocatello to buy one player at Kentucky."

For years, Tarkanian has told sportswriters and broadcasters that those columns and his continuing criticism resulted in the NCAA's vendetta to drive him from coaching. That may be true, but it also is true that sources at the NCAA point to the testimony of Tony Morocco as the root of the deep mistrust the organization has for Tarkanian and his program.

Morocco, an assistant coach who moved with Tarkanian from Long Beach to UNLV, had been fired by Tarkanian after his first year at UNLV. Several UNLV players told Tarkanian that Morocco was undercutting the coach by questioning his decisions and encouraging players to do the same. Morocco was doing a similar thing with the coaching staff, telling Tarkanian, for example, that Rickey Sobers was a disruptive influence on the team. On Morocco's advice, Tarkanian asked Sobers to transfer after the 1973–74 season. When Morocco left, Sobers stayed and played so well he became a first round NBA draft choice. He also earned his diploma.

But before Tarkanian decided to fire Morocco, he kept the assistant coach closely involved in the day-to-day discussions of the NCAA's investigation of the Rebel program. One day after practice during that first season at UNLV, Tarkanian, Morocco, booster Wayne Pearson, and Assistant Coach Dan Ayala sat in the basketball office and commiserated about the NCAA's dogged pursuit of the coach. Ayala was taking jabs from the other three for "being used" by the NCAA's Bill Hunt during one of the investigator's visits to Las Vegas. Ayala had, at Hunt's request, taken the NCAA staffer to several hotels around town and introduced him to the executives that were friendly to the basketball program and often "comped" the coaches at shows and meals. Now Hunt was using that information to allege that athletes, not the coaches, were the ones being comped.

As Ayala told the others where he'd taken Hunt, Pearson added that he had heard two NCAA investigators—David Berst and Hale McMenamin, a former FBI agent—had scheduled a repeat visit to Las Vegas.

"I remember Tony looking at all of us and saying he had an idea that could end this NCAA thing quick," Pearson said, speaking for the first time on the subject eighteen years later. "He suggested that we plant drugs in the investigators' rooms, then wait for them to come back and call the police. We all laughed at him. It was such a stupid idea."

The idea never was talked about again. Three months later, Morocco was fired. On McMenamin's next trip to Las Vegas, the boosters were baffled by his actions.

"He kept checking into a new hotel every night," Pearson said. "He'd pack up and check out the next morning."

Years later, Tarkanian, Pearson, and others discovered that Morocco had become the NCAA's top source in the UNLV inquiry. In his new role with the NCAA, Morocco decided to warn the organization to tread lightly in Las Vegas because there was a move afoot, he told them, to set them up with drugs. First he claimed the statement was made by Ayala. Then he said it was made by Tarkanian.

The NCAA's distrust grew to the point that Berst's own memos indicated he believed he should call the FBI each time he came to Las Vegas because he feared UNLV boosters would one day carry out the drug threat.

"When I heard that, I was so mad," Tarkanian said. "The drug thing was Morocco's idea. Two other people heard it. Then he went to the NCAA and blamed it on me."

Bothered by Morocco's cooperation with the NCAA, athletic department fund-raiser Davey Pearl called the former coach. "I said, 'Tony, the word is out that you spoke to the NCAA a little too much,'" Pearl said. "I didn't say anything other than that. 'No, I didn't,' he said. I told him, 'If you did, if I were you, I'd stay out of Las Vegas.' He got the shit scared out of him. You know, he was always running around, he was half a tough guy. But all I had to do was tell him that, he shit in his pants. I'm telling you, he was scared."

Morocco called Berst with word of Pearl's "threat." Driven by the belief that the desire to win in Las Vegas was so great that Tarkanian and his friends would consider such drastic measures, the NCAA took no chances and cut UNLV no slack.

After nearly three years of stalking UNLV, the NCAA delivered its fifty-four-page list of allegations on February 25, 1976. Tarkanian took exception to each of the ten allegations the NCAA made against him. And on each, his lawyers delivered sworn statements and documents which supported and underscored their position.

The reason for Tarkanian's confidence in preparing his defense could be found in two large legal-size boxes containing UNLV's response to the violations alleged by the enforcement staff. Each violation had been given its own file, and inside each file was evidence gathered by the Nevada attorney general's office. Some of the files were five inches thick, filled with statements investigators from the attorney general's office obtained from every individual the NCAA named in its charges. The State of Nevada paid either to fly those people to Las Vegas to be deposed or sent an investigator to their homes for the same purpose.

"I thought the evidence for our side was overwhelming," Tarkanian said.

In the many interviews and speeches he's given on the subject since 1977, Tarkanian often uses one example to paint how awful this picture was. It involved an allegation that he had arranged for a player named Robert "Jeep" Kelley, a highly recruited guard from Pittsburgh, to fly home free in November 1973. The NCAA also alleged that Tarkanian reimbursed Kelley in cash for his return trip.

Kelley had returned to his home after quitting the UNLV team a week before the first game of his freshman year. According to the NCAA, Tarkanian had arranged the trip by telling Kelley to call Frank Denton, the owner of American Tour and Travel Service, a Las Vegas agency that operated gambling junkets. When Kelley called Tarkanian three days later and asked to come back, the NCAA alleged, Tarkanian agreed and told Kelley he would reimburse him for his return flight whenever he finally showed up at the basketball arena. Although Tarkanian argued that it was "ludicrous" to think he would arrange a free flight for a player to quit his team and then pay for his return, the NCAA stuck to its allegations.

To prove its case, the NCAA turned to Berst, who said he had a conversation with Kelley in 1975 during which Kelley complained that he had been unhappy at UNLV and wanted to go home, but that he then changed his mind and wanted to return to UNLV. Berst said it was Kelley who told him that Tarkanian had made all the arrangements. Berst had no credible evidence, documentary or otherwise. Just his unsigned memo of a conversation he had with Kelley.

When Berst finally sat down, Tarkanian's lawyers, fully confident that they had him on this one, laid the following evidence out for the committee:

• A sworn affidavit from Kelley in which he stated that he did not meet Frank Denton until 1974; that he had sold his season tickets—a practice allowed by the NCAA at the time—to purchase the commercial airline ticket that he used to leave Las Vegas; that the flight he took home was not part of a gambling junket, but was on a commercial airline; that he was never reimbursed any money by Tarkanian or anyone connected with UNLV; and that his return flight to Las Vegas was paid for by his former high school principal, Dr. James E. Robinson.

• A deposition from Dr. Robinson in which the principal stated that he authorized the school treasurer to write a check for the airline ticket. The money was drawn from a special fund at the school which was established years earlier and was to be used for the benefit of current or former students.

• A sworn affidavit from Spencer Watkins, Kelley's high school basketball coach, in which Watkins stated that he and Robinson made the arrangements for Kelley's return to Las Vegas and the purchase of the plane ticket.

• A letter from Garin F. Veseley, Kelley's high school athletic director, in which Veseley stated that he used the money provided by the high school and purchased an airline ticket for Kelley on November 30, 1973, for Kelley to return to Las Vegas, as authorized by principal Robinson.

• A copy of the Schenley High School payment order requesting the issuance of a check for $135 to be made payable to cash "in payment of traveling expenses, RJK," to be charged to the special account and dated November 30, 1973.

• A canceled check drawn on the account of Schenley High School at the Mellon National Bank and Trust Company, made payable to cash in the sum of $135 and dated November 30, 1973.

With a little extra swagger befitting their confidence, UNLV's attorneys grabbed the last file in the box and tossed it on the table like a trump card. The file contained records from Frank Denton, which showed that the companies with which he was associated conducted no aircraft flights between Las Vegas and Pittsburgh and no flights at all on the dates before, during, or after the day Kelley left Las Vegas. To prove it, Denton offered the Committee on Infractions copies of his agency's flight manifests for the time period that Berst said Kelley reported accepting a free flight. There was no way Kelley could have gotten from Las Vegas to Pittsburgh on one of his planes, Denton said.

But just like in the casinos, it seems the dealer always wins. UNLV's trump card didn't play. The committee decided to believe Berst. Verdict: Tarkanian was guilty as charged.

"I have to tell you," Lois Tarkanian said, "that one really shattered my faith in the NCAA. It shattered my faith in the values we grow up with. I always thought that if you were honest, you'd eventually win. That taught me my belief just wasn't right. I remember going to the commercial airport with a bag of oranges and a couple of apples to give to Jeep for his flight home. He was the first player ever to leave one of Jerry's teams, and it was like a part of the family was leaving. I gave him the oranges, we hugged, and I cried. Then I watched him get on that plane. I know it was no charter. But they thought they had enough evidence. I was hurt by that one."

The reason Kelley changed his story when interviewed by UNLV's investigators, Berst asserted in his statement to the Infractions Committee, was because Tarkanian had threatened the former player. This major charge—which was made more believable when the committee learned of Morocco's drug allegation and the call from Davey Pearl—was based on telephone conversations Berst said he had with Kelley. During those conversations, Berst said, Kelley reported receiving repeated calls from Tarkanian during which the coach promised to arrange a professional tryout for Kelley if he denied his previous statements. Berst also quoted Kelley's aunt, Frances Parker, as saying Kelley "feared for his life" after Tarkanian called. But UNLV provided telephone records showing it was Kelley, not Tarkanian, who was making the many phone calls. The information proved that during the six months Kelley reportedly feared Tarkanian, he called the coach twenty-six times—and reversed the charges. Lonnie Wright, Kelley's closest friend, even signed an affidavit swearing that he and Kelley had dinner at the Tarkanians' home at least three times during that six months and "there was never any tension" between the two. And though Berst told the Infractions Committee that a frightened Kelley had called the NCAA to report the threats, telephone records suggest that Kelley was merely returning Berst's call.

The believability of Kelley's statements to the NCAA was a key tenet in UNLV's defense. Their importance grew when it was discovered that Morocco, who had recruited Kelley to UNLV, had arranged the meetings between the player and the NCAA. Throughout the infractions Committee hearings, Berst repeatedly denied that Morocco was his primary source. At one point, a transcript of the hearing shows, Berst even told the committee that "Tony Morocco would not be interviewed as it relates to anything."

Although UNLV's lawyers didn't believe Berst, it wasn't until the Infractions Committee handed down its verdict that Tarkanian finally discovered the truth. After reading that the NCAA had suspended Tarkanian from coaching, Morocco called Tarkanian, admitted he had agreed out of anger to be the NCAA's source, and asked for forgiveness. Morocco then called the Nevada attorney general's office and volunteered to give a deposition as UNLV prepared for its appeal to the NCAA Council.

In his deposition, Morocco said that once Berst sought his help in the Tarkanian investigation, he arranged to pick Kelley up at his home, take the former player to lunch, and then get him to "talk trash" about Tarkanian. After lunch, Berst sat and listened as Morocco and Kelley "discussed negative aspects of our stay at Las Vegas." Morocco also stated that it was he, not Kelley, who made the bulk of the allegations against Tarkanian during that meeting, but that he asked Berst to shield his identity by naming Kelley as the NCAA's informant. "The discussion actually consisted of a series of events to which I would make reference and to which Jeep would briefly respond," Morocco said in his statement. "I was clearly doing nearly all the talking and Jeep merely responded to my discussions." Morocco said he also arranged for Berst to interview several other witnesses, including Frances Parker, who was angry when Kelley quit the UNLV team as a freshman. "I called Mrs. Parker and made it clear that I had a strong dislike for Tarkanian and the university and very much reinforced her own bitter feelings toward them," Morocco swore. "I strongly encouraged Mrs. Parker's bitterness and suggested that she might want to speak with the NCAA since she felt that Jeep had been unfairly treated by the university and Tarkanian."

In a deposition taken four years later during Tarkanian's legal case, Berst acknowledged that it was Morocco who arranged and hosted the hour-and-a-half meeting between Berst and Kelley at the

Monroeville, Pennsylvania, Howard Johnson's, where Morocco had taken a job managing a rental car counter after being fired by Tarkanian. Berst also admitted that he had visited Morocco at the Howard Johnson's "five or six times," had called him another ten times, and had undersold the involvement of the disgruntled ex-coach to the Committee on Infractions. Asked by Tarkanian's lawyers if he had "interviewed anybody in the UNLV case who told you more about possible violations than Tony Morocco," Berst conceded, "I don't think so."

Morocco's hiring had been recommended to Tarkanian by Sonny Vaccaro, who later would serve as Nike's liaison with college basketball coaches. But when Vaccaro, who had known Morocco since childhood, heard that Morocco was the NCAA's chief witness against Tarkanian, he decided the NCAA ought to know a little bit more about his friend. Vaccaro decided to write NCAA investigator McMenamin a confidential letter "explaining Tony's background" and warning the NCAA that Morocco shouldn't be considered a credible source. In the three-page letter, Vaccaro took McMenamin through his friend's coaching career—which included brief stops at Trafford (Pennsylvania) High School, the University of Iowa, St. Francis College, also in Pennsylvania, and the University of Arkansas before he landed a spot on Tarkanian's staff—and described how each of those jobs had ended with Morocco criticizing his former employer.

"Mr. McMenin [sic], as a former FBI agent and knowing what it takes to make a character analysis of a human being, you can follow probably more so than I a situation which exists within this individual which shows his instability, envy and disloyalty wherever he has been," Vaccaro wrote. "As I look back at all of this and my part in helping Tony obtain new jobs and be accepted by new people, I feel a partial responsibility in what has occurred. If my providing this information can in any way prevent one more program or one more human being from being unjustly hurt in the way so many have in the past due to Tony's actions, then I will feel my sharing this was worthwhile."

Lew Schaffel, a New York lawyer who now is part owner of the NBA's Miami Heat, also offered Berst his opinion of Morocco. "If you're going to base your case on Tony Morocco, I think it would be a shame," Schaffel told Berst, according to Schaffel's recollection of the conversation.

Vaccaro's letter and Schaffel's warning were ignored and the NCAA chose to build much of its case around the many allegations made by the disaffected ex-coach. Berst, in fact, even increased the friction between Vaccaro and Morocco when he mailed Morocco a copy of the confidential letter Vaccaro wrote. "That was a total breach of the faith and trust which I had placed in individuals who had asked for my cooperation," Vaccaro would say later.

To this day, Lois Tarkanian carries her rosary beads if she knows Morocco might show up. "Hiring him was a mistake Jerry's still paying for," she said.

While the allegation involving Kelley's flight is the easiest for Tarkanian to describe in detail, it is far from the only time his lawyers caught NCAA investigators shading the truth. In another instance, McMenamin told the Committee on Infractions that Ron Vitto, then a Las Vegas sportscaster, had filmed a practice in which a recruit, Jerry Baskerville, had participated. Since recruits cannot participate in practices, the incident would be a rules violation. McMenamin, reading from his notes, quoted Vitto as saying he had broadcast the footage on his "5 P.M. and 10 P.M. sports shows" the night of the practice. McMenamin explained that he didn't have the videotape because the broadcaster was reluctant to talk with the NCAA. That reluctance, McMenamin wrote in his memo, stemmed from the fact that Vitto said he "was born and raised in Las Vegas" and "depended on the university to make a living." UNLV, though, produced an affidavit from Vitto saying he never filmed a practice involving Baskerville. It also proved Vitto was born and raised in Los Angeles and did not move to Las Vegas until he was an adult. The practice when the violation was alleged to have occurred was on a Sunday. UNLV provided programming reports showing that KLAS-TV Channel 8, the television station for which Vitto worked, did not broadcast his show on Sundays during the year of the alleged incident. Furthermore, regular newscasts on KLAS-TV at that time were broadcast at 6:00 P.M. and 11:00 P.M. Monday through Friday. If the recruit truly did participate in the practice—and UNLV coaches denied that he did—it could not have appeared on television as McMenamin said it did. In a minor victory for UNLV, the Infractions Committee told McMenamin it believed he'd missed the mark and threw the charge out.

After three hearings—the last of which came less than twenty-four hours after Tarkanian's team had upset San Francisco in the 1977 NCAA Tournament—the Committee on Infractions decided that UNLV had committed thirty-eight violations. Tarkanian was named in ten of them.

In August 1977, UNLV appealed the committee's decision to the NCAA Council. It did so, though, with little hope of reversal. No school had ever won an appeal up to that time, and no school has won one since. UNLV contested the factual basis for most of the allegations for which it was deemed guilty, criticized the NCAA proceedings, and attacked the credibility of Berst and McMenamin. "The University has good reason to believe, supported by uncontestable facts, that information provided by the NCAA investigators to the Committee on Infractions was either false, misleading or, at best, grossly inaccurate," UNLV wrote in its appeal.

If the Committee on Infractions was working hand in hand with the investigators, surely the NCAA Council, the organization's most powerful body, would set it all straight, Tarkanian thought. The coach was given only twenty minutes to state his case, the university thirty minutes. To ensure that every conceivable advantage had been given to the enforcement staff, documents released during congressional hearings show the council—after UNLV's representatives, NCAA staff, and Tarkanian had been asked to leave—quietly invited Berst and McMenamin back into the "closed-door" deliberation of the appeal. There, while Tarkanian and UNLV were locked out, the two investigators were allowed to "clarify" certain issues, as Berst later testified in Nevada District Court. The two obviously were persuasive. The council upheld the Infractions Committee's findings, ignoring the evidence about the behavior of the investigators.

Once its appeals within the NCAA's system had failed, UNLV was ordered by the NCAA in 1977 to suspend Tarkanian. The NCAA had never ordered a head coach suspended before Tarkanian and has not since. In response to the NCAA's demand, UNLV president Baepler appointed Brock Dixon, a university vice president, to review the case and spell out the university's options as they related to Tarkanian. After his in-house hearing, Dixon wrote that the facts supporting the NCAA's charges were "clearly in doubt." He also stated that the NCAA's "standards of proof and due process were inferior to what we might expect.

"In almost every factual situation delineated by the NCAA, the university's own investigation has been able to find a substantial body of conflicting evidence, some of which has been heard and considered by the NCAA and some of which has been brushed aside. By joining the NCAA we delegated to that organization the establishment of governing standards and their enforcement as well. We are allowed and encouraged to make our own investigations but this is in no way a substitute for the investigative functions of the NCAA itself. We must live by our commitments to the NCAA, its standards and its machinery. We must accept their findings of fact as in some way superior to our own. In this instance we could wish for standards of due process and evidence far superior to that which we have observed, but given the terms of our adherence to the NCAA we can not substitute—biased as we must be—our own judgment on the credibility of witnesses for that of the infractions committee and the Council."

Baepler informed Tarkanian by letter that he was being transferred from his job as basketball coach. The president justified the decision by claiming the university voluntarily joined the NCAA and as a result essentially permitted the organization the right to punish its coach. Forget the fact that the coach was a state university employee and the rights generally afforded other university employees were violated by the NCAA, Baepler said. "The University is simply left without alternatives," he wrote to Tarkanian.

The next day, Tarkanian took this plethora of evidence about the NCAA and its handling of his case and headed to court. Though his complaint was with the NCAA, he sued UNLV because it was the university that officially had removed him. During the hearing, a staff attorney for the Nevada attorney general's office testified that the investigation conducted by his office "found no factual basis for the NCAA charges." That said, Tarkanian won an injunction against the university, blocking the suspension.

So desperate was the NCAA to reel in this shark that the organization gladly filed a motion and became a party to this legal battle, spending more than $1 million over the next ten years while willingly exposing its seamiest side to public scrutiny in court-rooms across America. The result was one of the longest and most fascinating sports-related legal battles ever waged, creating the best public record available on the NCAA's enforcement program.

"Can you believe they were willing to go through all that just for me?" Tarkanian said, a smile creeping across his face.

Only once during that stretch, in late 1982, did the NCAA show any hint of surrender. A lawyer for the NCAA called a lawyer friend of Tarkanian's—specifically bypassing the coach's attorney of record—and asked if there was a penalty that the coach would accept in exchange for dropping all legal challenges. The NCAA offered to put the school on six months' probation, in lieu of Tarkanian's suspension. Tarkanian rejected any sanction that sounded as if he were admitting guilt. The NCAA then came back and asked if it could call the sanction six months' "monitoring" instead of probation. "There was a definite offer made to end the high cost of all the litigation," the Tarkanian family friend, who asked to remain anonymous, said. "I advised them to take the settlement." Feeling confident and heeding the advice of his own attorney, Tarkanian rejected the friend's recommendation and the deal. Both sides agreed never to reveal that the conversations had taken place.

"I probably should have done it," Tarkanian said years later. "But I figured if they were making an offer, it was because they must think they might lose and I wanted to beat them so bad."

Six weeks after Tarkanian's suspension was ordered, Congress entered the fray as well, beginning an eighteen-month-long investigation of the NCAA. During those protracted battles the NCAA attempted to flaunt the authority of both the Nevada court system and Congress. While defending itself in court, the NCAA issued daily press releases—despite the repeated warnings of the judge against doing so—recounting the most negative information revealed that day about Tarkanian. Nevada district judge Paul Goldman, in chastising the NCAA, said its refusal to abide by his order to stop its daily press releases, which it distributed to national media, during the Tarkanian trial "clearly was an attempt to wield its powerful connections with the press to win the case through the media if it couldn't do so in court."

When Congress was attempting to subpoena documents for its investigation, the NCAA originally ignored the subpoena, then issued a veiled threat to universities that might consider participating in the hearings. Committee chairman John Moss fired off a letter to then NCAA executive director Walter Byers reminding him that "to endeavor to influence, intimidate or impede any witness before a congressional committee is a felony." Berst had even ordered that an unflattering picture of Representative Jim Santini, the Nevada congressman who requested the hearings, be placed in the UNLV case file that was released to the public. In the picture, Santini is wearing a UNLV beanie and sitting on press row at the 1977 Final Four.

To both Congress and the courts, the NCAA's attitude could best be characterized as arrogant. At its worst, the organization's behavior bordered on criminal. But in those public forums, the NCAA's enforcement system in general—and its treatment of Tarkanian in particular—was shown to be malicious, slipshod, inaccurate, one-sided, and bigoted.

Tarkanian, well known for his inability to see anything beyond a ninety-four-foot-long basketball court, began to get the picture that he was in trouble when former North Carolina State coach Norm Sloan warned him at a summer basketball camp that he "better look out."

Sloan, Tarkanian, Louisiana State University athletic director Joe Dean, and Bill Wall, onetime president of the National Association of Basketball Coaches, were debating whether coaches should be fired for rules violations. Sloan's program, with the fabulous David Thompson, had just completed a one-year probation for four administrative rules violations. As Sloan argued against suspending coaches, Tarkanian suggested he was wrong. "Well, I've got news for you," Sloan recalls telling Tarkanian in his recently released autobiography, *Confessions of a Coach.* "You're going to see this whole thing in a different light before long based on what I've been told by Bill Hunt of the NCAA. He tells me they're not only going to get you, they're going to run you out of coaching."

Sloan later was asked about the conversation when he was subpoenaed to appear before Congress. He said that in 1973, then NCAA investigator Bill Hunt told him the organization was after

Tarkanian. He told Congress the conversation with Hunt took place just after Sloan's Wolfpack basketball program had come off probation.

After he was sworn in by the House Committee on Interstate and Foreign Commerce's subcommittee on oversight and investigations, Sloan was asked by John McElroy Atkisson, counsel to the subcommittee, to recall his discussion with Hunt.

ATKISSON: It was in your office, then, in this personal meeting between yourself and Mr. William Hunt that you discussed Mr. Jerry Tarkanian, is that correct?

SLOAN: Yes.

ATKISSON: Can you in your own words relate to us the sum and substance of that conversation?

SLOAN: I can give you the substance of it. I was rather upset about our probation and was stating it to Bill Hunt and explained why, that it branded me, and David [Thompson] and the university in a manner we could never erase, and I didn't think it was justified. That was—I was kind of going on about it. He said in effect, "Yes, I know what you are talking about. It throws you in"—and he named some schools and named a coach, Jerry Tarkanian. When he mentioned Jerry he became a little emotional, I thought, and said in effect, he said, "We are not only going to get him, we are going to run him out of coaching."

Atkisson asked Sloan how he could tell Hunt had become "a little emotional." "He stood up and his face got red," Sloan said. The coach said Hunt had told him, "Jerry and some of his friends were going to arrange to have drugs planted in the motel rooms and prostitutes in the motel rooms and therefore discredit the NCAA and the investigators."

Hunt had a little more trouble remembering exactly what he said to Sloan, but he was careful to avoid telling the committee he absolutely did not say the NCAA was out to get Tarkanian:

ATKISSON: Do you recall ever discussing that case [UNLV] or Mr. Tarkanian with Norm Sloan, a North Carolina basketball coach?

HUNT: I do not believe I have. I do not recall.

ATKISSON: You are saying that you do not recall having had the conversation but not—You do not say affirmatively that you did not have it, but you just don't recall, is that correct?

HUNT: That is correct.

ATKISSON: If you did have it, is there any possibility that you would have referred to either your or other people's desire in the NCAA to drive Tarkanian out of coaching?

HUNT: I really do not believe that is possible.

ATKISSON: You qualified it. You mean it is unlikely?

HUNT: No.

ATKISSON: Wholly impossible?

HUNT: The answer is no.

"It seemed like for five or six years every time I picked up the phone or went to a clinic I had one of my former players or another coach telling me that they'd just talked to the NCAA and I was in trouble," Tarkanian said. "Some of those people even signed affidavits showing that they were threatened. But I guess that doesn't bother the NCAA. It didn't bother the Gestapo either."

Roscoe Pondexter, a 6'6" forward who played for Tarkanian at Long Beach State, was one of the first of his former players to call Tarkanian with the news that Berst and his fellow investigators had either attempted to intimidate them or guaranteed that the investigation would end with the coach's demise. Pondexter had gone to a junior college for one year before posting a dramatic increase in his college board scores, allowing him to transfer to a four-year school. Tarkanian did not permit him to play at the beginning of the first year after his transfer because he admitted to having concerns over the increase in Pondexter's scores. During that year, Berst cornered Pondexter twice, each time asking for a little dope on Tarkanian.

"Berst told me that they had enough evidence on me and my test scores to declare me ineligible," Pondexter said in a 1988 interview. "But he said that if I gave him evidence on Coach [Tarkanian] I would be able to leave and go to any other school without sitting out a year. He said he wanted Tarkanian out of coaching, and he was going to make sure that happened. He told me that Tarkanian was a man who shouldn't be in basketball. He said, 'Tarkanian is bad for the game. Personally, I don't like the man.' He said, 'I'm out to get Tarkanian.' He later told me, 'I've got you now. I got all the stuff against you. You're dead ... Roscoe, if you help me get Tarkanian and Long Beach, I won't submit enough evidence to convict you and you'll still be able to play. I'm going to get Tarkanian if it takes the rest of my career.' This made me feel like I should make up something [on Tarkanian] to keep him [Berst] off me."

Pondexter said he repeatedly told Berst he didn't know of any rules violations, and, as Berst promised, he was later declared ineligible. But Helen Gallagher, a hearing officer appointed by a U.S. District Court judge, ruled there was not enough evidence to support the NCAA's suspension of Pondexter, and he was ordered reinstated.

Sports Illustrated's Rick Telander contacted Berst about Pondexter's comments for a story about Tarkanian. He reported that Berst "seemed really nervous and kept telling me to try to understand the NCAA policies and that I would have to talk to his attorney." Berst later told reporters, "As far as my supposedly saying things like 'I'll get Tarkanian if it's the last thing I ever do,' golly, I don't use language like that." He also said he had not treated the case against UNLV and Tarkanian any differently than any he had worked on before or since.

"Berst had lied so much and didn't report facts and when all this was presented to the NCAA, it just amazed me that they wound up giving him a raise instead of reprimanding him," Tarkanian said. "At that time, Walter Byers was in charge and Walter Byers was certainly not a fair man. This proved it."

As the investigation dragged on into its second year, UNLV attorney Mike Leavitt and the attorney general's office began clipping together the affidavits given to them by former players in what became known as the "Pink File," so called simply because the only file folder label Leavitt had with him during the infractions hearing was pink.

UNLV lawyers figured that by presenting what they considered to be damning evidence of unprofessional behavior, the Committee on Infractions would look more skeptically at the memos filed by the NCAA staff.

The reaction was precisely 180 degrees opposite of what they had expected. Byers and the committee rushed to the defense of the NCAA investigators and openly chastised UNLV for hinting that anything improper or unethical was done. UNLV's defense includ-ed, according to Byers, "unreasonable and unfair attacks on the integrity of the people who happen to work for me," and he thought "the representatives of UNLV were aggressively trying to discredit the commentary" presented by the enforcement staff. In 1976, when a member of the NCAA Council raised some general questions about the growing concern among coaches about the NCAA's staff work on infractions cases, Byers told him that such criticism was "for the most part, if not exclusively, the result of one coach's [Tarkanian's] increasing attempts to discredit the NCAA."

The picture of how ugly this would become was crystal clear for Tarkanian when he learned that Berst had occasionally referred to Tarkanian as a "rug merchant," a bigoted reference to the coach's Armenian ancestry. "I have utilized the words 'rug merchant' regarding Jerry Tarkanian, and I have used that term ... I cannot give you an approximate number of times," Berst admitted to the congressional subcommittee in 1978. Berst said his reference—par-ticularly when he told NCAA staff members and members of the Infractions Committee that Tarkanian could easily be recognized "as the one who looks like a rug merchant"—was really uttered in a curious spirit of "affection."

"He said that he said it in a spirit of affection," Tarkanian said, shaking his head. "I don't think anybody believes that. Berst obvi-ously was very prejudiced against me going into this situation. Throughout our case he repeatedly cut corners, made up his own reports that were proven to be false. He probably did all that out of affection, too, huh?"

The issue of Berst's bigotry came up in court as well. "The name of the plaintiff is Tarkanian," Judge Goldman admonished Berst. "The name of the chief justice of the state of Nevada is Noel Manoukian and the name of the governor of the state of California is George Deukmejian. All are Armenian and there isn't a rug mer-chant among the three."

Berst has generally refused requests to discuss the UNLV case, his comments regarding Tarkanian, and his role in the investiga-tion. But he did consent to an interview with *CBS Sports* before the 1991 NCAA championship. After Tarkanian told the television audience that although he presented the committee "with affi-davits, tape recordings, and canceled checks," he had "no chance" of beating Berst and the NCAA, Berst retorted, "That is totally false. Those affidavits had to be false. Once the credibility of some of that information was undermined, then I think that probably worked in my favor." He declined to elaborate.

Ironically, Tarkanian said pride in his heritage contributed, at least partially, to the strength that allowed him to plow through his seventeen-year struggle with Berst and the NCAA. In 1917, Turkish forces invaded Armenia and slaughtered 2 million of its citizens. Tarkanian's grandfather, a village official, was forced to watch Turks behead his son and then was himself beheaded. Ignoring the pleas of other villagers that she flee, Tarkanian's grandmother sewed gold coins into her daughter's slip and sat her atop a horse along with another child. As the horse reached the top of the hill, the young girl who would become Tarkanian's mother looked back on the village. There the Turks were herding dozens of villagers into a church, bolting the door, and setting it afire. The story was told and retold to Tarkanian as he grew up. "We have been fighting a long time," he said. "And we don't give up."

Tarkanian said he "could understand" Berst's bigoted comments because he'd lived with such words for years. What he couldn't forgive, though, was the "witch hunt" that had allowed Berst to make up new rules—and new quotes—to fit his needs. The best example of that occurred in October 1976, when Berst interviewed New York playground basketball coach Rodney Parker. Parker, a schoolyard hoops junkie featured in Rick Telander's book *Heaven Is a Playground,* was a close friend with two players Tarkanian was recruiting. Months earlier, the NCAA had sent UNLV its official letter of inquiry. Five of the NCAA's allegations stemmed from Berst's belief that UNLV had paid for Parker and recruit Rudy Jackson to visit Las Vegas. After receiving its official letter of inquiry, UNLV's responsibility under NCAA rules was to try and determine the truth of the allegations. While UNLV was plowing through its internal investigation, Berst went back to several key figures, including Parker, to ask if the university was taking a defensive posture while interviewing them. Based upon this interview with Parker, Berst asked the Committee on Infractions to find UNLV guilty of covering up violations rather than getting to the truth.

Court records show that Berst specifically told the committee four separate times that Parker said Assistant Attorney General Lyle Rivera, who handled UNLV's internal investigation, asked his questions in a "general manner." That was done, Berst alleged, so Parker would not have to reveal damaging information that could lead to the finding of a violation and thereby be "put in a bind." To back up this very serious claim, Berst read from a memo he prepared after the Parker interview. Berst's memo, entered into the court record, was central to his allegation that UNLV was violating the spirit of its NCAA membership by trying to hide violations from the Infractions Committee. By quoting Parker, a credible source, as saying UNLV was not trying to get at the truth, Berst could damage the credibility of everything else UNLV would claim.

Berst wrote that he "specifically asked Parker whether University representatives had asked him who paid his travel expenses to Las Vegas or about being reimbursed by Welch for his expenses. Parker reported he did not think the University's representatives asked him these questions or at least the questions posed were general enough so that his answers did not get himself or anybody else 'in a bind.'" Berst's interview with Parker took place in the New York office of Parker's lawyer, Lew Schaffel.

What Berst didn't know was that throughout the interview, Parker was taping their conversation; the tape recorder was hidden in his briefcase. Berst himself made no notes, instead relying on his memory when he typed his memo about the meeting a month later according to his later court testimony.

The transcript of that conversation from Parker's tape paints a dramatically different picture than does Berst's memo:

BERST: I mean, how, you know, were they trying to slam-bang you, or just put it down in front of you and let you help them out, or did they really want to know what the truth was?

PARKER: Well, basically, I think they really wanted to know what the truth was. I just told them, you know, exactly what happened and how it happened. They didn't try to lead me in any way.

Berst also repeatedly asked Parker if UNLV attorneys were taking shots at Berst or any other NCAA investigator:

BERST: Did they ask you about the NCAA investigator, that being me? It ain't going to hurt me either way. What the hell, life's life.

PARKER: I don't think they were leading in that direction. I mean, I don't think they like you very much, but I don't know about, I really don't know whether, I don't know how they feel about you. I think they were more interested in the facts, the same way you are.

BERST: Did they make you feel like somehow I am a bad guy? In other words, when they talk to you, am I a bad guy?

PARKER: No. No. I know, I know they're interested in the truth, but I don't know if they, you know, I'm not sure how they feel about you. They never said.

With the tape rolling, Berst admitted that it appeared, from his conversation with Parker and others, that UNLV was doing as it was required. "From what I've heard, they tried to find out the facts … What I figured was that they would probably come to you and make a deal for whatever the circumstances are in order to protect the school from getting in a jam. I figured they'd probably got you to sign a statement saying the NCAA is a bunch of bad guys and I put words in your mouth, and that kind of stuff. That's really what I figured probably happened to you, and I don't get that out of this conversation. Sounds like they asked you better questions and tried to figure out whether it was going on or not."

Relying on his notes, Berst then accused UNLV four times of hiding the truth and of asking questions in such a way as to keep Parker from being put in a bind. It should be noted that not once during the hour-long interview does Parker use the words "in a bind," even though Berst specifically attributed that quote to him several times.

The NCAA had spent months investigating Parker's involvement with UNLV and Rudy Jackson before declaring Parker a "representative of the university's interest," a euphemism usually used by the NCAA to describe boosters. According to the *NCAA Manual*, a school is responsible for the actions of anyone who "has been requested by the athletic department staff to assist in the recruitment of prospective student-athletes or is assisting in the recruitment of prospective student-athletes." If Parker was a representative of UNLV's interest, that would mean the NCAA rules regarding recruiting with which UNLV had to comply also would apply to Parker. Had UNLV asked Parker to work on its behalf in guiding Jackson to the Rebel program and then paid his one-night expenses for doing it, as was alleged, it would have been a rules violation. At the infractions hearing, Berst expressly told the committee that, during the October interview, Parker said the reason he accompanied Jackson to Las Vegas on Jackson's official visit was because the UNLV coaches asked him to do so. When UNLV attorneys specifically asked Berst at the hearing if Parker had "definitely said the UNLV coaches had requested he make the trip," a transcript of the hearing shows Berst responded, "Yes." But once again, Parker's tape told a different story. A review of the tape shows that at no time during the interview did Parker make or even imply the statement attributed to him by Berst. In fact, Parker explicitly said that he made the trip to Las Vegas because Jackson, not Tarkanian, asked him to. "Rudy wanted me there, you know, to help him out," Parker told Berst on the tape.

Berst also formally accused Tarkanian of bankrolling a trip for Jackson and Parker to attend the Dapper Dan Roundball Classic in Pittsburgh. In the interview he taped, however, Parker denied UNLV had paid for the trip and Berst admitted he had no reason other than intuition for making the allegation:

BERST: I think there is an allegation in there about them arranging to pay the expenses for you and Rudy to go down to that game. I don't really know that. That just makes sense to me that they would have, but nobody's told me that. The only guy that could know that for sure is you, and you didn't tell me that. That's, you know, that's one I don't know. So when we get to that question, I'll just say, you know, I—it just seemed like a reasonable, logical thing to happen based on other information.

PARKER: I've been going down there every year, and they never paid for it.

To underscore its defense, UNLV provided each member of the committee with a copy of the transcript and offered to make a copy of the tape for the enforcement staff. The transcripts were ignored, the copy of the tape never requested.

"You would have thought they would fire somebody who did

their job that bad," Tarkanian said. "But they wanted to throw him a parade."

The Parker incident underscored what definitely would prove to be the worst case of NCAA "justice." It didn't matter how many affidavits, how many taped transcripts, or how many depositions UNLV presented, the fact that the NCAA had no standards of evidence allowed the Infractions Committee to repeatedly accept hearsay from NCAA investigators while more legally recognized evidence—depositions, affidavits, receipts, and other documents—submitted by UNLV was ignored.

Tarkanian and his lawyers were continually amazed at how off base the NCAA was in its efforts to crucify the coach. It seemed the organization was willing to ignore what UNLV lawyers believed was an airtight defense of its allegations. On one occasion, McMenamin accused Tarkanian of asking Harvey J. Munford, a part-time UNLV instructor, to give a B grade to center David Vaughn. McMenamin charged the grade was falsified because, he said, Vaughn never attended Munford's class, "The Role of Black Development in America." McMenamin, reading from a memo never shared with the university, told the Committee on Infractions that Munford told him Tarkanian had enrolled Vaughn in the class "with the understanding that the student would not have to attend class or complete any work." McMenamin said Munford had volunteered the information, never answering the obvious question of why an instructor would admit to a total stranger that he had committed the academically professional sin of falsifying grades. According to court records, that was the extent of the NCAA's evidence: an unsigned statement from McMenamin recalling his conversation with Munford.

In Tarkanian's defense, UNLV's attorneys came back with:

• A sworn affidavit from Munford stating that he had never made such a statement to McMenamin and had never made an arrangement with Tarkanian or anyone else from the UNLV athletic department for Vaughn or any other student to receive special treatment or grades. Munford said that he did tell McMenamin that Vaughn did well in the class even though he didn't feel Vaughn attended as often as he could or should have. Munford also stated that he informed McMenamin that he had worked with Vaughn on his own to help him in the class and that although most of the class members received As, with no Ds or Fs and only one or two Cs being given, Vaughn received a B, a grade actually below the average of the class. Munford also stated that Vaughn had turned in the term paper required of all students.

• An affidavit from Vaughn stating that Tarkanian had made no special arrangements with his teacher and that he had attended classes and done the required work.

• Letters from five students, none of whom were athletes, stating that they saw Vaughn attend class and that it was easy to notice him because he was almost seven feet tall.

• A statement from Temma Rosenberg, a student in the class, that she had typed Vaughn's final paper for him and had been present in class when he had orally presented the paper.

Because the allegation attacked the professor's integrity, Munford was allowed to defend himself. On appeal, his attorney presented the NCAA Council with:

• Results of a polygraph test in which Munford restated the points made in his affidavit. He said he had made no special arrangements with Tarkanian concerning Vaughn or any other student. The analysis of the polygraph showed Munford was telling the truth.

• A voice analysis that supported Munford's polygraph test.

The Committee on Infractions and the NCAA Council ignored all those documents. Tarkanian was found guilty of the charge by the committee, and the finding was upheld by the council.

Congressional investigators, after reviewing NCAA records of the charge and UNLV's defense, called the Infractions Committee's verdict "curious," especially given the testimony of two committee members who said when one person's word is pitted against another's and neither is present so that his demeanor can be observed by the committee, "The issue will be resolved, absent other evidence, in favor of the accused." Former committee chairman Arthur Reynolds said as much when he appeared before the congressional subcommittee: "It is well understood by the enforcement staff that where a violation is not admitted by the institution, the staff must carry the burden of proof and they must satisfy the Committee that the available evidence supports the finding of violation."

In its final investigative report, the congressional subcommittee wrote: "Curious, then, that when UNLV's basketball coach Jerry Tarkanian was accused of suborning a bogus high grade for a student-athlete in a course it was understood he would never have to attend, on the strength of a statement to the infractions committee by investigator Hale McMenamin of his recollection of conversations he had with the instructor involved, and nothing more, Tarkanian and the instructor were convicted. In fairness, Professor [Charles Alan] Wright testified that he voted against this finding. The other members of the infractions committee appearing before the subcommittee simply could not remember, in this most celebrated of all infractions cases in the history of the NCAA, just how they had voted, though obviously a majority of the panel, evidently unswayed by Wright's own subjectively high standards, did vote for the finding. The subcommittee is astounded that the infractions committee could have resolved this particular issue against the accused, in favor of its own investigator, and with a straight face professed to adherence to any sort of evidentiary standard or sense of burden of proof. We do take comfort in Professor Wright's statement, referring to this UNLV finding, that, 'I do not believe that a finding would have been made in that episode if it came before us today.'"

Of all the incredibly bad work the NCAA did in this case, this is the charge that still bothers Tarkanian the most. He said Wright's concession to Congress has done nothing to reverse the public black eye he received in the press. With great fanfare, the NCAA used that charge of academic fraud to besmirch his reputation, Tarkanian said, while few people ever heard Wright say the finding was wrong. Despite Wright's pronouncement that Tarkanian would not be convicted of the charge "if it came before us today," the academic dishonesty allegation is the one that reporters use most regularly when explaining the major rules Tarkanian was found to have violated.

"This has hurt me more than anything else because for years, every time we went into the tournament or every time we'd be doing something great, invariably, someone would write up about that academic fraud," Tarkanian said. "But never would they mention how Charles Alan Wright said what he did. This was something totally manufactured. There wasn't any facts to support it. And it is something I've had to live with for a long time. That's probably been harder on me and my family than any other charge that we've had."

Sometimes it seemed the charges defied logic. Still, the university was required to spend taxpayers' dollars to chase the NCAA's allegations. NCAA investigators accused Tarkanian of arranging for David Vaughn to stay free of charge at the Flagship Inn in Flagstaff, Arizona. They even provided a date when Vaughn was supposed to have received the free accommodations. But while attempting to find out if the allegation was true, UNLV attorneys could not locate a Flagship Inn in Flagstaff. In fact, their inquiry with the Flagstaff Police Department showed no motel by that name ever existed in Flagstaff. The NCAA staff admitted it had no more information and agreed, after UNLV had spent more than a week and thousands of dollars checking it out, to drop the charge.

Convinced that this system was stacked against them, Tarkanian and his lawyers requested the right to bring witnesses to its hearings. Tarkanian himself wanted the right to face his accusers. He believed that if the Committee on Infractions was allowed to listen to what his accusers had to say rather than what the NCAA investigators claimed they had said, he would be vindicated. In an early exchange of correspondence, NCAA administrator Warren Brown made it clear that witnesses would not be a part of the NCAA hearing process. Even though UNLV offered to pay the costs of transporting witnesses to the hearings, the request was denied by the committee. It was clear that only the "accused" and not the "accusers" would be cross-examined before the committee, prompting two courts to note that "every fundamental principle pertaining to the plaintiff's due process rights was violated by the NCAA."

In the end, all the witnesses in the world wouldn't have mattered. In court testimony taken during Tarkanian's lawsuit, several members of the Infractions Committee admitted that their long-standing relationship with Berst and other NCAA staff members was the reason they gave more consideration to the staff memos than to UNLV's collection of affidavits and documented evidence.

Harry Cross, a University of Washington law professor and member of the committee, testified that the file boxes full of documents presented by UNLV "did not weigh as heavily as what staff had told us" when he was making his decision. He said the basis for that greater faith in the staff was a "great trust and confidence" that "had developed over the years." Chairman Reynolds, after admitting the staff provided "no evidence" other than its unsigned memos, also said he "gave great weight to their integrity as I had experienced it over many years." And University of Kentucky law professor William Matthews, another committee member, even went so far as to say he had his mind made up against UNLV before the hearing even began. When asked if he had made his decision prior to the hearing, "I did believe that was the case," Matthews said from the witness stand.

The attention given Tarkanian's case worsened his national reputation, to be sure. But it also took its toll on the NCAA, whose backside suddenly was exposed to an increasing number of newspaper columnists. In 1978, the *Chicago Sun-Times* declared Tarkanian the "most important" college coach of the year. "Granted there may have been better ones, particularly at De Paul, Marquette, and UCLA," the newspaper wrote. "But none of these fine gentlemen ever may have the lasting impact Tarkanian has had on the way that morality is legislated in their sport." The *Los Angeles Times*'s Jim Murray wrote this after the congressional hearings were complete: "The National Collegiate Athletic Association as a governing body in collegiate athletics occupies the same spot in the hearts of its subjects as the Gestapo in Warsaw. The NCAA deals in more hearsay than Rona Barrett."

As the headlines and the evidence mounted, so did the legal opinions.

Clark County (Nevada) District Court judge James Brennan, who was the first to hear the case and who ruled against the NCAA, said this in his trial court opinion:

The case against Tarkanian was incredible. The evidence the NCAA presented was 100 percent hearsay without a scrap of documentation in substantiation. The evidence shows that every fundamental principle pertaining to the plaintiff's due process rights were violated. The Committee on Infractions and its staff conducted a star chamber proceeding and a trial by ambush against the plaintiff. The plaintiff was denied the specific charges against him and the facts upon which such charges are based. The plaintiff was denied the right to present evidence and call witnesses in his behalf. And most important, he was denied the right to be confronted by witnesses against him and cross-examine them. The Committee on Infractions allowed a staff investigator, who, the evidence clearly shows, swore he would get Tarkanian if it was the last thing he ever did, to act as investigator, judge and jury. The record is replete with lies, distortions and half-truths. The evidence clearly shows Berst as a man possessed and consumed with animosity toward the plaintiff. There is no legal credible evidence to support the findings and action of the NCAA.

While hearing the case, Brennan took special exception to Berst's handling of his duties: "A review of the sworn statements in evidence shows that David Berst had an obsession to the point of paranoia to harm the plaintiff. The record is replete with lies, distortions and half-truths of David Berst in this case to the extent that anything he may have presented to the Committee on Infractions was totally devoid of credibility."

Not to be outdone, Judge Goldman, who next heard the case, put it this way:

This case presents a classic example of how misperception becomes suspicion, which in turn becomes hostility, which leads, inevitably, to a deprivation of one's rights. In short, the NCAA now seems to say: If you want to play ball, you must join us, obey rules and surrender any claim you may have under the Bill of Rights. This court disagrees with that attitude, as any fair-minded person must. At least one of the NCAA's investigators [David Berst] inspired, authored and drafted—in whole or in part—the NCAA preliminary investigation; the authority to issue an inquiry to UNLV; the Official [letter of] Inquiry; the minutes of the Committee on Infractions wherein the committee's rules appeared; the Confidential Report of the Committee; the Findings and Penalties imposed by that Committee; the Expanded Confidential Report (with the enforcement division's comments) used by the Council on appeal; and the order of the Council and the widely promulgated press releases about the supposed violations of NCAA "legislation." In sum, what started out as an association whose members met and acceded to certain lofty goals ended up as the NCAA-bureaucracy which looks upon its friends (sycophants) with feigned pleasure, and its enemies (those who still recognize the U.S. Constitution) with barely concealed malevolence. Regrettably, both the full-time investigators and part-time Committee on Infractions and NCAA Council members acted and thought, not like Caesar's wife, but rather as arrogant lords of the manor. The NCAA, incredibly, sought to equate "time" with "due process." The reasoning of the NCAA was, apparently, that since the infractions committee's and the NCAA Council's presentations were time-consuming, Tarkanian and UNLV were afforded due process. NCAA practices might be considered "efficient," but so was Adolf Eichmann and so [was] the Ayatollah.

During the trial, Goldman wrote that in his opinion NCAA lawyers even attempted to argue that this case was out of the jurisdiction of any court. They made that claim after quoting the *NCAA Manual*, which states that the Infractions Committee's decision "shall be final, binding and conclusive, and shall not be subject to further review by the Council or any other authority." As arrogant as the NCAA was, it still seemed hard to believe the organization would tell a judge that its decision was above the law. Goldman said that assertion was "laughable." He said the clause in the *NCAA Manual* "illustrates the arrogance" of the organization. "Even the NCAA's insistence on the use of the word 'legislation' instead of 'rules' gives us a view of the NCAA's view of itself and its power," he wrote.

The NCAA attempted to discredit the opinions of Judges Brennan and Goldman, claiming Tarkanian had a "home-court advantage" in the Nevada judicial system, apparently ignoring the fact that that charge could be levied at the NCAA as well. Tarkanian said his case proved the NCAA's home-court advantage "is worth more than a lay-up. Hell, it's a slam dunk."

But the opinion that really mattered didn't go Tarkanian's way. In a 5–4 decision issued in December 1988, the U.S. Supreme Court rejected Tarkanian's argument that the NCAA, which has through its own constitution the power to force a university to suspend a coach or face expulsion from the organization, must provide those it punishes with basic due process rights, including the ability to face one's accusers. What the court was asked to decide was whether the NCAA is an arm of the state—or a "state actor"—because it essentially has the authority to force a state university to discipline a public employee. If the court had decided the NCAA does carry out actions usually reserved for the state, then the NCAA would be required to treat those whose lives it affects with the same legal rights as the state would.

"If the NCAA wants to have the power that it has and it wants to deal with state schools, it's not too much to ask that [it] afford due process in the manner in which it affects the property and liberty of someone whose rights it may cut off," Tarkanian's attorney Sam Lionel said after arguing the case. "Americans have grown to expect decent and fair treatment and that's not the NCAA's way of doing business."

The court's majority didn't agree with Lionel's legal thesis, deciding that the NCAA was a voluntary association and therefore could not be a state actor. If NCAA members don't like the rules, the majority held, they should either fight to change them or quit.

Supreme Court justice Byron White, a onetime all-American football player at the University of Colorado and the only former college athlete on the Supreme Court, noted in his minority opinion that it was a "given" for purposes of the Supreme Court's review that the NCAA hearings "provided to Tarkanian were constitutionally inadequate." Although the NCAA asked the U.S. Supreme Court to overturn the Nevada Supreme Court's finding that Tarkanian's due process rights had been violated, the court refused even to look at the issue. Legally, White wrote, that left the Nevada court's determination that NCAA hearings lacked due process as the final legal authority on the issue.

Ironically, several court watchers have pointed out that Tarkanian likely would have won his case if it had been heard a year earlier. President Reagan's appointment of conservative jurist Anthony Kennedy to replace the more moderate Lewis Powell earlier that year provided the NCAA with the swing vote to support its position.

NCAA watchers point out, just as ironically, that Tarkanian might also have won if the same case were filed today. NCAA members decided in 1985 to require all member institutions to include a clause in coaches' employment contracts making violation of major NCAA rules cause for immediate dismissal. If being found guilty by the NCAA's Committee on Infractions of rules violations can lead to the firing of a state employee, then the organization surely has become a state actor and must protect the rights of that employee, several lawyers said.

In response to the national uproar created when it won the Tarkanian case, the NCAA appointed a committee to study its enforcement process and offer changes. In October of 1991, that committee suggested several major reforms—including mandatory tape recording of all statements and sharing of all evidence—that Tarkanian had begged for. When the committee's recommendations were announced, Berst bit his tongue, saying only that the changes, if adopted, might make the enforcement staff's job more difficult.

"All those years, I said they needed to do those things and they said they couldn't," Tarkanian said. "Now that they're going to have to change Berst is worried that it's going to be tougher on him. Now that they've got to be a little more fair, that's tougher. Too bad. When they can't run over people, they're going to have to do their job better. I'm glad to see that they're moving into the twentieth century.

"I'm glad the things that I did have had some impact. I'm glad a lot of the changes were made. I know a lot of them were made because of my fight. Certainly, it's taken its toll on me. It's something I wish I'd have never gotten into. But after all the knocks I've taken, I'm really happy that this much came out of it. I think it's going to be a lot fairer for coaches in the future. I think I left behind a more closely scrutinized enforcement staff. I don't know how good it's going to be yet, but the investigators are going to know people are watching. The rules are such that they're going to have to be a lot fairer than they used to be.

"I've always said we need an organization like the NCAA, we need an enforcement staff, and they should be able to enforce the rules. And they should be able to suspend coaches that violate the rules. I'm in total agreement with all that. But you need an NCAA enforcement program that's fair. That's all I want."

Tarkanian said he believes the NCAA battle he fought for most of his adult life is his greatest gift to the game of basketball. "Being the winningest coach of all time, that's great," Tarkanian said. "But fighting for what's right, that's better. They've made a lot of changes at the NCAA. They need to make more. But I feel like I made a difference. Sure, my reputation will never be the same. I did what I thought was right, though."

6

A New President, a Bad Omen

Tarkanian survived the NCAA battle with everything but his reputation intact. He had his job. His team had gone 20–8 and 21–8 during the two years of NCAA probation. His fans and university had stood solidly behind him.

Then came the year he'd like to forget. 1980–81. The probation, which had kept the Rebels from playing televised games or in the NCAA Tournament, combined with the persistent rumors that he was going to be fired or was headed to the pros, had cost him several recruits. As the team lacked depth, Tarkanian had abandoned the running game the year before. The 100-point games that once were Rebel trademarks now were Rebel landmarks. Tarkanian couldn't manage to find a starting lineup that could play together. Injuries riddled what was already a shallow bench, and suddenly the Rebels had gone from a program once ranked first to a team that was establishing firsts.

Tarkanian, who had won every home game when he was at Long Beach, suffered his first loss to Long Beach when the 49ers dumped UNLV by twenty-seven points, 104–77, in Anaheim. Tarkanian lost two games in a row at home for the first time in his career. His team lost five of six games, something a Tarkanian team had never done.

But it still appeared as if UNLV could get an NIT bid as it prepared to play its final game, a home contest with Wyoming. Three more firsts were set that night. Rebel star Sidney Green played his first-ever scoreless game. Wyoming became the first team to beat UNLV at home by more than twenty-five points, winning 97–70. And Tarkanian, with no chance of postseason play, had the first—and only—team of his long career that didn't win at least twenty games. The Rebels were 16–12.

He was so distraught over the team's performance that he contemplated resigning, quitting coaching altogether. He didn't eat. He didn't sleep. His wife didn't even stay in the same room with him. "What can you say about our UNLV basketball players so far?" Tarkanian wrote in one of his mid-season columns. "It's been a nightmare—horrendous—with elusive, brief flashes of brilliance heavily outweighed by mental lapses, mis-thrown passes, numerous turnovers and escaped intensity." When the season was over, Tarkanian said good riddance. He canceled the awards banquet for the team, saying he only threw banquets for teams that had played hard and showed dedication. "I always felt at a banquet you should say nice things about people," Tarkanian said. "I didn't think I could get up there and say nice things without being a hypocrite."

In part because basketball is so much a part of his life, losing for Jerry Tarkanian is intolerable, almost physically painful. His aversion to defeat is much greater than that of others in his profession. That desire to win, former players and assistants say, is what makes him willing to outwork coaching competitors.

Not only does Tarkanian like to win, he likes to be around winners. Rather than being intimidated by the success of others, he gravitates to it. It is this attitude that has allowed him to attract great assistant coaches, many of whom have gone on to become successful head coaches. "When you're around people who like to win, it's infectious," Tarkanian has said.

That's why he was elated to learn, in 1984, that the university's new president, Robert Maxson, was coming from the University of Houston. That fifty-year-old university was, like UNLV, a new kid on the block in the city of higher education and, again like UNLV, had used athletics to build its lightly regarded academic reputation. The school's basketball program, with coach Guy Lewis and stars Akeem Olajuwon and Clyde Drexler, had gone to three straight Final Fours. The football team had won the tough Southwest Conference and played in two Cotton Bowls. Carl Lewis anchored a great men's track program, and the golf team averaged one national championship every two years over a two-decade stretch. Despite news reports that Maxson was the leader who would change UNLV's image as a "basketball school," it looked as if the university Regents, who had been swept off their feet by this 5´8" rail of a man with a Southern charm that was as thick as his painfully slow Southern drawl, had made a choice that would benefit Tarkanian's basketball program. The timing could not have been better for Tarkanian, whose team appeared to have recovered from probation and was on the way back up.

Though Houston football coach Bill Yeomans later was fired for massive NCAA rules violations, Maxson's relationship with him was admittedly "close," as was his relationship to Lewis. Tarkanian also was told that Maxson had coached high school basketball in South Florida and had bragged about being a two-time conference Coach of the Year. And Tarkanian heard Maxson say he had worked in the desegregation movement while at Mississippi State.

Shortly after Maxson arrived on campus, Tarkanian received a call from a friend in Texas telling him he "was fortunate to have a guy like Maxson on his team" since the new president felt so strongly about athletics. Within weeks after Maxson moved to Las Vegas, the Tarkanians invited him and his wife to a barbecue at their home for a night out with several boosters. Though they were as different as night and day—Maxson a man of manicured nails, Italian shoes, and monogrammed shirt cuffs; Tarkanian a man who chewed his nails and wore Nikes and short-sleeved shirts—the two seemed to hit it off famously. Tarkanian thought this was the whole package. A president from a major Division I school with a winning tradition who had a background in basketball, understood and was sympathetic to the needs of the black athlete, and had a close friend who had gone through an NCAA investigation. The only thing that would have made Maxson look any better was if he were Armenian.

"Right after he got here, we had lunch with Brad Rothermel at the top of the Dunes," Tarkanian said. "He [Maxson] told us how much he supported athletics. We talked about the Southwest Conference, about coaches he knew that I knew. One of my best friends from junior college coaching was Jim Killingsworth, who was then coaching at TCU [Texas Christian University]. He told Eddie Sutton stories. I thought, this guy really knows sports. This was great."

The Regents thought they had found the whole package as well. Although his academic credentials didn't ring with tradition, Maxson was a skillful politician who always seemed to say the right thing about academics and the potential of UNLV. He worked well with the media—always speaking in sound bites and using catchy phrases—and was willing to spend time raising money, a quality that seems more important than academic credentials at many universities today. He was precisely what UNLV needed at the time—an image maker in a city built on image at a university struggling with its image. The Regents were so excited by Maxson they offered him the job—reportedly in violation of state laws—without even interviewing the four other finalists.

"We became a new university the day Dr. Maxson stepped foot on the UNLV campus," Regents chairwoman Carolyn Sparks said. "He was brought in to salvage a university just like Jerry was brought in to salvage a basketball program. The day Dr. Maxson said this is going to be a great institution of higher learning, all the people who had wanted this to happen over the years suddenly had someone in a point position of leadership, and I think it turned the community around. The Regents had to make a decision about what they were going to do with UNLV. Are we going to let it bumble along the way it has been or are we going to have a search, find a president, bring him in, and make an academic institution out of this and I think that was the decision they made. We could have gone another twenty-five years the way we were if there hadn't been a change in leadership. He made us believe."

They believed he had just the right mix of charm and ego, though some worried from the beginning that ego was the greater of his characteristics. "Bob Maxson has an ego the size of the Frontier Hotel," said former *Review-Journal* sports editor Bob Sands, a Maxson disciple. "Maxson is very, very slick and he can handle himself so well. He is as good as I've ever seen in political in-fighting. With his slick, southern Mississippi/Texas drawl, don't ever let that kid you because the guy will get inside of you and make a move on you. He's tough."

Maxson was born and reared in Watson, Arkansas, a little farming community not far from the Texas border. His Southern Baptist father, who stayed in school only through the sixth grade, owned a 120-acre cotton farm that he worked mostly with his two sons. Maxson said he was "bored in the summers, with no neighbors close by." So he took to athletics and, as a sophomore, made the varsity basketball team. As important as basketball was to him, religion was more important to his parents. When a storm forced a Friday night game with a rival high school to be rescheduled for a Wednesday night, Maxson recalled, "My father wouldn't allow me to play." He had to attend Wednesday night services."

He graduated from high school and enrolled at the nearest four-year school, the University of Arkansas at Monticello. He received his bachelor's degree in education there in 1958 and, shortly thereafter, received a call from his high school basketball coach, who by then was working in South Florida. There was an opening in the Palm Beach County School District for a junior high basketball coach. Maxson packed his belongings and made the drive. Two years later, he was offered the head coaching job at Pahokee High School and, in his second season, was named Coach of the Year in the Sunshine State Conference. One of his students was Sylvia Parrish, whose father was mayor of Pahokee. The two took a liking to one another and later would marry. Boca Raton High, a more prestigious school in a more wealthy neighborhood, called and offered him the head coaching job there. He accepted and, in three years, was named Coach of the Year once again.

Maxson's coaching talents were surpassed only by his political skills, said Phil Mallon, a former teaching colleague at Boca Raton. "He had worked himself into favor with people, and knew who to know," Mallon said. "He was very smooth. If I ever did hear anything that was construed as negative it was more those who, they didn't have the same verbal fluency and they would say, well, you know, he's a very smooth guy and he could con anyone."

Neither man had ever heard of the other at the time, but it

looked as if Bob Maxson might one day be competing with Jerry Tarkanian for recruits at rival universities rather than the spotlight at the same school. But Maxson decided to get out of high school coaching and into higher education. While working at Boca Raton High, he attended nearby Florida Atlantic University and received a master's in educational administration. Then he, Sylvia, and their two children left for Mississippi State, where Maxson was a research assistant and a doctoral candidate. He took his doctorate in educational leadership and headed for Montgomery, Alabama, where he taught education at Auburn University's extension campus. In 1973, the year Jerry Tarkanian headed for UNLV, Maxson became dean of the school of education at the little extension campus. After a brief stop at Appalachian State University in Boone, North Carolina, he began a six-year stint with the University of Houston system. His star continued to rise, and he was considered a leading candidate for the presidency at the well-established University of Rhode Island when a headhunting firm gave his name to UNLV's Regents.

It didn't take a genius, Maxson admits, to see that UNLV was the better bet. While Rhode Island was worried about maintaining the status quo, UNLV was a university on the go. It was also a good time to get out of Texas. The depressed oil market had left the state's financial future in jeopardy, and Houston was facing budget cuts. At the same time he saw in UNLV a campus on the verge of explosion. The construction crane, he could see, might soon replace the Rebel as the school's mascot. Additionally, fractious relations between administrators and faculty had led to a request by the previous president, Leonard Goodall, to order mental examinations for those faculty considered miscreant. The Regents, unbelievably, granted the request. Goodall also announced his plans to change the sacrosanct provisions of tenure, leading the faculty to consider unionizing. Goodall said openly that the university wasn't that good. Morale was at an all-time low. Enrollment had dropped for the first time in years. The university, Maxson knew, had nowhere to go but up. In a city longing for acceptance, in a region where explosive growth was inevitable, Maxson found wealthy business leaders—most of whom sent their children out of town for college—who were just beginning to understand the value of a "real" university in Las Vegas and were willing to reach for their wallets. With the expansion that was obviously in UNLV's future, Maxson knew that the school would be constructing many buildings that one day could bear the names of these benefactors, forever locking them in as patrons of the university.

With the right mixture of politicking and "perception manipulation," Maxson knew he could have Las Vegas eating out of the palm of his hand. He set himself an aggressive schedule, quickly becoming famous for his early-morning and weekend meetings with business people and politicians who could help him advance his cause, his daily business lunches, his open-door policy, and his never-ending attendance at as many as five university-related events a day. He became a media darling, posing for pictures and doing TV interviews with his sport coat draped over his shoulder in an effort to look like Everyman. Maxson regularly took visitors on walks through campus, where he proudly told the listener everything he knew about any student who walked up. He prides himself in his ability to squeeze tight when he grabs your hand for a handshake, working hard to prove there's more than mental power in his small body. He has refused to take a vacation and, though some have said that decision is a sign of insecurity, he ignores the criticism. His wife even made light of the situation on the family answering machine. "Since you know Bobby won't take a vacation," the message says with a little chuckle, "you know we can't be far away. Leave a message and we'll call right back."

Maxson immediately became a fixture in the city's establishment, showing up in the right places at the right time. In Las Vegas, that also means coming early to Rebel basketball games.

But if the arrival of Tarkanian's dream president was to be an academic-athletic marriage made in heaven, it didn't take long for Maxson to request a separation. His first month on campus, he called Brad Rothermel to his office and asked what it would take to fire Tarkanian.

"It [the meeting] was in his office and the words were in effect of, you know, is there something that could be done to make a change in the basketball program, the head men's basketball situation?" Rothermel recalls. "I don't think it was as strong as 'What can we do to get rid of Jerry Tarkanian?' Although that's what was meant. I looked at him and I said, 'Here the guy is winning, we won the conference each year. He wasn't violating any rules, as far as I could tell, he was creating winners and he was doing it within the budgetary framework that was created for him.' I asked him [Maxson] whether or not he was aware of rule violations in the program. And he indicated that he was not. So I asked why in the world he would want to get rid of one of the best coaches in the country without good reason. He didn't answer. I can say it was pretty clear in my mind at that point that he knew where I stood on Jerry and I knew where he stood."

Maxson bristled at Rothermel's revelation:

"If Brad said I said that to him, he's not, he's not being straight up," Maxson responded. "But you need to understand, when I tell you that I didn't have a conversation on something, that doesn't mean I don't feel that way about something. In other words, if I tell you I had no conversations about a person's comments, if I, when I say I didn't have any conversations with Brad on this or on that, no matter what the subject, that doesn't mean, I'm not saying I didn't have certain feelings about it, I'm just saying that those are certain things that I don't discuss. I haven't done an evaluation on Jerry with another employee. It's just that simple."

"Why would I make that up?" said Rothermel, who resigned as athletic director in 1990 but continues to teach at the university. "If you look at the dynamics of the time and you were going to get in a position you had to select one or the other, because I was also interested in remaining in the position I held at the time, then you've got to make a decision who's more powerful of the two. At the time, there was no question about it. The president was noticeably jealous of Jerry. He was jealous of how much money he made and of Jerry's popularity in the community. Probably one in ten people can identify Maxson while nine in ten can identify Tarkanian. If you get to know Bob Maxson, you'll know that bothers him."

Rothermel's answer to Maxson in 1984 drew an immediate line in the desert sand.

Rothermel said Maxson made it clear to Rothermel that he didn't think much of Tarkanian and the image his program was projecting. Maxson acknowledged that an article which appeared in *People* magazine while he was interviewing for the UNLV job in 1984 solidified his thought that the image being projected was not what he would tolerate were he to become president.

"I was on an airplane to Seattle," Maxson remembers, "with Houston boosters and our team was in the Final Four there. My wife was reading this magazine and she said, 'I think you better look at this, you won't believe it.'"

The magazine profiled Tarkanian and included lengthy criticism from several of his former players at Long Beach about the coach's less-than-aggressive attitude about academics. But the thing Maxson remembered most was the cover of the team's media guide, which was reproduced in the article. On the cover, UNLV's starting five were pictured with three scantily clad showgirls.

"It upset me," Maxson said. "We're a university. We may be in Las Vegas, but we're not gonna say, 'Well, we're in Las Vegas so we're different from other universities.' I said this is not an image that we will project. It's not the image I want for the university. I regarded this in poor taste, totally inappropriate. I also stopped a poster from being sold that had a stripper posing with our cheerleaders. That just doesn't belong on a college campus."

Within days after moving into his new job, Maxson called the sports information director and instructed her never to use those types of images again.

Later that fall, the men's basketball team played in the Great Alaskan Shootout. "I remember, one of the big things about that tournament is that each team is divided up and goes with other teams to people's houses for Thanksgiving dinner," Rothermel said. "The next day, Bill Guthridge, Dean Smith's associate head coach [at the University of North Carolina], came up to me and asked how the athletic department was relating to the new president. I asked why he wondered, and he told me that he and the president of UNC had gone to the same house as Maxson for Thanksgiving and that Maxson had said how the basketball program was a shambles, it was out of control, but that he'd got it under control, he'd got Tark under control."

"I would hear things like that constantly," Tarkanian said of the Alaska story. "I never paid much attention to it because I had seen how stories could be changed by adding a word here or there. And I knew some people like to talk big to make themselves seem more important. That's what I figured he was doing and that was fine with me."

"By that time, I knew we were in trouble," Rothermel said.

"Actually, I should have known things weren't going to work out when he told me he'd tried out for the men's basketball team in college and got cut. He went to college at the University of Arkansas at Monticello. Heck, there couldn't have been more than ten guys who tried out for the team."

Las Vegas is a city known more for marriages and divorces than for honeymoons. Those close to Tarkanian, like Rothermel, sensed the end of the honeymoon with Maxson early. They read quotes from Maxson in which the president said he "will not hesitate to make the tough decisions when it is in the best interest of the university. This university is bigger than any one of us. We must never forget that. No one person or group is bigger than the university."

"I remember showing that to Jerry and saying, 'Who could he be talking about? He's talking about you,'" Lois Tarkanian said. "He'd only been on campus two months when he uttered those words. Other people pointed that out to Jerry, too. But Jerry, he just ignored us all. He thought Maxson was wonderful."

Without Rothermel's help, Maxson was going to have to do this his way. He turned to his strengths, politicking and working with the business leaders, the media, and the academic core of the university.

Las Vegas was a dramatically different city in 1984 than it was the day Tarkanian showed up eleven years earlier. Most of the casinos, many of which had been individually owned and linked to the mob in the past, now were owned by corporations. Though it can be debated whether corporate America is morally superior to the mob, the fact that decisions were now made in boardrooms and not back rooms definitely worked to Maxson's advantage. He moved well in those circles, much better than most educators. And certainly much better than Tarkanian.

"Everybody knew he was networking," Tarkanian said. "We used to laugh about it. He used to love the limelight. He would almost insist on being on television at halftime of our games. On television, he'd say what a great coach I was, then he'd run up after the game and tell me what he said."

When Maxson worked his way into those boardrooms to meet with the city's new power elite, Maxson constantly shared with them a vision, one that's hard to knock. It was a picture of a "great urban university" that would educate their employees and their employees' families. No longer, he promised, would they have to go out of state for a first-rate education. What Maxson wasn't saying at the time, but what became part of the dialogue later, was that this vision couldn't be reached with Jerry Tarkanian dominating the headlines.

Asked if the university could ever become truly great with a basketball program and a coach who were the source of so many negative headlines, Maxson's top assistant, John Irsfeld, was quite candid. "I don't think so because you know you've got to have the world's agreement to be what you want to be or you can't be what you want to be. If you declare yourself without the agreement of the world, then that's considered to be crazy. We could have made all kinds of strides academically, but if we don't get the agreement of the world, if something stands between us and convincing people that we were making those strides, it had to be dealt with."

Said John Unrue, UNLV's vice president for academic affairs and Maxson's second-closest confidant: "If the conduct that we have seen had continued over there [in the basketball program], it would have been increasingly more difficult for us to have achieved the kind of academic standing that we want to achieve."

As time went on, Tarkanian's prominence became downright bothersome. When Maxson, Tarkanian, Brad Booke, and Danny Tarkanian were returning from their 1990 meeting with the NCAA Infractions Committee in Chicago, a fan ran up to Tarkanian in O'Hare Airport and asked if he would pose for a quick picture. No problem, Tarkanian said. The fan then thrust his camera at Maxson. "Will you take a picture of me and Coach Tarkanian," he asked with no clue that he was talking to the university president. As Maxson wiped a quick scowl from his face, Booke grabbed the camera and offered to do it, sparing Maxson the moment.

A few months later, attorney Roy Smith, who had been working with the university lawyers in defense of NCAA allegations, took a trip to the NCAA's headquarters in Kansas City with Irsfeld and Booke. "It became apparent that the attention Jerry and the team get is very irritating to them," Smith said.

"During the two days, several people who had noticed his [Irsfeld's] credit card or asked where we were from had commented on how great the basketball team was," Smith recalled. "Finally, as we were flying back, a thunderstorm over Dallas had forced us to circle the airport. A Delta stewardess asked what we did, and we told her. She said, 'I don't know anything about your university, but you sure have a great basketball team.' Irsfeld had had enough. He exploded. 'Do you know we've got the largest supercomputer in the world? Do you know we've got dozens of valedictorians going to UNLV?' He just snapped. His feelings were hurt because an airline stewardess said she knew nothing about UNLV except basketball. If they're trying to create the Harvard of the West, that's fine. But they have to remember where it all started."

On campus, though, the attitude Maxson was projecting toward athletics was being hailed by the academics, many of whom had grown tired of working for "a basketball school." Maxson was singing their tune, and it was the hottest act not appearing on The Strip.

"I remember in the spring of 1984 being invited to sit in and listen to a man who might be our new president," Irsfeld said. "I looked at this guy and I remember making notes to myself that he looked like a cross between Andy Griffith and Robert Ludlum. But this guy was deadly serious. He said in that meeting, I remember very clearly, 'If I were your president, my primary objective would always be to enhance the academic reputation of this institution and every decision I would make would be guided by that principle.' I walked out of that room saying to myself, 'If that man is our president, the time will inevitably come when he and Coach Tarkanian are head to head. I knew that if somebody was going to take charge of this institution with the idea that the academic reputation was primary, that meant that what was already primary was going to become secondary. That meant basketball. It was an exciting time for those of us on the academic side. In my heart of hearts, in my dreams of dreams, and I know I could get killed for saying this, what I'd really like is to have us a good strong Division III athletic program."

As important as it was for Maxson to win over his academic colleagues, it was more important that he get the town's heavies to weigh in on his side in this still officially undeclared tug-of-war. Just as he did with the professors, Maxson said everything the VIPs wanted to hear. He wanted to change the university's image, he told them. Then he could start changing the university. Some of what he said was even true.

"Every first-class city has a first-class university," he would tell them over and over again. "What we have here is a good university, a diamond in the rough. Together, we can make it better."

"UNLV's image is much better nationally than it is here," he said with a straight face on another occasion.

With an equally straight face, he proclaimed, "This university will be the cultural center of a great city." This he said to Las Vegans who only a handful of years earlier required applause prompts in their symphony program. The only "cultural" event that didn't require such prompts, it seemed, was the Rebel basketball games.

"The ambition I encountered most immediately among Las Vegans was the desire to shed the Bugsy Siegel image," Maxson told the *Los Angeles Times* in 1987. "If the time had come for Las Vegas to take itself seriously as an American city, then the improvement of UNLV was an obvious place to begin. A lot of people loved UNLV, but they were also vaguely ashamed of it."

Almost overnight, the city responded. Pride in the university, not just its basketball program, began to bubble.

As Maxson surveyed the desert landscape, the targets for immediate attention became clear. Editors and owners of the city's two newspapers became regulars on Maxson's power lunch circuit. The president of Summa Corporation, manager of the Howard Hughes estate, and the largest private land owner in southern Nevada got his own numbers on Maxson's speed-dial phone. Executives with the Valley Bank and First Interstate Bank started receiving invitations to everything that was happening on campus. Curiously, the one guy he never called for lunch was Tarkanian, the man whose life's work had given UNLV the name recognition that attracted Maxson.

But the relationship that proved to be most valuable for Maxson was with Steve and Elaine Wynn, the self-proclaimed "Mr. and Mrs. Las Vegas."

"I want to enhance the reputation of this institution," Maxson told the Wynns, as he did everyone else. "I think we can be one of the top five urban institutions in the country within the next ten years. But we must rescue ourselves from the image we've had."

The words sounded familiar to Wynn, who himself had spent the past several years working on an image make-over—both for himself and his city.

The son of a bingo operator and compulsive gambler from Maryland, Wynn first visited Las Vegas at age ten, when his father had arranged to operate a bingo parlor on the second floor of the Silver Slipper casino. Wynn's father, though, made a habit of gambling away his business profits on the craps tables of the half-dozen casinos in the city that was known as "Mob country."

"One thing my father's gambling did was that it showed me at a very early age that if you wanted to make money in a casino, the answer was to own one," Wynn once told a reporter. The bingo parlor went under in three weeks' time, but Wynn had decided Las Vegas was the town to which he would one day return.

The bingo parlor a flop, father and son went home to Maryland. Wynn attended the University of Pennsylvania and worked weekends at his father's parlor in Wayson's Corner, Maryland. When his father died in 1963, Wynn became general manager of the bingo business and bided his time until he could take his money and his new wife, Elaine, to Vegas. It only took him two years to get that chance.

Wynn took $10,000 of his own money and $20,000 he had earned in the bingo business and joined a group of "investors" who planned to turn the Old Frontier Hotel into the New Frontier. Court records later would show much of the group's financing had come from the Detroit Mafia family. A year later, a federal grand jury investigating the Detroit family's role in financing the purchase summoned Wynn to testify. It would not be the last time Wynn's name or his money would be linked to organized crime.

Along with his 3 percent interest in the hotel came a job as assistant credit manager. And along with the reputation he was building as a sharp young businessman grew a friendship with Nevada's most powerful banker, E. Perry Thomas. To this day, Elaine Wynn refers to Thomas as "my adopted father." Thomas and his Bank of Las Vegas were making money, big money, at the time by playing with the cash Hughes had decided to invest in Las Vegas. The banker decided to set Wynn up in business, arranging for more than $650,000 in loans that would allow Wynn to buy Best Brands,

Inc., a liquor distributorship owned by Schenley Industries. With the money and Thomas's backing, Wynn was able to become *the* liquor distributor in a town of hotels that bought lots of liquor.

Then Thomas arranged a real sweetheart of a deal for the young Wynn. Thomas found a strip of land that Hughes had leased to Caesars Palace—land Caesars' president Billy Weinberger had often tried to purchase—and arranged for Wynn to buy it. It was the first piece of Hughes's property that had been sold in Las Vegas and Wynn bought it for a mere $1.1 million, all on credit arranged by Thomas. Wynn told Weinberger he was considering building a small casino there to pick up stragglers before they made it into Caesars. In almost no time, Weinberger offered him $2.25 million and the investment that had cost Wynn nothing had earned him more than a million dollars.

With this money and the $51,000 profit he made by selling Best Brands, Wynn began buying stock in the Golden Nugget, a casino that the Securities and Exchange Commission had stopped Thomas from buying a year earlier. Between 1969 and 1973, Wynn bought 912,000 shares of stock for $1.2 million. After the influential Thomas paid a visit to Buck Blaine, the Nugget's president, Wynn was elected to the board of directors. Wynn immediately began documenting cases of stealing within the casino and then threatened the sixty-three-year-old Blaine with a lawsuit for mismanagement if he didn't relinquish control of the company.

By August 1973, Wynn was in control of the Golden Nugget. In seven years, he had taken his $30,000 investment and parlayed it into a cushy job as chairman of what would soon be the hottest casino corporation in Las Vegas.

As he continued to try and expand his company, Wynn found investigations of his personal life and wealth were making headlines. His move to open a Golden Nugget in Atlantic City led to hearings during which his associations in Las Vegas drew great scrutiny. The New Jersey Casino Control Commission was provided with copies of federal grand jury testimony gathered in a 1979 investigation of drug trafficking involving the Genovese crime family. In that testimony, Shirley Ann Fair, a onetime prostitute who became a federal informant, told the grand jurors that shortly after she moved to Las Vegas in 1977, she became friends with Michael Dennis Jones, a Golden Nugget employee who was suspected of being a major cocaine distributor in the Las Vegas area.

Fair said she began regularly attending parties at Jones's home with Jones, Louis Cappiello, a Wynn employee who has been charged with cocaine possession and indicted but not convicted for murder, and Neil Azzanaro, Cappiello's best friend. Also attending at least two of the parties was Steve Wynn, she said. Fair testified that during an August 1977 get-together, she saw Frank DeAngelo, who later was indicted for cocaine trafficking, hand Wynn a clear plastic bag containing cocaine. She also testified that Wynn then handed DeAngelo cash.

During her grand jury testimony, Fair was questioned by Assistant U.S. Attorney Phillip Pro, now a U.S. District Court judge in Las Vegas. "Specifically talking about this party that you attended at Mr. Jones's house in August of 1977, do you recall a specific transaction between DeAngelo and Mr. Wynn for approximately one ounce of cocaine?" Pro asked Fair.

"Yes," she responded.

"In a clear plastic bag?" Pro asked.

"Yes," she said. "It was a clear plastic bag with a zip lock. They were sitting on the couch and Mr. DeAngelo gave Mr. Wynn the cocaine and he just handed him like a wrapped package of hundreds; so I don't know how much it was."

On December 31, 1977, Fair told the grand jury, she attended a New Year's Eve party at Jones's home. She testified that Jones gave each of his fifty guests—including Wynn, Azzanaro, DeAngelo, and Cappiello—one individually wrapped gram of cocaine as a gift.

Of the eleven people named by Fair in her testimony, nine were indicted, including several of Wynn's closest friends and Golden Nugget employees. But the grand jury chose not to charge Wynn. At the drug trafficking trial, Jones was convicted, Cappiello was found not guilty, and the charges against Azzanaro were dropped.

Although Wynn later provided gaming investigators with five affidavits from people who swore that he was in Sun Valley, Idaho, on New Year's Eve 1977, Fair passed a lie detector test that was witnessed by a Division of Gaming Enforcement investigator. Wynn claimed Fair's charge was "outrageous" and said he had "never set eyes on her."

The Division of Gaming Enforcement also obtained statements from two other women who claimed Wynn used cocaine in their presence. Kathy Thomas told investigators she had seen Wynn use cocaine at the home of one of his employees and again on the Golden Nugget corporate jet. Thomas later recanted her statement. Fair and the third woman, who told investigators of drug use, Golden Nugget blackjack dealer Anita Cosby, refused to testify during Wynn's Atlantic City licensing hearings.

In that 1981 hearing, Wynn said he had never used drugs, including cocaine. He told the New Jersey Casino Control Commission that he had offered to help Nevada law enforcement authorities, had hired "snitches" to report on drug dealings, and went to the federal Drug Enforcement Administration for help in setting up drug abuse programs.

But DEA investigators who worked with Fair on the cocaine trafficking case filed a lengthy confidential report that listed Wynn by NADDIS number 894134, which had been assigned to him years earlier. NADDIS, the acronym for the Narcotics and Dangerous Drug Identification System, is an identification program set up by the DEA. NADDIS records show that Wynn, although never indicted or convicted, had been suspected in narcotics investigations dating back to his employment with his father's bingo parlor.

The Genovese crime family and Wynn made news again in 1991 when Las Vegas police arrested two convicted felons—Elia Albanese and Carmine Russo—with ties to the Genovese family, after they had been "comped" for a three-day meeting with three other alleged Mafiosi at Wynn's Mirage Hotel. By law, all felons who come to Nevada must register with police within twenty-four hours of arrival. The casino host who comped the mobsters in July 1991 also had been investigated for entertaining numerous high-rolling members of the mob when he worked for Wynn's Golden Nugget Hotel in Atlantic City.

During another hearing into mob activity in the casino industry, Wynn's Atlantic City hotel was investigated for laundering millions of dollars in drug money for the mob. The President's Commission on Organized Crime quizzed Wynn about a series of deposits totaling $2.5 million that were made at the Atlantic City Golden Nugget in December 1982 by Anthony C. Castelbuono, a New York lawyer. On one day, Castelbuono brought $1,187,450 to the casino's cashier's cage in denominations of $5, $10, and $20 bills. The bundle weighed 280 pounds and was stacked nearly six feet high. Castelbuono then proceeded to lose $300,000 while gambling but was able to walk out with $983,000 in fresh $100 bills. Within a week, one of Castelbuono's associates deposited $1 million in a Swiss bank that also launders heroin profits for the Pizza Connection heroin ring. The transaction was central to a May 1985 federal indictment of nine reputed mobsters, including Castelbuono, for laundering drug money.

Wynn told the President's Commission that he was convinced Castelbuono was "legitimate." He said he even visited Castelbuono in New York and, on the lawyer's advice, invested $50,000 in silver through a firm also used by Castelbuono.

After the Atlantic City investigation and the ensuing negative publicity did its damage, Wynn, whose long hair and Rebel army cap once had become symbols of his position as the young buck in a city of stallions, began a metamorphosis that was noted by many of his competitors.

"Suddenly, he's clean-cut, talking about how important it is for Las Vegas to project a more positive image," said one longtime casino owner. "And then Elaine goes over and gets involved at the university, helping to raise money and talk about education. Suddenly, everybody loves them."

The Wynns also introduced their close friend and financial partner, Michael Milken, to Maxson and UNLV. Milken, who donated $75,000 to a UNLV scholarship fund at a ceremony hosted by Maxson, has been criticized by the *Wall Street Journal* for embracing education in an attempt to restore his tarnished image. The junk bond king dumped millions of dollars into the Milken Family Fund to reward top-notch teachers in Nevada and California public schools.

Milken provided the capital for several of Wynn's major business moves—including the building of the $630 million Mirage and a run at a takeover of the Hilton Hotels Corporation—through money earned on the sale of the now infamous junk bonds that robbed thousands of Americans of their life's savings. Wynn had met Milken in July 1978 when Wynn was looking for money to finance his expansion into Atlantic City. After an hour-long meeting in Milken's Beverly Hills office, the financier arranged for Wynn to visit the New York offices of Drexel Burnham Lambert and put together a financing package. Just like that, Wynn was in. "Mike said, 'The gaming industry needs a white knight,'" Wynn likes to tell reporters when recounting his relationship with the imprisoned Milken. "They need somebody they can believe in, who's not just capable, but stands for integrity. Bill Harrah is that kind of guy. If someone emerges like that, the marketplace will give him everything he wants. He told me, 'You can be that guy, Steve. You've got an unblemished career.'"

Wynn built his Atlantic City Golden Nugget with the high-risk bonds, just part of the nearly $1 billion he borrowed as Golden Nugget chairman during the 1980s. The biggest chunk was the $630 million to build the Mirage, considered the class of the Las Vegas Strip. The hotel's gold-tinted exterior and theme-park atmosphere are in stark contrast to its garish, neon-lighted competitors. It fit perfectly in what Wynn hoped would be the new "resort image" that Las Vegas could sell to vacationing families, not just gambling adults.

When Milken, who Wynn declared "the most towering figure to bring about change in corporate finance in the history of America," went to jail and Drexel Burnham Lambert declared bankruptcy, Wynn said it appeared the building of such lavish adult play-grounds had suffered "a major setback." As Milken's troubles became daily reading in American newspapers, Wynn came to his defense. "My loyalty to Mike Milken is based on who the guy is, not what he's done for me," Wynn told reporters. "I love him and I'm proud he's my friend and I like what he stands for. I owe him for that."

Milken's efforts on Wynn's behalf had allowed Wynn to start changing the image of the gambling industry and, thus, Las Vegas. At first, Wynn and others made subtle changes, such as referring to their profession as "gaming," not "gambling." Then, as the image campaign became more serious, Wynn began funding efforts in other states to approve lotteries, casinos, or riverboat gambling. Each time one of those efforts was successful, "gaming" became less distasteful and Las Vegas became more attractive.

Like Wynn, Maxson needed a financial sugar daddy to help in his university image-building campaign. The mechanism already was there in the form of the UNLV Foundation, he thought. But he discovered the foundation, which was being run off campus with a large staff and no real direction from the university, had become almost like a shadow government at UNLV. Although it was supposed to raise money for academics, foundation staffers spent most of their time selling season tickets for the basketball program and sending the money to the athletic department—not just the basketball program. Within two months of his arrival, Maxson had private meetings with each of the casino owners, bankers, politicians, and millionaires who made up the foundation's board. He convinced them that the organization needed to be run from an office on campus, under the supervision of a senior vice president and that its mission, like the university's, should be the enhancement of academics. It was a compelling argument, and when he knew he had the votes Maxson fired the foundation's executive director, slashed its budget by 75 percent, and cut staff from six to two. He then took the basketball season tickets that were funding athletics and used dozens of them for his academic fund-raising efforts. Now high rollers could contribute to the university's academic programs—and still get their basketball season tickets.

The move was vintage Maxson. He had used the opportunity to network with the power brokers, sell them on his idea, and fire a disagreeable employee who knew them better than he. By the time the dust had settled, Maxson had established the base that would allow him to raise $1 million every twenty-nine days for the university—a paltry figure in comparison to most universities its size—and provide the support he needed when the day arrived for that ultimate showdown with Tarkanian.

"I can't overstate the significance of it [taking over the foundation]," Vice President Unrue said in 1991 as he looked back at Maxson's early days. "Because when this president was able to gain the support of and increase the support, I should say, of the foundation, which is a very powerful group, we saw a far more level playing field [with basketball] than there had been in the past. I'm not sure that any president at UNLV prior to this president had a sufficient constituency that would guarantee or ensure his survival had he taken on Coach Tarkanian. Bob came in in the shining armor and saw, I think, that there's a limit as to how far a president can go with this [basketball] program and survive and that, in my judgment, is a fact. I think that this president, who represents this institution, has reined Jerry in."

Maxson's takeover of the foundation and his high profile in the community left a few feathers ruffled. Just eight months into his presidency, newspaper columnist Don Digilio announced that the president's habits were grating on several other university administrators. "Is the honeymoon almost over for UNLV President Bob Maxson?" Digilio asked in his column. "Among the community, the answer would be no. The dapper, glib Maxson seems to still be charming local residents, but on campus the word is quickly spreading that yes, indeed, the honeymoon is definitely a thing of the past. Some administrators and faculty members are privately saying Maxson is more concerned with his public image than with students or with issues closer to the operation of the university."

The column prompted a series of hard-hitting letters from Maxson supporters, led by Elaine Wynn. "I am one of the local residents who has been charmed by Maxson, but I am also impressed by him," she wrote. "I find it particularly insulting when it is implied that I, along with other friends of the university, the Board of Regents and the governor, all of whom vigorously recruited Bob Maxson, may have been duped by a sweet-talking figurehead."

The Wynns were so impressed, in fact, that they endowed the Distinguished Professorship in Entrepreneurial and Leadership Studies with a $2 million grant so that if Maxson ever were to leave the presidency, he would have a teaching job at UNLV as long as he desired.

For several years, Maxson has taught one course at the university. Even that is part of his political and public relations strategy. The class, titled "Human Dynamics and Organizational Leadership," allows Maxson to invite business leaders, media executives, and politicians to be "Distinguished Guest Lecturers." The Wynns, *Las Vegas Review-Journal* editor Sherman Fredericks, Governor Bob Miller, and members of the state's congressional delegation are regulars.

"Bob Maxson is a great politician," Elaine Wynn says. "Don't let anyone tell you different."

Like a good politician, Maxson began taking credit for the works of others almost immediately. During an interview published after he had accepted the job but before his arrival on campus, Maxson said his three priorities were to boost faculty salaries, build a school of engineering, and develop a scholarship program for valedictorians in southern Nevada."

Once those things occurred, Maxson claimed it was because of his leadership. Not so, records show. One former university administrator said, "Those things were in the works and he walked in and took credit for them. Some of us stood there and shook our heads."

Fact: Plans for the Engineering School had been in the works for two years before his arrival, university records show. Fund-raising dinners with members of the aerospace industry had been held as early as 1982 and checks for construction of the new school were rolling in early In 1983, eighteen months before Maxson made his statements.

And records indicate the valedictorian scholarship concept—and funding for it—already were in the works and wasn't his idea either. Memos from the UNLV Foundation show the idea had been discussed months before Maxson's arrival. A February 10, 1984, internal document written by Charles Parrott, associate director of the foundation, quotes foundation board member Art Ham, Jr., as saying he wanted the $1 million gift offered by Margaret Elardi, owner of the New Frontier Hotel, to be "directed to Nevada High School valedictorians so that they will go to UNLV."

Maxson didn't even interview for the UNLV job until three months later.

But a glowing bio written about Maxson by John Irsfeld includes this anecdote about the scholarship program: "When President Maxson first announced his intention to begin such a program, his wife, Sylvia, asked, 'How are you going to pay for that?' 'I don't know,' he said. 'But we will.' His belief in the self-fulfilling prophecy was rewarded in this case, as it seems to have a way of doing with Maxson. 'I've always had a horseshoe in my pocket,' he says."

Irsfeld's creatively written piece was done under the pseudonym Guilford Doubleday and, after being rejected by airline magazines from American Airlines and Delta, was tucked away in the drawer where Maxson's staff keeps the puff pieces written about "the boss."

Still, if you ask Elaine Wynn why Maxson has been so good for the university, she's quick to tell you: "He set up a scholarship program for all the valedictorians in the state to come here. No one had ever thought like that. The program has been one of UNLV's great success stories." Dick Etter, chairman of the board of Valley Bank, echoed Wynn's sentiment: "The valedictorian scholarship idea was really great thinking. That's what Maxson brought to UNLV."

After the $1 million grant Elardi made to the university proved to be less than was needed, the Wynns started paying for the program, which is now known as the Elaine Wynn Valedictorian Scholarship.

The one thing Maxson can take credit for was his decision to establish and fund a well-oiled public relations office at UNLV and put it under his direction as he embarked on "an aggressive campaign to improve UNLV's academic image." This was, Maxson concedes, by design. Then he gave the PR office orders to produce "50 news releases a month," according to a Self Study Report filed by the university. He started spreading the word that UNLV already was becoming a better university, even though it was virtually inconceivable he could have that impact in so short a time.

"You're very perceptive," Maxson said when asked about the immediate focus he put on public relations. "This place had done a terrible job of promoting itself. The PR off of this campus was horrible. I think what we had were pockets of excellence around the campus and individual scholars and individual scientists that were highly respected in their discipline which would be a very small segment of the higher education community. But nobody knew about them. Nobody was bragging on them, trying to make them look like the norm, the standard on campus. When I first got here we talked a lot about promotion. I am reluctant to use the word 'hype,' but what we did, there's no question, we promoted the place like you would promote a product. And this was all planned, I mean they were calculated decisions, if you may. "

Like a good salesman, Maxson chose, appropriately, to focus on his local market first. The negative press over the tumultuous final year of Goodall's tenure had left many in the community wondering exactly what really was going on at UNLV.

"There are about 750,000 people who live in the community,

Maxson said. "But only about 20,000 of them go to UNLV. So most of those other people, what they know about us is what we tell them. And if we tell them we're not very good, if we tell them we're struggling, if we tell them we're problem-ridden, then what's the perception of UNLV going to be?

"My plan was to change the perception and then let reality catch up. Sometimes you have to tell people what reality will be rather than what it is."

That, Maxson learned quickly, was what the people of Las Vegas, people who love to win, wanted to hear.

Maxson thought his prophecy had been fulfilled when, in 1989, *U.S. News & World Report* declared UNLV one of the "up and coming universities" in the West and a "Rising Star in American Education." The magazine accorded UNLV that honor again in 1990 and a third time in 1991 after polling more than 2,300 college presidents, deans, and admissions officers.

But that award is based on perception, not facts. It is the result of an opinion survey, not a statistical analysis. By hyping the magazine's recognition—Maxson even had bumper stickers printed with the "rising star" slogan—the president hopes that perception can carry the university until truth becomes so.

Even Tarkanian was taken in. "He's improved the university tremendously," he told one reporter in 1990. "He's done a great job. Our kids have to stay eligible, and some of them have a difficult time.

"Every time I went out to speak, I always talked about what a great university it was," Tarkanian said. "I always praised academics, even though I didn't know much about it."

But there usually is one thing even the best PR plan eventually can't overcome—reality. The reality is, UNLV is a very, very average academic institution. This "Rising Star in American Education" is actually a phoenix barely climbing from the ashes. The star, facts show, is not as bright as Maxson would have people think.

Take a look, as some Las Vegas researchers did recently, at the academic statistics, not the academic hype of UNLV, for the period of 1980 through 1990, with emphasis on the period after 1984, the year Maxson arrived.

Universities are rated primarily on a handful of factors: academic reputation, student selectivity, five-year graduation rates or averages, student satisfaction, student-to-faculty ratio, and the percentage of faculty with doctorates.

UNLV has never been rated, based upon academic statistics, by any recognized rating entity. After reviewing the data, it is easy to see why. Here's how, internal documents show, the university stacks up in those categories:

Academic Reputation is measured by historical academic statistics. UNLV is only thirty-four years old, and there has not been sufficient time to develop an academic reputation. That's obviously no one's fault since the average age of highly rated, "academically reputable universities" is 168 years.

One of the quickest jumps into that select "academically reputable" category belongs to UCLA, which became top rated in less than seventy years. There are distinct similarities between UNLV and the UCLA of thirty years ago. Both were located in explosive demographic regions. Both quickly established national recognition through high-profile athletic programs. Both benefited from the increased student applications stimulated by that national recognition. There the similarities end.

UCLA capitalized on the windfall enrollments and tightened admission standards to academically reputable levels. In other words, as more students heard of UCLA and began applying to the school, administrators chose to accept fewer of those who applied, allowing them to take only the cream of each year's crop of applicants. During the 1980s, UCLA accepted between 33 percent and 43 percent of freshman applicants. In 1990, UNLV continues to accept 80 percent of its applicants. In fact, the statistics show that under Maxson's reign, enrollment percentages have deteriorated, moving more closely to those of Maxson's previous employer, the University of Houston system. The four University of Houston units average approximately 91 percent acceptance rate.

In comparing the achievement levels of the academic and athletic sides of the university, researchers documented a well-known parallel: all but five schools that have made the NCAA basketball tournament since 1939 from five to twelve times—as UNLV did—have been included within the academic ratings of colleges—UNLV, Oklahoma City College, University of Texas at El Paso,

Western Kentucky, and Utah's Weber State. The other schools took advantage of the increased applications from their athletic success to become better academically.

According to the academic researchers, one of the most significant deficiencies uncovered in an April 1990 Evaluation Committee Report of the Northwest Accreditation Committee involved the lack of a comprehensive, integrated academic master plan. Repeatedly, UNLV had been requested by the committee to produce "a master academic plan." Three commission evaluators who visited UNLV in 1987 commented on "the apparent lack of an up-to-date academic plan. The steps and means for achieving the goals of the entire university, not just its discrete units, should be set forth in clear and concise terms, with priorities identified, for a period of time of at least three years, with an updating to occur annually. It is preferable that this plan be developed before any new major programs are implemented.... The Committee notes that UNLV is considering introducing a significant number of new doctoral and professional programs without a fully integrated university academic and resource plan ... but sustained commitment is not at all evident or assessed."

The report went on to say: "It appeared to the Evaluation Committee [1990] that major new programs were being proposed and/or developed without institutional priorities being identified ... With UNLV experiencing fast growth and without an up-to-date master academic plan to refer to, it was not easy for the Evaluation Committee to determine to what degree the institutional goals and objectives were being achieved. Related to this, academic planning for the University of Nevada System is admittedly weak, and solid institutional research is lacking for both UNLV and the System."

Student selectivity represents acceptance and admission rates at universities being rated. The average acceptance rate for the highest rated universities is 36 percent; the average acceptance rate for all rated universities is 62.6 percent. UNLV's current acceptance rate is more than 80 percent. The academic researchers found that, surprisingly, the acceptance rate had actually gotten worse under Maxson's Rising Star. Prior administrations of UNLV had kept the rate at a level of 71 percent to 78 percent.

Graduation rates or averages represents the percent of enrolled freshmen who graduate within five years. UNLV's graduation rate ranks 203 out of 204 colleges in its category for 1990 and ranked 202 out of 204 in 1989. The average time to complete a degree at UNLV is 6.5 years. The UNLV graduation rate has changed little since Maxson's appearance. Over the past five years it has moved from a beginning 19.5 percent, to 16.1 percent in 1989 and 20.8 percent in 1990. Most puzzling is the 79 percent graduation-rate figure the administration claimed in its response to *Money* magazine.

Academic researchers said these facts are a sad commentary on the "Rising Star" hype created by an administration that seems to enjoy spending most of its time and money creating more and more "glitz" and "image making" to cover up little if any substantive change.

Though Maxson often has been critical of the graduation rates of UNLV athletes, the Evaluation Committee Report from the Northwest Association of Schools and Colleges states: "the program [Intercollegiate Athletics] can point with some pride to the fact the graduation rates for student athletes is higher than that of the general student body."

Student satisfaction is measured by reports, surveys, complaints, and dropout rates. UNLV's attrition, or dropout rate, is among the highest in the nation. The dropout rate after one year of college is essentially the same as it was five years ago—more than 40 percent. The overall campus crime is alarming. According to the 1990 Uniform Crime Report, released August 11, 1991, one of every thirty-eight students committed a crime on campus. Since the 1987–88 academic year, student surveys show a growing dissension on campus related to a host of problems, such as the lack of progress with library facilities, slow administrative process, and student support functions. According to the budget reports, UNLV spent more money on postage than on public safety.

The student-to-faculty ratio of academically reputable and highly rated universities is 13.6 to 1. UNLV's student-to-faculty ratio has ranged from 17.5 to 1 in 1979, to 30 to 1 in 1980, to 22 to 1 in 1984—an average of 23.1 to 1. In 1990, UNLV's overall student-to-faculty ratio was 22.9 to 1.

The percentage of faculty with doctorates is another key component in ranking universities. Approximately 96 percent of the faculty of highly rated universities have earned their Ph.D. UNLV maintained a 78-plus percentage rating through 1983. There has been an overall decline since then. The average percentage of UNLV faculty having earned a Ph.D. in 1990 was 51.5 percent. Puzzling is the fact that the UNLV administration claimed 81 percent Ph.D.s in response to the 1992 edition of *Peterson's*, a respected educational publication.

The statistics and the hard data show that the facts do not match Maxson's public pronouncements.

"This 'great' university is a fraud," stated one current part-time faculty member. "Everyone has a vested interest in keeping it up. In many departments, sixty percent of the classes are taught by part-time faculty. Almost all freshman English classes are taught by part-timers. No one has ever evaluated my teaching or even evaluated my exams. In one class I chose not to use a text. They said fine. There were no academic standards placed on me. I was appalled at how bad this was. For one class, I asked for a syllabus that was used before and was told they had never used one before."

"Well, if getting rid of Coach Tarkanian wasn't about academics, what was it?" said Esther Langston, an associate professor of social work. "Was it about ego? I felt for many years this debate was about ego, not academics."

Maxson, one faculty member said, went out of his way to make unfavorable comments about the academics of the men's basketball team. "He never attacked Jerry by name," said the faculty member, who assisted in compiling the inside information about the university's academic standing. "He'd talk academics, then say, 'We need our players to graduate.' Then as an aside he'd say, 'You realize we've only had so many of our players graduate.' Tark is such a strategist in basketball, but on this one, he was had. At the end of the game, Maxson got people to raise questions about the basketball program without ever letting them raise questions about the quality of what he called 'his' university. Everyone in this town wanted so much for their university to be good, so they just lapped up what he said like puppy dogs, not stopping to think if it were true or not."

These aren't the numbers Maxson brags about. They're not the numbers that find their way onto the pages of those fifty news releases. But they are facts.

As the community started responding to his call for a cleaner image, Maxson decided it was time to make some changes in the athletic department, which was matching him headline for head-line, but often for opposite reasons. Although he was unhappy with Tarkanian and the men's basketball program, he knew meddling there was politically impossible. Football was a different matter.

Coach Harvey Hyde was starting to prove the decade-old logic of the University Rebels Club to be sound. Hyde, who grew up across the street from Tarkanian in Pasadena and was a childhood friend, had been a successful junior college coach in California. Like Tarkanian, he had moved into Division I and was quickly develop-ing a reputation for winning. Using revenues generated by basket-ball and his affable manner to raise private funds, Hyde appeared finally to have UNLV on track to become a two-sport school. Future NFL stars Randall Cunningham and Ickey Woods led the Rebels to their first ever appearance in the Associated Press Top 20 and the *Los Angeles Times* predicted Hyde's program would be "the next West Coast football power." In 1983 and 1984, the team posted records of 7–4 and 11–2, winning the Pacific Coast Athletic Associa-tion Championship and going to the 1984 California Bowl, where it registered UNLV's only postseason football win, 30–13, over Mid American Conference champion Toledo.

"We were starting to get respect, starting to get good recruits, starting to put it together," said Hyde. "It was exciting."

But an anonymous letter sent to several UNLV opponents sug-gested they look at the academic eligibility of a specified list of Rebel players. Those allegations were turned over to the confer-ence, which found that UNLV had played seven ineligible athletes during the '83 and '84 seasons. UNLV was forced to forfeit eighteen wins, give back its conference championship, and send the Califor-nia Bowl title to Toledo. Maxson called a press conference and said this "source of embarrassment" would be dealt with.

"I get my list of who is eligible from the [university's] NCAA faculty rep [Tom Schaffter], who is appointed by the president," said Hyde, who today hosts Tarkanian's radio show. "What was at issue was an interpretation of an NCAA rule on junior college transfer credits. It was something I had no reason to understand. That's what the faculty rep is for. If they tell me a kid is not eligible, I don't play him. My job is to coach football. His job is to keep tabs on who is eligible. But rather than blaming him, they blamed me.

Maxson called me in, with Rothermel and another guy. He tells me, 'Harv, I really appreciate your being strong. You'll surface from this. You've got momentum, you know, you'll come through all this. Now it would be very difficult for me to have another faculty rep accept the position like this if the faculty rep was the one blamed for the error. It would be hard on me if we did that.' So, I agreed to not speak up and tell people who it was that was supposed to have caught that problem. I agreed to let it be my fault. I fell for it."

Hyde began to sense that there could be problems in his future when Maxson committed at a football team banquet to "fully support" the program, then turned around and ordered that the football budget be slashed by $200,000 days later.

"I asked Brad [Rothermel] if he would mind me writing the president a memo on that," Hyde recalls. "I told him I needed more than his vocal support at events. I needed support from him administratively, more than just banquets and things. I told him budget was the number one thing. Without money we couldn't compete. He didn't respond to the memo. But Brad said it was something he didn't appreciate at all." In retrospect, if you look at it, I was the warm-up for what they did to Jerry."

Fresh from taking the blame for the forfeitures and watching his recruiting budget go by the wayside, Hyde became the brunt of increasing criticism when several of his players ran afoul of the law. Each of the arrests made the newspaper, and, as the number mounted, the stories started getting better play. Maxson eventually had had enough. He told Rothermel to fire Hyde. Rothermel refused. So Maxson called Hyde in and did it himself.

"Clearly, that was an athletic director's decision," Rothermel said. "My position was, having been an athlete, having been a coach, having been around the athletic department environment, that while some people would like to hold coaches accountable for the actions of their players twenty-four hours a day, I don't. If one of my staff goes out and commits a robbery, should I be held responsible for that? I told the president that Harvey was doing a good job. He was doing what we were asking of him. But the president wanted to make a change. He didn't like the stuff in the newspaper. But if you go back now and look at all charges against his players, most all of those were dismissed."

Tarkanian also had pled with Maxson to spare Hyde, making many of the same arguments as Rothermel.

As time went on, Tarkanian began taking Hyde to receptions as his guest, showing support for his friend. When the University of Wisconsin came to Las Vegas for a game, Tarkanian and Hyde made the rounds at several major booster events, once showing up at the same time Maxson was there. Word filtered back to Tarkanian later that Maxson was unhappy that he was so openly supporting Hyde instead of him.

The whole incident widened the gap between Maxson and Rothermel and Tarkanian.

"I told the president Harvey Hyde was the last coach he would fire while I was athletic director," Rothermel recalls.

He was right.

7

The Big Mistake:
Lloyd Daniels

The post–Harvey Hyde football program at UNLV has been a disappointment. The Rebels have had only one winning season since and regularly lose to their Division IAA sister school, the University of Nevada-Reno. Maxson, some in the community said openly, had blown UNLV's best opportunity to become respectable on the gridiron.

UNLV was a basketball school again, and Tarkanian's Runnin' Rebels did their best not to disappoint. On the court, they were getting better every year. More significantly, the off-court image was getting better, too. The construction of the Thomas & Mack Arena, which opened in 1983, gave UNLV the finest on-campus facility in the country. It was a recruiting tool unlike anything Tarkanian had been able to use before, and it came just in time. The postprobation years proved to be a mere blip on the screen of time. From 1983 through 1986, the Rebels went 28–3, 29–6, 28–4, and 33–5, including four straight NCAA Tournament appearances. Though they didn't make it to the Final Four, they were always right on the brink.

In 1987, that changed. With Freddie Banks and Armon Gilliam leading the way, the Runnin' Rebels went 37–2 and to the Final

Four. Everyone talked about how Tarkanian finally would get the credit he deserved as a coaching genius. This team, which had spent much of the season ranked Number 1, was built around Banks, a high school all-American from Las Vegas; Gilliam, a 6'9" junior college transfer who hadn't played basketball until his junior year in high school; Eldridge Hudson, a onetime high school star who had destroyed his knee; Gary Graham, a "complementary player" who was never highly recruited; and two other junior college transfers, Mark Wade and Gerald Paddio, who weren't even ranked among the best at their positions while in junior college. It was a typical Tarkanian team, filled with players others had passed on.

"People always say Tarkanian wins because he gets all those great players to come to Vegas," said former University of California coach Pete Newell. "While that was a team that was ranked Number One for most of the season, Tarkanian didn't even have Top Twenty talent. That should tell you something about the coach."

UNLV's return to the Final Four gave the national media plenty to write about—and most of it was surprisingly good. There were always the stories about Tarkanian's battle with the NCAA. But now there were stories about his focus on the overall student-athlete. Newspapers from coast to coast ran pictures of the five cap-and-gown-clad seniors—Banks, Gilliam, Hudson, Graham, and Leon Symanski—who were graduating that spring. The players were actively involved in the community. And the spotlight was so bright it produced dozens of stories about Maxson and his commitment to help change the university's image to that of a serious academic institution.

Though the team lost to Indiana in the semifinals, this looked like a dynasty in the making. Some of the nation's most talented juniors—Don MacLean, Shawn Kemp, Chris Mills, and Derrick Martin—had UNLV on their wish list. Each was a good student as well, Mills a 3.0 high school student and Martin a 3.5. These were the players UNLV never was in the running for in the past. Things were going good—almost too good. Everyone, including Maxson, seemed happy with the team's commitment to academics. Obviously that was recognized by potential recruits, many of whom wouldn't have considered UNLV previously. Maybe there was hope that Tarkanian would produce that "image" the president so desired.

But on the way to the top, the bottom fell out. During the previous season, Tarkanian had received a call from Arnie Hershkowitz, a teacher at Westinghouse High School, and Lou d'Almeida, a wealthy New York businessman and summer league coach, who posed a simple question: How would you like Lloyd "Swee' Pea" Daniels, the best player to come out of New York City since Lew Alcindor, to play for your Rebels?

Tarkanian let it be known he was interested and that he would have assistant coach/recruiting coordinator Mark Warkentien get in touch.

There were complications, to be sure. Because Daniels had left high school before becoming a senior, UNLV couldn't pay for his official visit. Hershkowitz said that was no problem. He would arrange to have Daniels flown to Las Vegas and come by the UNLV basketball offices. Two weeks later, Daniels showed up in Tarkanian's office just after the Rebels played Memphis State on national television. It was a meeting that would alter the lives of Tarkanian and those around him, yet no one knew it at the time. In a career built on long shots, Tarkanian was getting ready to take his biggest gamble. The success he had experienced over a lifetime of dealing with academic misfits had, to date, been remarkable. So, like a player on a roll at the craps table, Tarkanian was getting ready to throw the dice and scream, "One more time."

Daniels stuck his graceful, long-fingered hand out to greet Tarkanian. Introductions weren't necessary. Daniels's reputation, like Tarkanian's, was legend. Though he has never stepped foot on a Division I college basketball or National Basketball Association court, Daniels's scrapbook is filled with stories from *Sports Illustrated*, *The Sporting News*, and every major newspaper in America. His life has even been profiled in John Valenti's 268-page book, *Swee' Pea and Other Playground Legends*.

In the most appropriate use of an overused cliché, Daniels was a product of the streets of New York. Born in 1967 to a single mother who died when he was only three, Daniels was raised by his maternal grandmother, Annie Sargeant Stevens, in the East New

York section of Brooklyn. School never became a priority for Lloyd. He didn't have time for it. He was too busy looking for a pickup basketball game—in a neighborhood known for some of the best pickup basketball games in America. He experienced success on the court in inverse proportion to his problems off it.

His consistent truancy led officials at Intermediate School 218 in Brooklyn to demand he repeat the eighth grade. High school coaches from the area, drooling at the opportunity to hand over their teams to Lloyd, were disappointed by the delay in his arrival at their level. The experience taught Lloyd that as bad as things got in the classroom, someone—usually a coach or a hanger-on—was always willing to come to his defense.

Although his high school career had been delayed by a year, Daniels was quick to remind onlookers that he was more than a legend. He was for real. As a freshman at Thomas Jefferson High School in Brooklyn, Daniels fractured his ankle and played in only seven games. Still, he scored thirty points in a second round playoff loss to Lincoln High. He showed that his legendary academic problems were for real, too. Despite receiving home tutoring while injured, Daniels failed all of his classes and dropped out of school.

He played that summer for d'Almeida's AAU team, the Gauchos, and d'Almeida then paid his tuition to attend Oak Hill Academy in Mouth of Wilson, Virginia, in 1984. D'Almeida, a wealthy businessman, had sent several other players, including Rod Strickland and Chris Brooks, to Oak Hill. Oak Hill is a private school so far from the streets of New York City—one writer began a profile of the town by saying, "There are a hundred stories in this naked city"—that it seemed the perfect environment for Daniels to straighten out his life. Six weeks after he found Mouth of Wilson, Daniels found trouble. He was kicked out of school for "a conduct violation" when he was found in a room where marijuana was being smoked. He denied having partaken of the drug, but Oak Hill coach Steve Smith decided it would be better for Daniels to leave.

D'Almeida decided to give Daniels another shot at a private school, enrolling him in the Larinburg Institute in North Carolina in October 1984. Daniels proved he hadn't missed a beat on the basketball court, averaging twenty-four points a game. But the biggest surprise was his sudden success in the classroom. He passed all of his classes that year, becoming a junior academically.

Feeling as if he had something to prove, Daniels again enrolled at Oak Hill in September 1985. This time, he lasted eleven weeks before Smith kicked him out of school as a suspect in "several stealing incidents." In his two stints at Oak Hill, Daniels never lasted long enough to play a regular season basketball game for the school. During this second stay at Oak Hill, he did begin practicing with the varsity, and it was during one of those practices that Warkentien saw the talent that had captivated the playground basketball world. Warkentien actually had made the trip to Mouth of Wilson to watch Chris Brooks, another recruit, who eventually ended up at West Virginia University. He left talking about Daniels.

After his second unsuccessful stop at Oak Hill, Daniels moved back to New York and lived with his paternal grandmother, Louila Daniels, in the Cambridge Heights neighborhood. He wanted to play for Cardozo High School in Bayside (his girlfriend went there), but was told by the Public Schools Athletic League that he must attend Andrew Jackson High School in Queens. It didn't matter to Daniels. He figured to score points no matter what jersey he was wearing. In his first game, he scored forty-three of his team's sixty-eight points against Eli Whitney, including a half-court bank shot to tie the game at the end of regulation. As the clock ticked away the last seconds of overtime, he did it again, this time hitting the game-winner. Lloyd Daniels was back, and New York City—along with scores of college coaches—took notice.

Four high schools in three years. A grand total of eleven credits. The box full of letters he had from institutions of higher learning all over the country—postmarks from Lexington, Louisville, Tuscaloosa, Providence, and Lawrence—validated Daniels's belief that the numbers that mattered most were 31.2 points, 12.3 rebounds, and 10 assists per game. Daniels's ability on the court was matched only by his uncanny knack for finding trouble off it. In a sad commentary on the state of big-time college sports, that didn't stop college coaches from groveling at his million-dollar feet.

"My NBA experience will prove invaluable, as I can now help develop future pro draft choices," then Providence coach Rick Pitino wrote in one of his several letters to Daniels.

Larry Brown, who would take Kansas to the national championship two years later, was so interested in Lloyd that he requested a meeting with him when the Jayhawks were in New York City to play in the NIT. Hershkowitz took Daniels down to the Essex House, an expensive hotel overlooking Central Park, for a late night meeting with the coach. After calling him from the lobby telephone, Hershkowitz turned around to find the usually dapper Brown bolting out of the elevator in his pajamas and a robe. "He knew who Lloyd was," Hershkowitz was quoted as saying in the book *Swee' Pea*, "and he wasn't about to keep him waiting while he changed into his clothes."

Daniels dropped out of Andrew Jackson February 20, 1986, the day after Jackson was eliminated from the play-offs. Like all good point guards, Daniels already had his mind on his next move. Before he played that last game at Andrew Jackson, Daniels was talking to college coaches about placing him in a junior college and helping him get his General Equivalency Degree. "It ain't worth goin' to no high school now," Daniels told John Valenti of *Newsday*. "I can't worry about it. I got goin' to college to worry about."

"Does Lloyd have the wrong perception about how the world works?" East Coast recruiting expert Tom Konchalski asked Valenti. "No. His perception of the system has been correct. It is the system that's not correct. Every time he screwed up, there has been a solution to his problem. How long will it be before he runs out of solutions?"

With d'Almeida looking out for him, the answer appeared to be never. D'Almeida and Hershkowitz first tried to help Daniels enroll at St. John's, where Coach Lou Carnesecca had taken Walter Berry, another New York City star without a high school diploma, and arranged for him to get a GED and go to junior college. Lloyd was Carnesecca's guest at several St. John's home games. But Redmen assistant Ron Rutledge, during his recruiting of Daniels, suggested he disregard the advice of d'Almeida, Hershkowitz, and Ron Naclerio (a third Daniels groupie), and start working with another man, Ernie Lorch, who had helped Berry. However, Lorch was aligned with a summer league team that competed with d'Almeida's squad, a competition that Daniels described as "bitter." Rutledge was unaware of the conflict, and that tactical error opened the door for new recruiters. D'Almeida, who had once coached future Rebels Sidney Green and Richie Adams, next recommended that Lloyd consider UNLV.

Ironically, Tarkanian used the case of Berry and St. John's to answer his critics years later: "His [Daniels's] situation is no different than Walter Berry's," Tarkanian told the *Los Angeles Times*. "This is what tees me off, the hypocrisy. Berry was not a high school graduate. He was admitted to St. John's without a diploma on a special program they have for New York City kids. Then the NCAA came in and said, 'Hey, this is not sufficient, he can't play.' So they sent him to a junior college, exactly like we did. Their backgrounds are exactly the same. And why is it that St. John's is so nice for giving Walter the opportunity and Lloyd shouldn't have the opportunity?"

Given Daniels's academic record, NCAA investigator Rick Evrard told *Newsday* in 1986 that Daniels "would be thoroughly investigated if his name appears on a college roster."

The mere fact that Tarkanian recruited Lloyd Daniels points to the very root of the coach's strength and his greatest weakness. Players seek him out and play harder for him because they know he doesn't stand in judgment of them as the rest of society does. Then again, maybe he should. Tarkanian was willing to look past Daniels's well-documented troubles to give him a chance—while also winning basketball games. But he looked so far past those problems he didn't see the obvious pitfalls—the guarantee of an NCAA investigation, renewed national criticism, and an erosion of his local support base—at a time when he could ill afford more trouble.

Even Tarkanian acknowledged that recruiting Lloyd could produce explosive results. "You've got to be a damn fool to think that anything with him wasn't going to be checked out, wherever he played," Tarkanian said. "I don't care what school he went to. And particularly being us, there was no way we would stick our neck out in any way."

Tarkanian twice had watched Daniels play during summer tournaments in Las Vegas. At the time Daniels was in his first two years of high school, but he was playing college-quality ball. "I remember after I got the call that Lloyd wanted to come to UNLV, I couldn't sleep," Tarkanian said later. "He was one of the best players I'd ever seen, as good as Magic Johnson at that stage, maybe better. I used to stay awake thinking about having Lloyd Daniels as my point guard. I wasn't even going to draw plays, just give him the ball and tell the other four guys to move around."

Thinking about Lloyd Daniels would continue to keep Tarkanian awake at nights.

Daniels wasn't Tarkanian's only risk that year. He also had visited and gotten a commitment from another bona fide star named Clifford Allen. While Daniels's problems appeared to be academic, Allen's ran a little deeper. The 6'10" Allen had been in and out of jail for most of his teenage years, and when Tarkanian finally signed him to a letter of intent, he had to go behind bars at El Paso de Robles, a detention center in Paso Robles, California, to get his signature. Allen had been sentenced there for robbery.

Tarkanian claimed Allen had reordered his life and deserved the chance UNLV would provide him. As proof, he pointed to Allen's academic record, which showed he had graduated tops in his class. "My first valedictorian," Tarkanian bragged, ignoring the fact that Allen had graduated from school in the juvenile detention center.

Allen showed up at UNLV in the fall of '86. He started missing classes from day one. Because he was missing classes, Tarkanian sent him packing. Allen later attended three different junior colleges before he was convicted of second-degree murder for the stabbing of a sixty-four-year-old guidance counselor in Milton, Florida. Allen, who committed the crime while in Pensacola for a tryout with that city's Continental Basketball Association team, told police he stabbed the man in a fight after the two had sexual relations. Allen currently is serving a forty-five-year sentence in a Florida state prison.

"You can't hold me responsible for what kids do after they leave," Tarkanian said. "Especially after I've kicked them off the team. If he'd have been able to stay with us and go to class, we might have been able to turn his life around. He never played one minute at UNLV and everyone blames me for everything he's done. If another student at the university is arrested two years after he leaves school, do you hold his professor accountable?"

The greatest irony of Tarkanian's efforts to sign Daniels and

Allen is in his timing. At the same time that his program was shedding its image as a home for wayward leapers, he reached even deeper into the pit of troubled talent.

"Tark got greedy," said former *Las Vegas Review-Journal* reporter John Henderson. "And the truth is, he didn't need either of them to go on and win the national championship."

Though neither Daniels nor Allen ever practiced with the Rebels or wore a UNLV jersey, the fact they were even signed to letters of intent provided Tarkanian with two Achilles' heels. The moves also provided Tarkanian's critics with ammunition aplenty for an assault on his ability to see the big picture. The more things change, they said, the more they stay the same.

"When all the [Daniels] recruiting violations started to surface, that was the beginning of a closer scrutiny of what was going on," said Elaine Wynn. "Was the incident with Jerry at Long Beach an aberration? Was it an isolated incident or is this really a pattern with this man? And all of the sudden, there's some allegations, and even if these people [the NCAA] are on a vendetta, if somebody is finding out that this has some merit to it, you know, maybe we shouldn't keep our head buried in the sand here. Maybe we need to take a look at this."

"The only thing Tarkanian did wrong in recruiting Lloyd Daniels," said Valenti, "is be unlucky enough to win."

Daniels had decided in January 1986 that UNLV would replace St. John's as his college of choice. He asked d'Almeida and Hershkowitz for help, and they were more than willing. In a meeting with Warkentien and Naclerio at the Nassau Coliseum, where Andrew Jackson was playing, Hershkowitz said that he had a friend from New York who spent winters in Las Vegas and who would be willing to pay for Lloyd's visit and give him a place to stay. Since Hershkowitz's friend had no connection to UNLV, everyone thought it would be within the NCAA rules for the friend to offer these perks to Daniels.

The friend was Sam Perry, a "commodities broker" whom Hershkowitz had met at the local racetracks. Perry, after Hershkowitz told him the plan was a go, called directory assistance and asked for the number at UNLV's basketball offices to set up the meeting with Tarkanian.

Everyone seemed convinced at the end of the meeting that

Lloyd was making the right choice. He would move to Las Vegas, where he would sign a letter of intent and begin taking remedial reading classes at the university. In the fall, he would transfer to Mount San Antonio College, a junior college in Walnut, California, where several past and future Rebels had spent time working on their grades. On April 11, 1986, Daniels signed his letter of intent.

Shortly after Daniels finally made the move, he was joined by a friend from New York, Steve Cropper, who said he was coming to Las Vegas to help with Daniels's academics. UNLV coaches thought Cropper's arrival was a good idea. They were starting to realize that Daniels's academic woes were worse than first suspected. He was dyslexic and, according to court documents, suffered from "cultural deprivation." One writer described Daniels as having "a jump shot like Larry Bird and a handle like Magic Johnson. The only thing he couldn't do with a basketball was autograph it."

Shelley Fischer, an academic adviser to the UNLV basketball team, was the first academic to work with Daniels when he came to Las Vegas. She wondered then and continues to wonder now how anyone thought he would ever make it as a college "student-athlete."

"I've been a teacher for twenty years, and he just didn't have the equipment for education, period," Fischer said. "He would have to be considered an invalid and start at ground zero and have the desire and the drive to want to do it. The kid never did. He wasn't even a long shot. I think you can take a long shot on somebody who has the basic equipment and you can say, well, let's give it a chance. He was a singular, one-dimensional person that in one area is terrific and everything else is a mess. I'm not even sure why they went out on a limb for him."

Fischer taught Daniels in a remedial reading course shortly after he arrived in Las Vegas. She said he didn't want to admit that he couldn't read and would pull a copy of a comic book titled *Off the Glass* out of his pocket to prove that he had mastered basic reading.

"There was an article [in the comic book] done about himself," Fischer said. "That's all he ever wanted to do was read it over and over again to me. He had it memorized. He wouldn't even look at the page, and he knew the names and the sentences. That's how he tried to prove he knew how to read. It was very sad, it was very pathetic."

Warkentien had by this time made Lloyd his personal project. He signed up for and attended Fischer's reading class with Daniels. He began to see that Daniels needed even more attention than he was getting at the university if there was any hope for success. That's when Warkentien's wife, Maureen, decided to get involved.

According to the story Warkentien told university investigators looking into allegations of impropriety involving Daniels, Maureen and Lloyd developed "a very close" relationship. Daniels would visit the Warkentiens' home when Mark was on the road. And Maureen started giving Daniels a little extra help with his school-work.

Warkentien said he sensed that Lloyd truly was interested in learning to read, even going so far as to once say Lloyd was "more excited about reading than about basketball." In statements taken during Warkentien's defense against NCAA charges, he said he and his wife even "called several 1-800 numbers on literacy" and were told they had to act immediately. "You can't wait ..."

As the university's recruiting coordinator, Warkentien was exceptionally familiar with the 400-plus-page *NCAA Manual.* If all that he had done to date was, in fact, within the rules, he knew Maureen's work with Lloyd would be considered outside of them.

Warkentien told investigators that he ordered his wife to start charging Daniels for her help. She argued that it wasn't fair. From that argument hatched Warkentien's idea to solve the problem—he and Maureen would become Lloyd's legal guardians, thereby allowing them to do things for him as their ward that they might not be able to as a basketball recruit.

Warkentien went to Tarkanian with the idea. Tarkanian told him it sounded good if it was approved by the university, the Pacific Coast Athletic Association, and the NCAA. Warkentien went to Brad Rothermel and asked him to clear it with the NCAA.

After asking the PCAA to seek a ruling from the NCAA on the situation, Rothermel was told by the PCAA in August 1986 that the NCAA "would allow a university staff member to become the guardian for a potential student-athlete." Based on that telephone discussion, in which no names were mentioned, Rothermel felt the university had taken the proper precautions.

Rothermel went a step further. Recognizing the volatility of the situation, he went to see President Maxson and told him that Warkentien wanted to become Daniels's guardian.

"Brad Rothermel came to see me and he told me they had this recruit and he told me about his sort of desperate situation that he had been sort of abandoned," Maxson recalled. "Brad came to me, I think, with what he thought he should have come to me, not the fact that this youngster was struggling academically, I didn't know anything about that. He came to me on the guardianship and as I look at it in retrospect, I probably should have known that he sensed this thing might become an issue or why would he be coming to my office to tell me of three hundred and fifty athletes they were recruiting I want you to know about this athlete? So, in retrospect, as I look back that was probably a pretty good signal that Brad thought that this might, this might raise some concerns. I tell you what, ninety percent of this is not a good commentary on me."

Steve Wynn said in his discussions with Maxson the president's participation in the decision-making process never came up. "I asked Maxson. He said, 'I found out [about Daniels's guardianship] when it was over,'" explained Wynn. "He inherited the end of it, as I understand it. It was Rothermel and Tarkanian. That's reasonable for me to believe. I know Maxson. That's not the kind of thing he would let happen. It's not the kind of thing he would turn his back to."

Told that Maxson did, in fact, have a chance to voice his objections to the Daniels guardianship, Wynn expressed surprise. "That's certainly the kind of conversation I'd like to have with Bob," Wynn said. "I don't understand exactly what he did and didn't know. I don't think it's cool to discuss it with you and, based upon what you tell me, form an opinion about him. I, in fact, have never been aware that Bob gave approval before the fact to the Lloyd Daniels mess. That would surprise me."

Though he didn't discuss his part in this fiasco with close supporters, Maxson today admits he "didn't ask all the questions I should have." Bells and whistles should go off when an athletic director visits a university president to talk about the handling of a high-profile recruit in the university's most high-profile program.

Maxson concedes that for some inexplicable reason they did not. It is a point worth noting if only because Maxson's role and responsibility in what has simply become known as "the Daniels thing" has never been part of the debate.

"If they'd ever told me, anybody, the president, the athletic director, anybody, that they didn't want Lloyd or that they wanted us to stop, we would have stopped," Tarkanian said. "I don't have a death wish."

With the approval of the president and the apparent go-ahead from the PCAA and the NCAA, Warkentien filed his petition to become Daniels's legal guardian. "The proposed ward has the potential to be a successful human being, student and athlete," Warkentien stated in his guardianship petition. "He has shown great promise in athletics and, given the right direction and encouragement, has the potential to be a successful professional athlete. However, the proposed ward, being eighteen years old, barely reads at a third-grade level. Without the guidance, support, encouragement, and counseling of a special guardian, the potential for exploitation of the proposed ward is great."

Warkentien also asked the court for permission to borrow money and obtain loans for Daniels as well as assist him in his financial affairs. The petition received court approval that October.

Several weeks after Warkentien became Daniels's guardian, UNLV was headed back to New York to play in the Big Apple NIT. Several newspapers and television stations had asked for interview time to talk about his relationship with Lloyd. They didn't have to say any more. Nervous that he might say the wrong thing, Warkentien called Maxson. "He's still at Mount SAC. Should we bring him back? Is it all right with the university if he comes back?" The president said yes.

Tarkanian then told several reporters about Lloyd's impending arrival and Warkentien's guardianship. No one seemed to care—until Tarkanian's comments to ESPN commentator Dick Vitale were repeated on national television. During the broadcast of a game between the University of Arizona and the Soviet national team, Vitale told the Daniels story. It raised such a stir that Lew Cryer, who was then commissioner of the PCAA, urged Rothermel to contact the NCAA in writing and specifically mention Warkentien and

Daniels. Rothermel did so and received a reply stating that, no matter how the court saw Warkentien's relationship with Daniels and no matter what the NCAA may have told PCAA officials, the relationship would not be exempt from NCAA recruiting rules. By that time, however, Warkentien had purchased an $1,800 motorcycle for Daniels to use while attending Mount San Antonio. "They [the NCAA] have said we should have specifically identified the student-athlete involved," Rothermel said in 1990. "And we didn't. It would seem like it shouldn't make any difference if your general question and your specific question are basically the same, but it may." Especially if the school asking is UNLV and the player is one of the best ever.

Daniels already had left Las Vegas and gone to Mount San Antonio College. Warkentien and others had determined a way that would allow Daniels to become eligible as early as the fall of 1987, despite the fact that he never earned a high school or GED degree. To accomplish this, Daniels had to complete eighteen credits that fall at junior college, then take several intersession courses and come to UNLV for summer courses. Combined with the credits he had received during his previous summer's academic work, it looked like Lloyd could become eligible a full year before the NCAA had said it would be possible. The only thing that kept Warkentien's idea from being "brilliant" was that it counted on a kid who had never completed a full year of high school to do two years of junior college work in fourteen months. Daniels couldn't pull it off, dropping several of his classes that fall. He did earn enough credits—including two for playing on the school's basketball team—to become a regularly enrolled student at UNLV in January 1987. By law, both of Nevada's four-year schools must accept any junior college transfer who has passed fourteen hours of classwork. Lloyd barely made the cut.

Finally, it seemed Daniels was on track to play for the Rebels. A month later, he was derailed. Daniels was one of fifty-four people arrested in a drug sting operation at a North Las Vegas crack house. He tried to tell police that he had come there to pick up tickets to a basketball game, but undercover officers reported he had attempted to buy a $20 rock of crack. Tarkanian had suspected Daniels of using drugs after his arrival in Las Vegas and had questioned him about his concerns. Each time, Daniels offered to take a drug test. Each time, Daniels was so insistent that Tarkanian believed him. This time, there was little doubt.

The next morning, Tarkanian and Maxson met in the president's office to decide what to do. They agreed the action had to be swift and sure. Both men announced immediately that Daniels would never play at UNLV. "He was there, it's on television," Tarkanian said of Daniels's arrest, which was filmed by a TV crew. "It's not like it was a case of mistaken identity." Tarkanian said the progress made through UNLV's stringent drug-testing program, which was instituted two years before the NCAA mandated such, would be undermined if he allowed Daniels to join the Rebels. "It would be hypocritical not to kick him off," Tarkanian told reporters the day after Daniels's arrest. "I don't want to make it look like we're giving him an out." Maxson decided that any athlete accused of a felony would be suspended pending the outcome of his trial. Even if found not guilty, his return would be at the discretion of the coach. "Because of who we are, we have to be purer and cleaner," Maxson said.

Ironically, while UNLV was being crucified for having recruited the troubled Daniels, Mark Freidinger, an assistant coach at the University of Kansas, called Warkentien about Daniels's availability even after the arrest.

Daniels's $1,500 bail was paid by Perry, the "commodities broker" who had helped him make the jump to Las Vegas. And his legal defense was going to be handled by David Chesnoff, one of Las Vegas's brightest young liberal lawyers. Chesnoff, who later also would represent Perry, was known for his defense of people accused in drug cases.

"I thought if a guy had a drug problem, it was bad for the president to throw him out," Chesnoff said. "I always thought a university was about diversity. Through diversity people learn, they learn not to hate each other. I'd like to see if they'd take a kid whose father owns a casino who had a drug problem. I think an academic institution should show a certain amount of progressiveness when it comes to problems. Lloyd used to say, 'I don't understand this president Maximum'—that's what he called him—'how can he say these things? He never met me.' See, Lloyd is not a bad kid. A couple of years ago, he asked me to take him to Tarkanian's house on Christmas day. He said, 'I'm sorry I let you down, sorry I caused you problems.'"

Chesnoff went to lunch with Maxson shortly after the arrest in an effort to understand the president's position.

"He said Lloyd's bad for the school," Chesnoff recalled. "He said, 'I feel sorry for him, but he may not be college caliber.' I said it's time for people to embrace, not castigate. I told him he shouldn't make Lloyd a sacrificial lamb if what he's trying to do is embarrass others. Maxson told me that if I did prevent Lloyd from receiving a felony conviction, they'd let him back on the team."

The Sunday before UNLV headed to New Orleans for the Final Four, stories in *Newsday* detailed a series of possible NCAA rules violations involving Daniels and UNLV coaches, boosters, and other "representatives of the school." The stories alleged that all the gifts Warkentien had bestowed upon the prized recruit were NCAA violations, regardless of his legal status as Daniels's guardian.

Warkentien responded only by saying, as he would later tell university lawyers, that he had become Daniels's guardian because it was the boy's last hope to make it in school. Without the tutoring of his wife, Lloyd was doomed to fail, he said. But there was a fatal flaw in Warkentien's altruistic logic. If he was becoming Daniels's guardian to better his academic potential, was it really necessary to give him a beat-up $200 car? Or buy him an $1,800 motorcycle?

It looked as if this grand plan to dress the superhuman Daniels in Rebel red had completely unraveled. Tarkanian, it appeared, had been given just enough rope to hang himself. Warkentien had made sure the knot was tight.

"I can understand if people want to criticize them for taking Lloyd Daniels," said Lois Tarkanian. "But let's be honest. If it hadn't been Lloyd Daniels that was used against us, it would have been something else."

That Tarkanian's dealing with Daniels was a watershed in the coach's ultimate demise is unquestioned. Across the city, Tarkanian critics and zealots alike wondered aloud about the coach's decision. Some were bothered by Tarkanian's attempt to introduce such an ill-prepared young man to college life. Others were critical of Daniels for his drug use and of the coaches for not knowing about it. And still others saw the guardianship as a thinly veiled attempt to skirt NCAA rules.

"Kids that are rough and tough and come from the wrong side of town are one issue, but a kid that's a known drug abuser enters into a whole consideration that needs to be dealt with," said Elaine Wynn. "He should not have been given a chance."

Her husband, though, was careful not to make drugs the issue.

"In and of itself, being on drugs ... well, currently that's a bad thing," Steve Wynn said. "Two years ago, if you went for rehabilitation, that's another thing. I'm not privy to Lloyd Daniels's whole story. I just watched him get arrested on television. But it could have happened to anybody. You know crack is an insidious little thing and affected a lot more people than ghetto kids. That's not the point. This had nothing to do with the drugs."

To Steve Wynn, the issue was the adoption of Daniels, an act he described as a "ploy" to beat NCAA rules.

"Lloyd Daniels shocked everybody," he said. "When we found out that they had tried a scheme of making the guy the guardian, everybody said, 'Whoa.' The manner in which it was handled was disrespectful of the university and the university's obligations that it voluntarily and freely assumed as a member of the NCAA system. The recruitment and the treatment of Lloyd Daniels was flagrantly out of line with the obligations that we had to assume. I just thought this was crazy. I didn't understand what anybody was thinking of. For them to go out and adopt a guy and think that it was okay and then proceed to do things under the flag of a ward, of a legal guardianship, it was preposterous. It was spitting in the face of the NCAA. We looked real, real, real stupid. He looked stupid. We looked like we were sneaky and dumb. The double whammy. I can just see them in the basketball office. What's the kid's name, Warkentien? He looks at Jerry and says, 'Now that I'm his guardian, I'll get him a car. I'll get him a Mercedes.' 'No,' Jerry would say. 'All right, then just a Porsche.' To do that while you're an official of the athletic program, if Jerry didn't understand the rules chapter and verse he should have. We're at a level of accountability here that you can't escape. If we're looking like we don't respect our commitments flagrantly, if we look stupid, it's embarrassing. We looked stupid."

Summa Corporation president John Goolsby said he thought

the Daniels case showed Tarkanian's disregard for the constant NCAA attention he should have known to expect. "In spite of all the scrutiny, he still took chances with marginal athletes like Lloyd Daniels," Goolsby said, shaking his head. "I think he's being criticized for doing things like that, knowing that he was under the magnifying glass. Why would he even try it?"

"What they've said is true," Lois Tarkanian said. "But as a former administrator myself, I question where was the administrative leadership? When we heard Lloyd would be coming back from Mount SAC, I argued with Jerry about having him come back. I liked Lloyd. He was always a sweet person around me, but I knew his academic needs were so great that it was too far a reach for us. I told Jerry we had the wonderful 1987 team where five of the six seniors would graduate, and it was as if he was in euphoria about it and couldn't get his feet on the ground. I knew how hard those seniors were working and how difficult it had been for them to keep focused and do all the necessary academic assignments. I didn't think Lloyd was at a point where he would be able to do that."

Lois remembers an evening when she was "literally begging Jerry not to" let Daniels come back. "'Why would you be so worried?' Jerry said. 'Even President Maxson told Mark it was okay.'

"I couldn't believe a president who talked academics would do that, so I asked Mark later that week about it. He told me the same thing. My question is, why didn't Maxson say no? When did Maxson ever give a directive to Jerry that Jerry did not obey?"

Tarkanian said it was obvious that the Wynns and others of Maxson's inner circle had been misled about the facts of the Daniels guardianship.

"This [guardianship] wasn't just some trick to get Lloyd in," the coach said. "Ask the Warkentiens. They'll tell you they really cared about Lloyd. Hell, he never even played for UNLV and they still are doing things to help him. They're still keeping in touch with him and helping him financially."

"He just called two days ago," Maureen Warkentien said in early November 1991. "I love Lloyd to death. He's always been wonderful around me and good to me personally. If I ever took him anywhere and we'd stop to get Cokes or something, he would always buy mine. He'd never let me pay. And he's really good with our girls. He likes to play with them. He still calls once or twice a month to check in and let us know what he's doing. He'll ask Mark for advice. He usually doesn't listen and does what he wants to anyway. When he calls, he always talks to me about the kids. When he visits, he'll always have some kind of present for them, stuffed animals or something like that. Lloyd's a good guy and a great friend."

"We took a chance on a few kids." Tarkanian shrugged. "That one backfired. But no one ever writes that Lloyd Daniels never had a scholarship, never played in a game, never even went to practice."

Whether Lloyd Daniels ever practiced or not, the decision to take that chance didn't just backfire on Tarkanian, it exploded. It gave Maxson his greatest opportunity to articulate to his growing number of supporters what he claimed was a difference between his philosophy on the student-athlete and Tarkanian's.

"I knew that Lloyd was a million-to-one long shot," Tarkanian said. "I figured if he came here for one year before he went to the NBA, we'd be lucky. There's nothing wrong with that. The way I look at it, if you bring a kid in who can't read or write—somebody nobody else would touch—and you keep him here four, five years, teach him to follow the rules, make him responsible for what he does, and at the end, if he can read and write, you've done him a favor. Even if he doesn't have the piece of paper [diploma], you gave him a chance to straighten out."

Tarkanian has applied that philosophy throughout his career and knows he's been chastised for it. "Every time I say something like, 'You can help a kid without graduating him,' it gets me in trouble," he told *Sports Illustrated* in 1987. "That's the biggest problem you've got with education today, the hypocrisy. You say what you think, you get murdered."

For all his wit, Tarkanian was always on the record that this was his philosophy. He was brought to the university to win basketball games, and he did so with student-athletes who were admitted by the university. He says universities are to educate, not just graduate. And education, he contends, can happen whether a diploma is achieved or not.

Maxson, though he never has talked with Tarkanian about the issue and shared his differing opinion, said Tarkanian was helping everyone but the university by recruiting questionable students.

"We should never recruit any student to UNLV that all indicators don't show that they have a good chance to graduate," Maxson said. "His theory is that, well, it's good for the kid, even if he just stays here a year. My theory is, it may be, but it's not good for the university. It's not good for the university to recruit people that you know cannot do college work. It diminishes the institution. He says if the kid helps them win a few games, it's good for the team. It's totally wrong. I think it is, it is absolutely wrong, categorically wrong, I mean, add any words you want, any adjectives you want to use. I think it is wrong to recruit any student to the university that you know is so academically ill prepared that they don't have a chance of being successful academically. I think moms and dads [of other students] can see the difference, and I think that a school has got to be careful that if you take the marginal kids, 'the kids that nobody else wants,' either because of academics or social problems they can't fit in, I think in the long haul you hurt yourself because those youngsters who are good students and come from those good homes and are strong socially don't want any part of that. Listen, parents want their kids around other kids that are like them. I think it's wrong to recruit anyone that you know doesn't have a chance to graduate. There are two reasons. Number one, I'm not sure that it does them any good. I will concede some of the argument of some side benefits, but I think mainly what it is is a false promise. I think it is exploitation. I think you're promising something, or at least implicitly there's a promise of something you can't deliver. And also, I think what makes it that wrong is when you statistically know what percent of the kids end up in the pros. In other words, it's not like you could say, well, look he's got a shot at a lucrative pro contract. I don't know the percents, but I understand it's something like only one percent or less than one percent, which is not overwhelming, so I'm not sure that it does the youngster any good. I'm not sure that it's not a false promise."

"That sounds good, when he talks that way, doesn't it," said Lois Tarkanian, who has her doctorate in education. "But his university graduates twenty-one percent of its students. And the percentage of graduates has declined all but one year since Maxson's been at UNLV. Does that mean he's exploiting the other seventy-nine percent? Does that mean he's offering them a false promise? The UNLV men's basketball program, according to figures released in *USA Today*, graduates not only a greater percentage than football and even women's basketball, but also almost twice as high a percentage as the university's general student body. And Maxson knows these figures as well as I. By not accurately reporting these figures, he's helped nurture the animosity toward the men's basketball program by some of the individuals on the academic side. That's abhorrent.

"I work in special education. I deal with people who have troubled educational backgrounds. Jerry's success rate is so high, higher than mine or anyone I work with in special ed. If he were in my field, he'd be honored. The federal government spends millions pouring money into helping kids improve their lives through education. Jerry does it on a basketball court. Jerry doesn't deserve to be run out of coaching. He deserves a federal grant."

Tarkanian said he is "disappointed" that the president harbored such strong feelings about his recruiting and never shared them with him. Maxson did, though, share those opinions with others, especially after Daniels became a national embarrassment.

"I have agreed with Bob that [Tarkanian] is not a disciplinarian," Elaine Wynn said. "He is a permissive personality. His style is to be the kids' friend, sort of. It's managed to work for him, in terms of wins and losses; it's not a particularly effective style when the chips are down. You lose control of your program. I can't say that I woke up one day and just arrived at that conclusion. It [the fact this was no longer tolerable] kind of emerged in the transition, just one more story, one more headline, one more. If [Tarkanian hadn't lost control] before Lloyd Daniels, that certainly was the final straw. At that point, I just thought that we were no longer acting responsibly. You can do a lot of things because that's always the way you've done them, and that can take you just so far. But then, when you get into hot water and you take a lot of innocent people with you— meaning the university—it's time to be accountable. That was the klutz move of the century. That's where they deserve to get fired, just the bad judgment, the stupidity of it."

Combined with the headlines that, in his opinion, proved all of his good work was being undone by this difference of philosophy,

Maxson was able to make a compelling argument that something had to give. He began calling his chief supporters, asking if they would stand with him were he to "take action" against the coach. The sobering answer he received was that while they would support him, the town likely would not.

Elaine Wynn said Maxson was faced with the tough choice of dealing with Tarkanian then—possibly by refusing to sign his rollover three-year contract—or riding the storm out until the time appeared more appropriate.

"What if you're the boss and you don't want to have to live with that length of time," Elaine Wynn said, explaining Maxson's options. "What if you had stuff pending, knowing the Lloyd Daniels investigation was going to come out, that might supply you with information that would give you cause to terminate, and then you could use that and not have to live out the terms of the three-year contract. It's a chess game."

"If they were having a chess game, they should have let me know, so I could have played, too," Tarkanian said. "It doesn't seem fair to have a chess game and not tell the other party that the game is being played."

"Isn't it interesting to find out you're regarded as pawns in a chess game rather than human beings?" Lois said. "If Jerry was not good for the university, he should have been told so, directly and honestly by the university president. Their reason for waiting to tell Jerry was not to improve academics or the well-being of the student body; it was for one reason only, [to] protect Bob Maxson. They cared more about his image than the lives of other human beings. He wraps himself in the flag of the university, but if that had been his major concern, why didn't he spend more time and effort in increasing the academic level and the graduation rate of the general student body? Maybe he could have brought it up to the same level as that of the men's basketball team."

Elaine Wynn said Maxson's strength in the community in 1987 wasn't great enough to put Tarkanian in checkmate:

"In a perfect world, if you are a perfect person and you don't have to consider all the ramifications of the decision, and we all deal with this every day in our lives, the correct thing would have been to have said, 'Coach Tarkanian, you've been great up till now, but we can't continue this arrangement because it's no longer working for the university. Your method is not my method and I don't respect it or approve of it anymore, so toot, toot, tootsie, three years down the road you're out of here.' Now, realistically speaking, aside from the litigation, you see what's happened in the press here, everybody rallies, it polarizes the community. In the long run it creates more ill will and antagonism, it creates distraction for the president, who really needs to be focused on more important stuff like academics. It shakes the confidence of the faculty. I mean the ripple effect of that little decision could have been much more disastrous than the rightness of making that decision for those reasons. And so you always have to consider consequences when you're making these decisions at the time.

"Now, I wouldn't presume to tell Bob Maxson what to do in that spot. So, when he called, all I could do is say, yeah, this is really tough. Yeah, Jerry is getting to be a real son of a gun. This is a miserable thing, and, so what are the options here. So if you do this, then what's going to happen there, and yeah, we got eighteen thousand people [at the arena] and we're selling out and a majority of those people have never set foot on this campus and they could you know, just call for your hide. So there was a scale. Jerry Tarkanian's popularity versus a new university president who was building his credibility, and it probably would not have been in his best interest to take that on at that time. The timing might not have been right. It's not that he wouldn't have been able to survive it, but he would have done a lot of damage in trying to get back on track."

Instead, Maxson decided to appoint a committee to investigate the *Newsday* allegations. A firing squad couldn't have been stacked any more against Tarkanian. On the committee, Maxson appointed John Unrue, his academic vice president, Paul Burns, the school's NCAA representative, Gary Jones, the president of the Faculty Senate, and Lew Cryer, commissioner of the PCAA.

In 1991 interviews, both Burns and Unrue admitted that at the time they were appointed, they believed the basketball program was "out of control." And Cryer was a candidate to replace Tarkanian's archenemy, Walter Byers, as executive director of the NCAA. Records show these three, with their obvious bias against the basketball program, set the tone for the in-house hearings.

"The deep feelings harbored against the basketball office by Burns and Unrue were there long before Maxson got here," said

Dominic Gentile, an attorney for one employee interviewed by the in-house committee. "Bob Maxson gave them the green light. It was plain that this committee had an agenda. In the minds of these 'academics,' nothing was more distasteful than the national recognition Jerry Tarkanian was getting. In their pettiness of their bruised egos, they had to cut down the tall tree so they could be in the sunshine."

Several of the attorneys representing those interviewed by the committee said its actions were "unethical at best." The committee summoned at least one witness under false pretenses, pressured witnesses, and asked some questions as many as a dozen times in one interview to get its desired answer.

"The in-house committee worked to deprive state employees of their rights," said attorney Steve Cohen, who represented another member of the basketball staff. "Their tactics mirrored those employed by the NCAA years earlier."

The in-house committee spent the summer and early fall questioning those who were quoted in the *Newsday* series. They determined that there wasn't much they could determine. Except, that is, that this was "scary business," as Unrue put it.

"The Lloyd Daniels case was the kind of benchmark or marking the decline of the present regime over there," said Unrue, who served as the committee's chairman. "So many things began to unravel from that point on. We were to investigate those specific allegations [in the *Newsday* series], and then it just seemed to me that Pandora's box opened up. We interviewed people who were alleged to have furnished cars for the players, and [in] the investigation that we conducted, we would ask a question and then some of the witnesses would say, Oh, yes, but then here was X, Y, and Z in addition to that.

"The thing about that investigation that was an eye-opener for me, and it really did trouble me tremendously because it gave me some perspective on what I will call for want of a better word, was the 'madness' that attends big-time athletics. I'm not going to mention names to you, but some of the witnesses who came before our committee were so frightened and so intimidated by somebody that they were literally terrified. I can tell you that there was actual weeping, weeping in some of our committee meetings and we found that as people in the university and in society extremely unnerving that it had come to that. People felt that their lives were in jeopardy if they told what they perceived to be the truth. I think that all of us began to think in different terms about this program and about the madness that attended it. I understand the fans are excited and we all want our team to win, but this was, in my opinion, an extraordinary distortion of values. I thought that we had reached a very, very dangerous point. As a committee we felt somewhat helpless because obviously we weren't a part of any kind of enforcement group."

Unrue failed to mention the only witnesses that said they were threatened were Ricky Collier, who flunked off the team, and Ann Mayo, a former academic adviser to the team whose animosity toward the basketball program was well known. The credibility of both witnesses later was severely questioned.

Unrue also said he could show no link between those who he believed threatened witnesses and Tarkanian. "I don't know whether I could say that the group Jerry was 'hanging out' with was the very group doing the threatening or making the threats, but I think that they were persons surely associated with the program," he said.

Just seven days before the committee made its report to Maxson about its concern for the health and welfare of its witnesses, it heard from Collier, the eleventh man on Tarkanian's team and the player quoted frequently by *Newsday* in the Daniels series.

It was Collier, transcripts of those meetings show, who cried before the committee and told its members several people in Las Vegas had threatened his life and tried to bribe him into silence. He said several boosters had provided him with handfuls of cash when he was riding the bench for the Rebels. One of those whom he claimed to have received money from was Tarkanian's friend Irwin Molasky, one of Las Vegas's most wealthy citizens.

Collier's revelation prompted this exchange with Paul Burns:

BURNS: You know he [Molasky] has the reputation of knowing people who might hurt other people. You know, he has ...

COLLIER: I know, because of how big he is.

BURNS: Yeah, he's supposedly had some connections with organized crime and so on. I don't know if he has or hasn't, but there's certainly stories.

The "stories" Burns referred to include a 1975 feature in *Penthouse* magazine linking Rancho La Costa, a posh San Diego resort that Molasky helped develop, with the mob. Under the headline "La Costa: The Hundred Million Dollar Resort with a Criminal Clientele," reporters Lowell Bergman and Jeff Gerth wrote that the 5,600-acre coastal complex was built with questionable loans from a Teamster Union pension fund and was "a gathering place of thieves and hoods." Molasky and his partner, Morris B. "Moe" Dalitz, sued *Penthouse* for $522 million. Dalitz later was ruled a "public figure" and dropped from the lawsuit. After fifteen days of deliberation, the twelve-member jury decided Molasky had not been libeled by the stories. Some writers stated the verdict meant the *Penthouse* charges were true, and obviously Paul Burns believed them.

Burns's mudslinging outraged Tarkanian. "Irwin is one of the most respected men in our community," Tarkanian said. "He's served on more committees and done more good work than anyone I know. He started the UNLV Foundation. It's really unfortunate that he's being dirtied up by people who don't know him. Burns was way out of line saying those kinds of things. But that's the way that committee was doing its work, trying to scare people."

Unrue and Burns said the experience of investigating Tarkanian's program gave credence to their belief that basketball was out of proportion at UNLV. It also allowed university administrators to start raising questions quietly about Tarkanian's friends and associates.

"No doubt the biggest weight around his neck was his associations," Maxson said.

"He certainly wasn't helped by his associations, in spite of their loyalty," said Steve Wynn. "I mean he's a complicated and a mixed bag kind of guy. His group of associates was the same way. He's got a strange taste in friends."

There were the questions about Tarkanian's most visible supporters—Molasky, Freddie Glusman, and Mike Toney. Glusman and Toney, both of whom had been licensed by the Nevada Gaming Contol Board and gone through exhaustive background checks, were seen as too loud, too obnoxious. They didn't fit "the image."

Then there were the questions about others—friends like Vic Weiss, Tarkanian's onetime agent who had negotiated his first contract with UNLV and, in 1979, was finalizing a deal that would have made Tarkanian the next coach of the Los Angeles Lakers when he was found dead in the trunk of a maroon-and-white Rolls-Royce, the victim of a gangland-style murder.

Weiss last was seen with Jack Kent Cooke, owner of the Washington Redskins football team, and Jerry Buss, who was buying the Lakers from Cooke. The three were holed up in a room at the Beverly Comstock Hotel in Los Angeles working on Tarkanian's multi-year deal. Weiss was to have met Jerry and Lois Tarkanian that evening to present them with the Lakers contract. He never showed. When he was found four days later, the only items police believe were missing were his briefcase and Tarkanian's contract. His $6,000 ring and diamond-studded Rolex watch were un-, touched allowing police to rule robbery out as a possible cause for his death.

In *Interference: How Organized Crime Influences Professional Football*, award-winning investigative reporter Dan E. Moldea quoted numerous police and organized crime sources as saying Weiss had been more than a car salesman, which is what Tarkanian said he knew his former friend to be. Sources told Moldea that Weiss was a bagman for Los Angeles Rams owner Carroll Rosenbloom, who had drowned in the Atlantic Ocean two months earlier.

"Weiss and Carroll Rosenbloom were definitely associated," Los Angeles Police Department detective Leroy Orozco, who investigated Weiss's still unsolved murder, told Moldea. "Weiss was definitely a bagman for some of the Vegas people. Weiss came up on some phone records at a place called the Gold Rush, a little jewelry shop in Circus Circus casino in Las Vegas. The Gold Rush was run by Tony Spilotro."

Spilotro, a well-known Chicago mobster, was found murdered and buried in a shallow grave in Indiana in 1986.

"There were reports that Weiss was involved in a major West Coast "layoff" gambling operation, that he had been placing large bets on NFL games," Orozco explained. (To "layoff" is to spread bets to many bookies, in order to prevent any one bookie from taking too great a loss or making too great a profit.)

Tarkanian, who was interviewed but was never under suspicion in the case, said he was "shocked" when he heard what police were saying about his longtime friend.

"I didn't even know that he knew Carroll Rosenbloom," Tarkanian said. "When his wife was interviewed after his death, she didn't even know most of what the police were saying. If she didn't know, how were any of the rest of us going to? I knew Vic as a guy who played football at Pasadena College. He was a little cocky, always bragging, saying he'd been recruited by Bear Bryant at Kentucky. We all wondered if he was legit. Then one time, I'll never forget, they were having an intersquad football game and he told me to come early because he was going to run the opening kickoff back. I was five minutes late and missed the kickoff. When I got there, it was 7–0. I asked a guy what happened and he said, 'This guy Weiss ran it back.' From then on, I was a believer. We used to ride to class together every day. I played on the softball team sponsored by his father's dry cleaning business. That team got thrown out of the league because we started so many fights. We were just kids having fun."

Tarkanian said he kept in contact with Weiss and grew to trust his business sense. "I remember the last time he came to Las Vegas, we were at dinner with like eight people at the Palace Court and he said, 'I've made all the money I need to make in my life. I can't spend it all.' He picked up the tab. He used to go to reunions and buy everyone's drinks. He was a big spender."

Police investigating Weiss's murder found he had left everyone believing the story of his supposed wealth. But when he died, all Weiss owned was a vacant lot.

Though he was never even remotely linked to Weiss's suspect past, Tarkanian found the death of his friend was used by those who wanted to raise questions about his "associations." The *Review-Journal*, in an editorial after Tarkanian resigned, dragged Weiss's death up again, stating the newspaper was concerned for its sources, given the dangerous associates the coach had made during his lifetime.

All of this brought back the same rumors and innuendo that the NCAA had used in 1977 when it presented the Committee on Infractions with the claims of former assistant coach Tony Morocco. It worked then. The NCAA found Tarkanian guilty and branded him a cheater. Now, it was working again. Confused by discrepancies in the testimony of Ricky Collier—the disgruntled player who the university later would decide had more stories than credibility—that he was threatened, the in-house committee recommended that Maxson turn the case over to the PCAA and the NCAA.

Maxson called a press conference for October 21, then went the day before and paid personal visits to editors at both newspapers—Mike O'Callaghan at the *Las Vegas Sun* and Bob Sands at the *Review-Journal*—to inform them of the committee's decision. He shared copies of the press release he would make the next day. All before even talking to Tarkanian. When he finally did meet with him, Tarkanian read Maxson's proposed release, which said there was some "corroborating evidence" to support *Newsday's* allegations. Tarkanian challenged the wording, and Maxson agreed to change it to indicate the committee had heard "conflicting testimony." Later that night, Rothermel received a call from Sands, the *Review-Journal* sports editor, asking why the wording had been changed from the release Maxson had given him earlier that day.

Tarkanian expressed shock and outrage. But he should have known this was coming. Earlier in the summer, Las Vegas businessman Harry Woods, who now owns Redell Sporting Goods, was having dinner at Café Michelle with his wife and a business associate from Dallas. Maxson and two friends—a man and a woman—were sitting at the adjacent table

"I overheard some conversation over my shoulder from the table right behind me," Woods said. "I looked over, and it was the president, Maxson. He was dogging it pretty good. His back was to me. He said, 'The NCAA's coming in and if they find anything, I'll have his ass out by fall.' The guy he was with told him, 'You better watch out.' There was no ifs, ands, or buts about it. He was talking about getting rid of Tark. I was so sure of it I called Tark."

Woods, who said he has met the coach only three times, called Tarkanian to give him the heads-up. They met for lunch at the Dunes Hotel.

"I was just trying to warn him," Woods said. "Tark said maybe I misunderstood him. He didn't believe me. He said the president had told him different himself. I told him, 'I'm not making this up. I heard it.' I walked away from there and told my wife I was embarrassed that I had even tried to tell him because he was so sure I wasn't right."

The warning didn't help. Tarkanian said he was "totally surprised" when he heard the president's decision to call a press conference. He pled with Maxson to change his mind or, at the very least, put the decision on hold. There were several reasons that a delay made sense, Tarkanian said. First, the committee had promised Warkentien and others that they would have a chance to refute any conflicting testimony before its work was done. That promise was never kept. Second, a list of questions given to Chesnoff, Daniels's attorney, were being answered by the former recruit. But because Daniels was then going through drug rehabilitation in a Kansas clinic, his response had been delayed. Chesnoff had called Unrue just days before the press conference to explain Daniels's situation and was told that it was no problem because "the committee is far behind schedule." And finally, Maxson's press conference, Tarkanian pointed out, was scheduled just three weeks before the fall signing period opened for recruits. Once they heard that the NCAA was being given a key to the city, recruits would flock in the other direction, Tarkanian predicted. Maxson told Tarkanian he had made "a commitment" to hold the press conference. The coach later learned that commitment was to the editors he had met with earlier in the day.

Maxson held his press conference, and Tarkanian's prediction proved correct. Rather than nabbing the best group of players he'd ever had, Tarkanian was suddenly scrambling for recruits who hadn't yet committed to other schools. Matt Othick, a Las Vegas high school star who would later start for the University of Arizona, told the local newspapers, "[I] really love Coach Tark. I really think he's the best coach in the country. All along, in my heart, I wanted to play for UNLV. But my father heard through the grapevine that the UNLV president was out to get Coach Tark. That played a big part in my decision." Tarkanian wasn't just losing recruits because of the NCAA anymore. Now it was his own president that was costing him talent. All but one of the blue chippers told him "No thanks."

Tarkanian's lawyer, Chuck Thompson, took Maxson to task in an interview the day after the press conference. "The whole Lloyd Daniels thing has been a grandstand affair [for Maxson]," Thompson said. "It's been my opinion that Bob Maxson's attitude has always been that this town wasn't big enough for him and Jerry. I don't know of a man with a bigger ego than Bob Maxson's. The press conference was totally unnecessary. Bob Maxson is too smart not to know it's not going to play that way, too. He's too smart not to know it's going to be detrimental to Jerry. Bob Maxson is a capable, charismatic, bright man with an enormous ego. Therein lies the problem for Jerry Tarkanian. When it [recognition] comes around the country, it's UNLV and Jerry Tarkanian and not UNLV and Bob Maxson." Thompson told reporters he had advised Tarkanian to take an NBA job offered to him earlier in 1987. "I told him, 'It's a matter of time before Bob Maxson cuts you off at the knees.'"

Thompson's statement enraged Maxson. But it also awakened many in the community to the possibility that Tarkanian lacked Maxson's full support.

A little more than two weeks later, Maxson was introduced during halftime ceremonies at the homecoming football game. The crowd booed, hissed, and hollered. It was apparent that his decision, while it may have provided him with the best opportunity to get rid of Tarkanian, also was costing him points.

Thompson said university counsel Brad Booke later said the only time he had heard Maxson curse was in reference to the crowd's response to Maxson's call for an NCAA investigation of the Daniels situation. "Booke said Maxson told him, 'I really stepped on my dick on that one,'" Thompson remembers.

Maxson, it seemed, took a lesson from the experience—the dagger that ultimately would do Tarkanian in better not have his fingerprints on it.

Tarkanian, though, didn't learn his lesson. Though he admits "Lloyd was my biggest mistake," he declares it so only because it didn't work out. "If Lloyd had worked out, it would have been one of the greatest sports stories of all time," he said.

Unfortunately for Tarkanian, Lloyd became fodder for award-winning investigative, not feature, stories.

8

Here Comes the NCAA: Round Two

Maxson wasn't the only one who noticed that his decision to invite the NCAA into a town that hates the NCAA might have been fatal. Joe Foley, a member of the Board of Regents and one of the president's most ardent supporters, asked Tarkanian to join Maxson for a short meeting and a photo session outside the president's office to project the image of harmony. Tarkanian showed up as requested, saying he did so out of loyalty to the president. Maxson even asked Tarkanian if he would allow John Irsfeld, his executive assistant and a novelist wanna-be, to ghostwrite Tarkanian's next newspaper column.

"I have been assured by UNLV President Robert Maxson and UNLV Athletic Director Brad Rothermel that no one from our university has requested that the NCAA undertake an investigation of our program," the Irsfeld-Tarkanian column stated. "Certainly, we accept the fact that if inconsistencies exist in information obtained by the UNLV committee, then the larger agencies would need to use their personnel to investigate further. There appears to be a strong effort by some to develop a wedge between athletics and academics at UNLV. In truth, Maxson, as well as several other faculty members, have met on many occasions with our recruits in a coordinated effort to convey the strong academic and athletic link which exists at the university. I did not agree that a press conference should have been held before the UNLV committee report was completed because I know full well how that type of announcement gets blown out of proportion. However, that type of disagreement exists daily in every educational and business institution. The man at the top makes the final decision. Other than the disagreement over the publicity of the press conference, Maxson and I have had no other disagreement concerning the handling of this matter. In fact, we are both united now in asking that the creation of a public controversy between us stop. It is important to the university and the community."

More important, it was important to Bob Maxson.

Tarkanian's lawyer, Chuck Thompson, was upset that the coach would "kiss and make up in a picture," then give up his column to "let Maxson spew that crap." "Jerry, by doing that, allowed Bob Maxson to live to kill another day," Thompson said. But Tarkanian was consistent in his belief that coaches don't fire presidents, presidents fire coaches. "If the president asks me to do something, I do it," Tarkanian said. "I always have. He's the president."

The picture and the column were only the beginning of Maxson's effort to distance himself from his invitation to the NCAA. He first attempted to blame the decision on PCAA Commissioner Lew Cryer, who Maxson said requested that the investigation be handed over to higher authorities. But Cryer, in an interview with the *Las Vegas Sun,* said that wasn't true. He said it was Maxson who had asked for the hastily prepared committee report, even though, Cryer said, the committee's work was not done: "He wanted a report, coming forth with what we had so far." Cryer then told Rothermel that he had advised Maxson against mentioning the NCAA and had told him there was no need for a press conference.

Maxson's predicament became even more sticky when the *Las Vegas Sun* printed the text from a letter the NCAA's David Berst sent him just two days after the press conference. "As you know, at the university's request, a preliminary inquiry of the men's basketball program at the university will be undertaken by the NCAA enforcement staff," Berst wrote. Maxson fired a letter back to Berst and another to Cryer, trying desperately to re-create the facts. "I was surprised to receive your letter of October 23, 1987, informing me that you are beginning a preliminary inquiry into the men's basketball program here at UNLV 'at the university's request.' Although I have made it clear that our institution does intend that the inquiry continue, there has been no request made of the NCAA. In fact, there has been no communication at all between this university and the NCAA regarding this matter." That last line contradicts a statement Maxson made to the *Review-Journal*'s Bob Sands, who quoted the president as saying, "I personally have been in contact with the NCAA about the study."

In a 1991 meeting with Tarkanian, NCAA Executive Director Dick Schultz confirmed the coach's suspicions. "He said, 'You know you can't blame this investigation on us'—your president asked us to come in," Tarkanian said.

The only group that wasn't thoroughly confused by all this was the committee Maxson had appointed and which was supposed to be wrapping up its work. Instead, the committee became an in-house advisory group to the NCAA's investigation.

With its hands untied to probe allegations outside of the Daniels' recruitment, the committee thought it was in for a fireworks show. And it started out with a bang.

During its first meeting after Maxson's announcement, the committee invited Ann Mayo, the onetime academic adviser to the men's basketball program, to a closed-door session. Committee chairman Unrue had become friends with Mayo over the years and had listened as she had leveled many charges against the program in private conversations. Now, Unrue wanted Mayo to put those allegations on the record.

If the charges the committee had heard earlier seemed unsubstantiated, Unrue was confident he'd found the person who could put the puzzle together. Mayo had been offered the job at UNLV in 1984 on the recommendation of Lois Tarkanian, who saw her academic credentials and thought she'd help beef up an improving academic support staff. Mayo had worked as an academic adviser to the Ohio State University football program and had what appeared to be the perfect résumé. She told friends she had been offered a job at the NCAA as an investigator—a fact sources said later was not true—but she was obviously familiar with the do's and don'ts of college sports. "I thought it would help build respect for the entire academic effort," Lois said.

It didn't take long for respect to turn to disrespect—in both directions. Players complained to Tarkanian about Mayo's attitude toward them, and Mayo began telling friends that she was "miserable" on the job. Almost immediately, the friction began to surface. Mayo had been hired to replace Mark Warkentien in dealing with the team's academic counseling. By relieving Warkentien of those responsibilities, Tarkanian was freeing him to become a full-time recruiter. When several players told Warkentien that Mayo was unavailable when they needed her, he took the complaints to Tarkanian. That caused a rift between them so wide that Tarkanian later would refer to them as "bitter enemies."

The backbreaker in the relationship, though, came just months after Mayo arrived. She left one afternoon to play golf with three other women in the athletic department when a player came to Warkentien with an "urgent" academic need. Warkentien helped the player, then let Mayo know later that he thought her timing was "incredibly bad." Again, he went to Tarkanian. This time Tarkanian berated Mayo for shirking her responsibilities. During a deposition taken by the university, Warkentien recalled Mayo saying, "I'll get your ass." She told Assistant Athletic Director Tina Kunzer that Warkentien was now on her "list," Kunzer said under oath. And Joyce Aschenbrenner, who Mayo testified was her closest friend at the university, told UNLV lawyers that "if there was some way for Mayo to undermine Warkentien, she would."

Based upon the continuing complaints, Tarkanian wrote Mayo a memo asking her to account for her time outside the office. Enraged by this attack on her professionalism, Mayo told Kunzer that she was going to "get Tarkanian" and that she would "bring down the basketball program," according to Kunzer's sworn statements. Then Mayo told Assistant Coach Cleveland Edwards, whom she once dated and described as her closest friend in the basketball office, that she planned to "get that bald headed Armenian mother fucker," Edwards said in his sworn statement.

By 1985, it seemed everyone in the athletic department was aware of Mayo's feelings toward the basketball program. So it came as no surprise when Rothermel received a complaint from Mayo alleging that Warkentien had arranged for three members of the basketball team—Richard Robinson, Jarvis Basnight, and Freddie Banks—to receive a grade for a tennis class without ever attending the class. Mayo said she knew this to be true because she had driven by the tennis courts and noticed that none of the players were present on the day of the final.

Mayo passed the allegation on to Rothermel, who made several calls and determined, without conducting a full investigation, that the charge was unfounded. He let her know that he found her "complaint to be invalid," and dismissed the charge as another in the troubling string of events arising from the Mayo-Warkentien personality conflict.

Mayo thought Tarkanian and Rothermel were attempting to sweep her concerns under the carpet. She told Aschenbrenner and Kunzer that the coach and athletic director now would be added to her "list." Feeling ignored, she started looking for new people with whom she could share her frustrations.

At a party off campus one weekend, Mayo pulled Unrue aside and shared the tennis-class allegation with him. Unrue called Maxson, who summoned Rothermel to his office first thing Monday morning.

"The president explained to me what Unrue had heard," Rothermel said. "The president asked me to investigate it. Now, Ann thought Unrue had conducted the investigation. That's how I know for sure she could not have driven by the class. First, she was on leave during the period of time when she claimed that she had observed them not being in the final of that class. But when I turned in a report saying it was not true and Ann accepted that report because she thought Unrue had done it, that gave her away, that's when I knew she couldn't have been there during that period of time. Had she really been there, she wouldn't have accepted the answer from anyone. She said what Unrue found must have been true. She didn't realize I was the one who presented the information to the president."

What Mayo didn't know was that Maxson and Unrue told Rothermel that she was the person raising the issue. She told others, including the in-house investigating committee, that Maxson

had promised "to keep my name out of it" and would create a scenario that would leave others believing the tennis-class allegation
came from the registrar's office.

Edwards, who now coaches at Marshall University, recalls
Mayo returning from a meeting with Maxson and boasting that the
president had offered to protect her job if she helped him bring
down Tarkanian. "It was about six months after she had been here,
she told me she had a meeting, said she had a discussion with Dr.
Maxson about if she could prove, did she know of any violations
that was [sic] going on in the basketball program," Edwards said in
that deposition taken by university attorneys. "And if she could
help him prove that there was, he would help her get a job." That
seemed consistent with the statement of former player Ricky Collier, who told the committee Mayo said in the fall of 1986 that she
was "getting out" of the basketball department and would soon
become a senior administrator in "another department." Either
Mayo had inside knowledge or a crystal ball because her transfer
didn't come up until the next summer and the job she was given
hadn't even been created when she made her statements to
Edwards and Collier.

"That's just not true," Maxson said when asked about Mayo's
claim of presidential protection. "I don't remember the exact, I
don't even remember the conversation, I don't even remember the
specifics of the conversation. She and John Unrue came to see me
and I did not know Ann at that time, I mean I knew who she was
but I didn't know her personally, didn't know that much about her.
I knew she was an academic adviser and she had her doctoral
degree from Ohio State. I'm going to tell you exactly what I remember about that conversation and I certainly remember the essence of
it, but I don't remember the details of it because you must remember that I have a jillion meetings in my office, and, even important
meetings, more important than that. I remember John and Ann
coming up, and I remember her expressing concern about activities
in the athletic department. Now, I remember that being the tone of
the meeting. And I know that's correct. I don't remember the
details, I don't even remember that she gave me any specifics. I
don't remember a single example, but I do remember her having
concerns. And what I told her was that just tell the truth and every-

thing would be all right. You're not going to be in any trouble if you tell the truth."

Mayo, who declined interviews regarding the NCAA inquiry, also originally refused to be questioned by the attorneys for those she accused. She later agreed to be deposed, but would discuss only the NCAA allegations—not the other unfounded allegations she made—after the attorneys pressed the university to take disciplinary action against her for noncooperation. In a short discussion for this book, she said Maxson's hazy memory has left her in a difficult position. "Now you might have sort of a clue why I choose not to discuss it in public at all," Mayo said after being told Maxson didn't remember the specifics of their discussion. "For me this is a no-win situation if the president doesn't remember that I went to discuss something with him."

Told that Maxson denies ever guaranteeing her job security, Mayo snapped, "I would like to ask him how he explains that there are quite a few people as of today who are no longer employed by the athletic department or who are leaving the employment of the athletic department. I am still employed as an assistant dean, as an administrator of this university, I'm a faculty member, I chair a standing committee of the Faculty Senate, I think that I am very well regarded amongst my peers. I just think that it's unusual that if I'm the one not telling the truth here, why I'm the one who still has the job and feels fairly secure about it."

Both Mayo and Maxson have said he had nothing to do with her transfer to the business department. And though Maxson denies ever promising Mayo job protection, Mayo's employment record at UNLV shows she has done quite well for herself since her conversations with the president began. Copies of her annual contracts show that she has gone from a $35,798 job as an "athletic academic consultant" to a $47,561 job as a lecturer of management in the school of business and economics. In three years, she received a 30 percent increase. During that stretch, she also received two sizable merit raises, both of which were approved by Unrue, whom she thanked for "getting me out of there [the basketball office]" during one of her appearances before the in-house committee.

Mayo told Edwards and fellow academic advisers Mike Alsup and Shelley Fischer that she knew Unrue and Maxson would act on

Young Jerry Tarkanian with his mother, Rose, father, George, and sister, Alice. *Tarkanian Collection*

Jerry and Lois play with sons, Danny and George, and daughters, Pam and Jodie, in those "early days." *Tarkanian Collection*

Tarkanian is carried from the court after his first junior college state championship at Pasadena. *Tarkanian Collection*

Tarkanian and his Long Beach team erupt in joy after the '49ers' first win in the new Long Beach Arena. The 1970 game was a win over Tulsa. *Tarkanian Collection*

Tarkanian and young Danny watch the last seconds tick off the clock in another win at Long Beach. *Tarkanian Collection*

Tarkanian accepts the NCAA's most prized trophy from Big Ten commissioner Jim Delany. *Tarkanian Collection*

Tarkanian and Larry Johnson, UNLV's number-one draft pick, talk as Johnson goes back in to a 1991 game. Johnson led the Rebels to a forty-five game winning streak. *Greg Cava*

Before each home game, the crowd is treated to an indoor fireworks show. *Greg Cava*

Larry Johnson throws his arm around assistant coach Tim Grgurich after a national semifinal game in Oakland. *Greg Cava*

Dennis Finfrock and his wife, Kay. *Greg Cava*

UNLV President Robert Maxson talks to Tarkanian on the bench of a 1989 game. *Greg Cava*

Don King and Mike Tyson want a shot with Tarkanian, too. *Greg Cava*

Former athletic director Brad Rothermel and his assistant, Tina Kunzer, watch a Rebel game. *Greg Cava*

Tark and ticket manager Le Riggle, who was fired by Dennis Finfrock in the wake of an investigation into ticket trade-outs. *Greg Cava*

Tarkanian lost sight of his towel when the Rebels lost to Seton Hall in the 1989 tournament. *Greg Cava*

Tarkanian and his legendary towel. *Greg Cava*

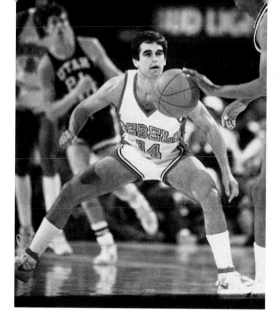

Danny Tarkanian played point guard for his father and held UNLV's all-time assist record. *Greg Cava*

Rebel fan Bill Cosby and Tarkanian at a basketball banquet. *Greg Cava*

The President, Vice President, and Secretary of Hoops. *Greg Cava*

The players hug Tarkanian as the final horn sounds in Denver. *Greg Cava*

Las Vegas fans went wild after the championship win. *Greg Cava*

Fans presented Tarkanian and his wife, who were on the way home after the championship game, with a cake at the Denver airport. *Greg Cava*

Golden Nugget Corporation President Steve Wynn, actress Whoopi Goldberg, and Wynn's wife, Elaine, enjoy a Rebel game. The Wynns supported Maxson's effort to encourage Tarkanian's "retirement." *Greg Cava*

Ricky Collier, a backup guard who flunked out of UNLV, alleged that boosters gave him cash. *UNLV Sports Information*

Tarkanian and Florida State coach Pat Kennedy embrace after the game that became better known for its fans than for its result. Richard "the Fixer" Perry (circled) had been sitting behind the UNLV bench. Athletic Director Dennis Finfrock spent an afternoon sorting through pictures by photographer Greg Cava to find this shot. *Greg Cava*

President Maxson changed the format of the championship celebration so that he could lead the team onto the stage and into the spotlight. *Greg Cava*

The team looks on as the 1990 championship banner—with no mention of the NCAA on it—is unfurled. The next day, the NCAA sent UNLV a list of twenty-nine charges stemming from Lloyd Daniels's recruitment. *Greg Cava*

During the first home game of his last season, Tarkanian asks the referee not to cut Louisiana State any slack. UNLV won in a 21-point upset. *Greg Cava*

This shot by Anderson Hunt bounded off the rim, ending UNLV's forty-five game winning streak and Tarkanian's dream of back-to-back national championships. *Greg Cava*

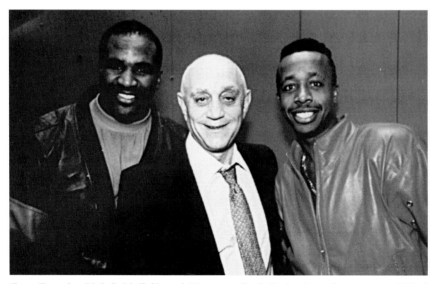

Fans Evander Holyfield (*left*) and Hammer flank Tarkanian after a game. Rebel contests are star-studded affairs. *Greg Cava*

"This is hard for me," Tarkanian said, his hand quivering, as he resigned. Maxson looks on. *Greg Cava*

Tarkanian's resignation brought reporters from across the country to Las Vegas. *Greg Cava*

Rebels Moses Scurry (*left*) and James Jones celebrate with Tarkanian as the clock winds down o
the 1990 Championship game. *Greg Cava*

her complaints because Unrue "had enough skeletons in his closet and she could take him out whenever she wanted to" and she "had enough on the president to bury him," according to depositions.

Mayo told the investigating committee that Warkentien had physically threatened her and that Tarkanian indicated he would fire her if she had, in fact, gone to the president with her complaints. She said "that's when the tide turned" against her in the basketball office.

Although Maxson and Unrue did not find the tennis-class allegation to be true, it was apparent that they had found the eyes and ears in the basketball office that would provide them, the committee, and the NCAA with countless allegations against Tarkanian and his assistants.

What they would have to live with, though, was an investigation of Mayo that showed her statements to be filled with inaccuracies and her motives to be historically vindictive. Through depositions taken by lawyers defending those she accused of wrongdoing, Mayo's closest friends claimed the list of people she vowed to "get" included a broad range of Las Vegans, including an administrator at National University in Las Vegas, who had reprimanded her for poor attendance in her job as an instructor, a member of the university Board of Regents, and several other members of athletic department staff outside of basketball.

In one instance cited by the attorneys, Mayo became irate after Kunzer decided to fire Frances Cox, UNLV's women's softball coach and one of Mayo's closest friends. Aschenbrenner said Mayo decided to go on a "personal attack" against Kunzer. Letters were sent to the president and calls were made to Rothermel attacking Kunzer's character. A few days later, Kunzer's estranged husband received a call from an anonymous woman suggesting that he might want to check the paternity of their child. "If I were you, I'd question the paternity of your son Steven, I would go ahead and ask Tina about it," Tom Kunzer remembers the caller saying before quickly hanging up. When Kunzer called his wife and asked what might be happening, she told him it sounded like Mayo. The next day, when Tom dropped Steven off at Tina's house, he called Mayo while he was there. The voice on the answering machine was the same as the woman who called him the day before, he told university attorneys. He said he had "no question" that Mayo was the caller.

Mayo was willing to share her thoughts on UNLV basketball with any investigator who called. She also was willing to travel far and wide to spread the word. At the request of PCAA Commissioner Jim Haney, who replaced Cryer in 1988, Mayo flew to California, where she met with NCAA investigators without notifying the university. By NCAA rule, if an investigator seeks to interview a university employee, the university is allowed representation at the meeting—but only if the interview is on campus. By bringing Mayo to California, the NCAA and Mayo no longer were bound by the rule. Several lawyers questioned the propriety of the move.

Mayo told friends that she planned on writing a book, *Swimming with Sharks*, about Tarkanian, Warkentien, and Rothermel and her experience with the basketball program. Aschenbrenner swore that every time Mayo became angry, she would blurt out, "Well this, this will be in my book." Mayo also told the in-house committee that she was keeping a journal of violations by the men's program. When pressed for copies of the journal, she at first said she sent it to friends in California because it was "too dangerous to have around." In a second statement taken by lawyers, she said the journal included only academic records and that she had shredded it with scissors because it "was of no importance."

Mayo defended her actions throughout her tenure at UNLV, saying, "Usually what happens in an NCAA investigation, somebody gets pissed off and starts talking, you know. At this place, that didn't seem to happen a lot before, but there's still time, you know. And while I'm made out to be a very vicious, vindictive person, I think that that's probably not true and I think that the people who are close to me would probably tell you that. I think that the one thing they will tell you is that I am a person very concerned about personal ethics and integrity. I teach business ethics in the college of business. I have a Ph.D. in an area in which I did a lot of my course work in ethics. But then I'm made out to be a very unethical person and I'm teaching ethics in the college of business and I teach an honors ethics seminar that's a university course. I have a lot of personal problems with how this thing has fallen out obviously. But those are all going to have to be resolved later."

"I'd love to sit in on an ethics class taught by Ann Mayo," said attorney Dominic Gentile. "I bet it would be interesting."

Despite all this, Brad Booke said Mayo's credibility didn't concern him. "None of the allegations ultimately made by the NCAA depends on Ann Mayo by herself," the university counsel said.

That's not exactly true. After spending more than three years investigating UNLV, the NCAA lodged twenty-two allegations— plus another seven charges of unethical conduct, one by Mayo and six by other staff and athletes—against the basketball program in December 1990. Mayo is the key source in three of those charges and is named as a witness in eleven. Her name comes up as a witness in more allegations than any other individual besides the coaches and athletic director, who were questioned on every charge.

At the end of her first meeting with UNLV's in-house committee, Mayo was asked if there was anyone who could corroborate her statements. She at first mentioned Aschenbrenner, who was out of town. Not wanting to wait, the committee asked her for another name. Mayo said she had just the guy the committee needed: Mike Alsup, who worked for her before she transferred to the business department.

Paul Burns, who also served as the university's faculty representative to the NCAA, rushed to the telephone and called Alsup. He told him that he had some "eligibility questions" that he wanted to discuss and asked if he could hustle over. No problem, Alsup said.

When Alsup showed up, Burns told him that he had deceived him because the committee worried that he might change his story if he had time to think about what he was facing.

"I'd worked with him [Burns] in certifying student athletes in the past," Alsup said. "He called and said, 'I've got a problem with a tennis player I need to talk to you about, something about a certification, can you meet me over at my office?' I said sure. He said, 'You have to meet me on the sixth floor [Burns's office is on the seventh floor of the administration building, adjacent to President Maxson's].' He said, 'My office is a mess, I'll just meet you down there.' I said okay. So I just showed up, thinking I was going to do something to some tennis player. I was shocked when I walked in.

"Unrue told me, 'You know, Mike, I was a young man once, just got married, just got my first job,' he said, 'so I know the kinds of things you're going through,'" said Alsup, who was just then experiencing those things. "'Your cooperating with us pretty much makes sure that whatever happens, you're going to have a job.' And he says, 'Now I don't want that to sound like a bribe. You know you cooperate with us and tell us some stuff and fill in the blanks, and substantiate what she said, and you're going to be okay.' But he left it open like a threat. You don't cooperate, you're tossed out. Never saying that ... but I mean that's what it was."

If that wasn't enough to make Alsup nervous, records show the committee allowed Mayo to sit in while he was being questioned. On several occasions, according to a transcript of the meeting, Mayo prompted Alsup by saying, "Oh, you remember that, don't you?"

According to a transcript of the meeting, Commissioner Cryer said: "She [Mayo] has indicated some things that have happened and there are other people in the department who may be aware of those and we don't want to leave her out there by herself because I believe everything she's told me and I don't have any reason to doubt anything she's said. But it's really important that [what you say] gives her credibility beyond this room because we have no question of credibility in this room. We need to support these people because they're being honest and truthful with us."

"When they told me they believed all the things that Ann has told them, they said that 'having her here, maybe she can help jar your memory,' and things like that," Alsup recalled. "And then they said, 'If you'd be more comfortable if she left, she can.' At this point, I was just glad to have somebody I knew in the room because I had no idea what this was going to be like. I had no idea what this was about, I didn't know what I was supposed to do. They said, 'Well, we'd like to have her here because you can substantiate all these things that she's said.' They told me, 'everything she says is true,' and they believed her. Now, at that point, what was I supposed to say?

"One of the parting things when I left was that they told me, 'Now, you can't tell anyone that you've spoken with us. That's the worst thing ... if you do that, it's going to be a big problem for the program and for all the people you work with. It's important that you don't tell anyone.'

"For more than three years, I carried that around. It felt really like I was betraying everyone because I really wanted to tell someone. I didn't tell my wife, didn't tell my parents, I didn't tell anyone. And I wanted to tell somebody. I resent the hell out of them for doing that to me. They ruined those three years for me. Now, I always say 'Hi' to Unrue and Burns and make them look me in the eye. I always address them. If they can avoid it, they don't look me in the eye. They can't."

In fact, Alsup did tell one person. Upon leaving the room, he hired Dominic Gentile. If he was going to be dragged into this mess, he wasn't going to be there alone.

"I'm afraid in our country we've reached a state where people have become passive," Gentile said. "With government doing things like waging a war on drugs, we have given government more and more ability to walk over people. That passivity has eroded our concern about people in power not telling the truth. We've let them say that in pursuit of a greater cause, they should be able to manipulate the truth. Examples of that are all over this NCAA case. Paul Burns deceived Mike Alsup, ignoring his right as a university employee to be treated honestly in university matters. What this showed was that those in charge of the day-to-day affairs at that university were willing to do anything in the name of their cause—getting rid of Tarkanian."

Mayo's partner in making many of the allegations against the basketball program was Ricky Collier, the backup guard who flunked out of UNLV in the summer of 1986. The fact that Mayo and Collier would work hand in hand was itself interesting. According to documents filed with the NCAA, Mayo wrote a letter to Tarkanian on March 1, 1985, saying the player had been "rude," "lied," and been "disruptive" and that she refused "to provide [him] academic support services, at least until an apology is rendered and most probably until I believe he is serious about his education." The coach then brought Collier into his office and ordered him to apologize to Mayo.

On July 22, 1986, Mayo again wrote Tarkanian complaining about Collier. "I had a call from Ricky Collier's Communications

101 instructor," Mayo wrote. "She asked if I knew if Ricky was back in town since his grandmother died last week (?) [*sic*]. She said he had missed class Friday, July 18, and Monday, July 21, and today, Tuesday, July 22. He also apparently missed the first day of class, so he has missed four of seven days of class. I happen to know that Ricky was in town Monday and Tuesday. But he did not attend class. He lied to me Monday when I asked him."

Collier needed to pass the class to remain eligible. When he did not, his mother came to Las Vegas for a meeting with Mayo. During that meeting, Collier later told investigators, Mayo told him that Tarkanian had asked her to "fuck up" his grades "so [he] wouldn't be here next year."

Then, on August 14, 1986, just three weeks after telling Tarkanian in a memo that Collier had skipped class and lied to her, Mayo wrote a letter of recommendation to the director of admissions at Westmont College, an NAIA school in Santa Barbara that had offered Collier a place to finish his college career. "After working with Ricky, I do believe that he has the capacity to succeed at college work," Mayo wrote. "I also believe he is motivated to graduate. I realize that Rick's grades might not indicate this. However, I also believe that there may have been some extenuating circumstances at UNLV which left Ricky unmotivated as far as his studies were concerned. Rick's tenure at UNLV has not been the happiest for him both personally and athletically. He has not had a great deal of support or encouragement from the basketball staff here."

So Collier transferred to the small school believing that Mayo was his friend and supporter. "She said I wasn't the best, but the most cooperative student she had," Collier told university lawyers. "She said there was no way I should have been ineligible." He left believing Tarkanian had "done me in." And he became, it was later discovered, the main source for the *Newsday* series that started the investigation.

As the in-house committee was looking into the *Newsday* allegations, it asked Collier if he would help unravel the confusion it felt surrounded the basketball program. Collier was willing to comply.

"Unrue and Burns are either very, very stupid or very, very shrewd," Gentile said. "They took a couple of people in desperate need of attention—Mayo and Collier—and made stars out of them. Once you've made a star out of someone, you own them forever.

They had an agenda even before they had Ann Mayo or Ricky Collier. Those two just helped as they tried to accomplish their goals."

On his way to meet with the committee, Collier would later tell investigators, he met with Mayo. "She said, 'Tell them [the committee] everything because they [the coaches] dogged you,'" Collier recalled. "She said, 'Don't lie to them, just tell them everything, tell them everything you know about anything.' I said, 'Well, why did they [the coaches] do that?' And she goes, 'Well, I don't know, they just didn't like you at all.' She goes, 'Tell them everything because the university fucked you, they screwed you over.'"

It was during that October 13, 1987, meeting with the committee that Collier said Tarkanian had threatened him, saying he could "end up wearing concrete boots in the bottom of Lake Mead ... He called me on the phone, he goes, 'Ricky, what the hell's going on?'" Collier told the committee. "I said, 'Nothing.' He said, 'Why'd you say all this shit in the paper? You know everybody in town's down on you. You know you could be killed.' He said, 'You screw me, if you screw me, I'm going to run your ass all the way to the lake.' I've been scared every day."

In a later deposition, Collier changed his statement—something he did frequentlyTarkanian ever made the statement.

Collier's meeting with the committee was the last before it decided, as Unrue said, that "the safety of some witnesses was in jeopardy." His stated fear gave the committee reason enough to turn the investigation over to the NCAA. But when Collier was later questioned by attorneys representing those he had accused, he said under oath that Tarkanian never had made a threat to him. In fact, he admitted he had repeatedly called Tarkanian trying to meet with him and explain what happened, but Tarkanian refused to talk to him without a third party present. He said he also called Tarkanian and Maxson looking for help getting a job.

Maxson acknowledged taking the call from Collier, whom he said the university planned to discredit during its defense in the NCAA allegations. "I just told him he had to start being honest, start telling the truth," Maxson said.

Collier also told the committee that he had been given $200 by booster and Klondike casino owner John Woodrum to sign an affidavit claiming that he had lied to *Newsday* when making his allegations about Daniels's recruitment. Collier said that Woodrum paid him the money by writing a "business check" and listing in the memo that it was for "moving furniture." University investigators, the NCAA, and lawyers for others charged in the case all have scoured the Klondike's bank accounts looking for the check. All of the checks were placed in order, and none were missing. There was no check made out to Ricky Collier and only one made out during that six-month period for $200. It was paid to a woman ...

Though the only evidence the NCAA had was the word of a discredited Ricky Collier—and a statement from his ex-girlfriend that Collier told her about it—the organization included the charge that he had been bribed by Woodrum in its list of allegations.

Collier made a laundry list of other charges to the in-house committee, including an incredible allegation that booster Irwin Molasky had walked up to him after a game—as a crowd of 19,000 fans was filtering out—and handed him $3,500 in cash. Collier had wrecked his car, gotten hurt, and was on crutches. He said Molasky gave him the money to fix his car. When asked about the allegation during his second meeting with the committee, Collier said it was actually $1,000 that Molasky gave him after the game. During a third interview, he stuck with the $1,000 figure, but said he had been given the money in Molasky's office. "He [Molasky] said, 'This is between me and you, I won't ever tell Coach Tark about this,'" Collier said.

"Give me a break," Tarkanian said. "Who believes that a booster is going to walk up after a game and hand a kid a thousand dollars. I don't know if Ricky Collier knows what the truth means anymore."

The NCAA apparently had some doubts, too. They didn't attempt to allege the Molasky gift as a violation.

Collier's story seemed to change every time he was interviewed. He told the committee on one occasion that after his arrest for unpaid traffic tickets, Assistant Coach Tim Grgurich called then district attorney Bob Miller (now Nevada's governor) and had him released without bail. During his second interview Collier said he got out when he called Judge Danny Ahlstrom, a UNLV basketball fan.

On another allegation, Collier said his first car at UNLV, a Toyota Corolla, had been purchased by money lent to him by a friend's mother. After a short break by the lawyers, Collier changed his statement, saying he had gotten the money by selling his season tickets to Tarkanian's friend Larry deBoef.

In all, Collier's four statements—two meetings with the committee and two taken by lawyers defending UNLV—include at least three dozen story changes. Most of his allegations were so wild that even the NCAA didn't take him seriously.

Mayo, too, leveled charges that proved unfounded. After she told the committee about the tennis class, she added an allegation that seemed to catch everyone's attention. She said that Danny Tarkanian, the coach's son and the team's point guard, had been given credit for a physical education summer school course that he did not attend. She was so sure of the charge that she gave the committee the name of the professor. Her specifics made the charge a joke. The grade that she was so sure had been fraudulently earned was a B in a course that the younger Tarkanian's transcripts show had been taken as a miniterm, one-credit class in January 1982.

"The reason that's so ridiculous is that I had taken the course in 1982, a full two years before she came to UNLV," said Danny, an Academic all-American and a Rhodes scholar candidate. "She was three thousand miles away at Ohio State at the time. It was a miniterm course, not a summer school course. I got a B in the course, and I had a GPA of 3.76. So why would I get a grade in a course that doesn't go toward my degree that doesn't keep me eligible that would lower my GPA? Why would I get a grade for a course when all it would do was hurt me?"

Danny was livid when he learned of the allegation during his 1989 interview with the NCAA. "That's a serious accusation of academic fraud against me, the professor, and the university," he said. "Forget athletics or anything to do with that. If you're the president of the university and you've got an allegation of academic fraud, wouldn't your first responsibility be to get to the bottom of it and not send it to an outside agency and let them sit on it for two years? I told [Regent] Carolyn Sparks that and she didn't do anything about it, making excuses for Maxson. When we questioned Paul Burns on it, he said they really didn't take her [Mayo] that seriously. How can they take her seriously on some things but not on others?"

Mayo also alleged that Shelley Fischer was tutoring Lloyd Daniels during the summer of 1986, just before Daniels left for junior college. Because Daniels wasn't yet a UNLV student-athlete, it would be an NCAA violation for anyone at the university to offer him academic help. Mayo said that Daniels and Fischer met each afternoon during the summer for two hours of extra academic attention. But Daniels was enrolled in Fischer's reading class that summer, which ended each day at 11:30 A.M. and his employment records show that he showed up for work each day at 1:00 P.M. and worked until six. There weren't two hours available.

The tutoring of Daniels and another player, Barry Young, were among the lesser allegations made by the NCAA. That list included the purchase of a pair of shoes for George Ackles during his recruiting visit, the telephone calls, and the hotel room incidental charges. NCAA investigators also discovered that Lois Tarkanian had paid cap-and-gown rental fees of $15 apiece for five players who graduated in 1987. And they learned that when Los Angeles high school star Don MacLean was leaving UNLV's NCAA regional game at Pauley Pavilion, Danny Tarkanian, who had known MacLean since junior high school, gave him a ride five blocks to his car.

In one of the many ironies in the case, the NCAA said it was the universitys responsibility to make sure that players and recruits paid any incidental charges incurred while in hotels, yet also said it was a violation if players gave coaches money from their scholarship checks to pay their rent and utilities. "In one charge they say we have to make sure players pay their bills and in the other charge they say we can't," said Danny.

A review of the allegations shows the fate of UNLV and Tarkanian hinged on two issues: Was the adoption of Lloyd Daniels approved by the NCAA and was Richard Perry a booster? If Warkentien's guardianship plan was approved by the NCAA, all the questions about the extra benefits provided to the player become moot. And if Perry was not a "representative of the universitys athletic interests," then any help he provided to Daniels or other players could not be in violation of NCAA rules.

In its defense of the guardianship, UNLV sent the NCAA a copy of phone logs from the Big West Conference (as the Pacific Coast Athletic Association renamed itself in 1988), showing that Brad Rothermel had called Assistant Commissioner Dennis Farrell for a ruling on the question. According to Rothermel's notes and Farrell's logs, Farrell called the NCAA and asked: "Can a coach become a legal guardian? Student-athlete enrolled in school. Mother died, can a coach legally adopt the kid?" Farrell's memo indicates that Rick Evrard from the NCAA staff responded "Feels a coach could adopt an enrolled s/a [student-athlete] ... or become a legal guardian. Would be acceptable only if they assume full legal responsibility. Should probably write to ad com [the NCAA's staff]." Rothermel, though, remembers Farrell advising him to write the NCAA "if we had any specific questions." The university claims that based on that response, it allowed Warkentien to file the guardianship petition.

The issue became even more muddy when Evrard, under questioning by UNLV lawyers, denied giving Farrell an "affirmative response." He said the query from Farrell asked if a student-athlete, not a prospective student-athlete, could become a legal ward. The latter is within the rules, the former is not, the NCAA said. When Daniels enrolled in junior college that fall, his letter of intent was voided, making him a "prospective" student-athlete again, the NCAA argued.

"If there's a mistake, it was between the NCAA and the Big West," said Chuck Thompson. "The information we received was to write the NCAA if we had other questions. We didn't have any questions, so why should we write the NCAA? We never tried to hide this. In fact, we're the ones who told Dick Vitale about it before he mentioned it on TV."

But the response UNLV hopes will work best in its favor is a comparison between the Warkentien-Daniels relationship and that of University of Arkansas coach Nolan Richardson and Divor Rimac, a 6'7" guard now playing for the Razorbacks. Richardson became Rimac's guardian during the player's junior year in high school, when Rimac was living in Arkansas as an exchange student from Yugoslavia. The NCAA ruled in March 1990 that Richardson did not receive a recruiting advantage by adopting Rimac.

"I'm not going to compare the two cases," NCAA spokesman Jim Marchiony told the *Review-Journal*. "But from what I know, with Arkansas, it was determined the relationship between Nolan Richardson and the young man was a relationship that had started well before this young man was a recruitable student-athlete."

Tarkanian doesn't buy it: "Most recruiting in college basketball today occurs during a player's junior year, so the fact that Rimac was living with Richardson has to have given Richardson an advantage. They said nobody called him during his junior year. Now what coach in his right mind is going to call Nolan Richardson's house and ask for the kid? Do you think they met more than three times during the recruiting season? Do you think maybe there were good meals and maybe clothes given to the kid? Do you think maybe he gave him money when he went out at night? Just living in his house was an extra benefit. You look at it and tell me how that can be okay and Daniels is against the rules. The only way that can happen is if it's UNLV."

Danny Tarkanian said his father was so stricken by the apparent double standard being used by the NCAA that he made it his personal cause to tell the story of Daniels and Rimac. "I get a sick feeling every time I think about it," Danny said. "When we were getting ready to play in the [1991] Final Four in Indianapolis, the team came out for its practice the day before. A Las Vegas television station had done a story about this thing, and I had brought a copy of it and was going to give it to some of the other television guys, Billy Packer, Dick Vitale. Before the practice, my dad told me Packer was standing over there and told me to go talk to him. In the middle of practice, he came over and asked if I'd talked to Billy and what he had said. You know, not many coaches get the chance to win back-to-back national championships. This was the moment that would cement him as one of the great coaches of all time and instead of worrying about the game, he's got his mind on this Nolan Richardson thing, this guardianship thing. It was sad."

While acknowledging in an interview with managing editor and top reporter Dan Burns of KVBC-TV in Las Vegas that "clearly, it's a recruiting advantage having a guy live in your house," NCAA Associate Executive Director Steve Morgan said there was no violation because the recruiting process hadn't started when Rimac moved in with Richardson. The NCAA, when it announced that Rimac's guardianship was within the rules, said it was so because the relationship was not related to athletics. "That's so untrue," Tarkanian said.

Rimac's father, a professional coach in Yugoslavia, had sent his son to Richardson's basketball camp and decided it would be good for Rimac to learn defense in America to complement the offensive skills he developed in Europe. An Arkansas spokesman said the preexisting relationship with Richardson was only part of the reason Rimac's father decided his son should live with the coach. The larger reason, he said, was that Richardson and his wife had recently lost their daughter, Yvonne, to leukemia and Rimac helped them compensate. "As far as I'm concerned, [Rimac] did us a favor," Richardson told the *Arkansas Gazette*.

The time with one of America's best college coaches apparently did Rimac a favor, too. The next year, he blossomed into Arkansas's top high school player, averaging twenty-three points and eight rebounds a game. He also shot 42 percent from a three-point range. He set a school record with 1,245 career points and scored fifty-one points in a tournament game in Oklahoma.

In his statement to university attorneys, Warkentien noted that he and his wife were struggling to deal with the cystic fibrosis that had stricken their young daughter. He said that Daniels had provided them with a welcome diversion and that although he became Daniels's legal guardian, the player never lived under his roof, unlike Rimac, who received free room and board from Richardson.

Additionally, UNLV argued, Warkentien's decision to adopt Daniels came after the player had signed a letter of intent binding him to UNLV and the papers were filed while Daniels still was in Las Vegas taking remedial reading classes at the university. Warkentien's efforts, UNLV said, were to try and keep Daniels in school, not gain a recruiting advantage. He didn't need an advantage because Daniels already had made it clear he wanted to become a Rebel.

"Our case is even better than Arkansas's because Lloyd already signed with us, was going to summer school, and both his parents had died," Tarkanian said.

On the Perry question, UNLV showed that Tarkanian and his staff never had met or heard of Perry before he showed up in the basketball office with Daniels after a Memphis State game. It would be difficult, then, for Perry to fall into any one of the five definitions of a booster listed in the *NCAA Manual*. That litmus test declares an individual a booster if he:

• Has participated in or is a member of an agency or organization that promotes the institution's intercollegiate athletic program.

• Has made financial contributions to the athletic department or to an athletics booster organization of that institution.

• Has been requested by the athletic department staff to assist in the recruitment of prospective student-athletes or is assisting in the recruitment of prospective student-athletes.

• Has assisted or is assisting in providing benefits to enrolled student-athletes.

• Is otherwise involved in promoting the institution's athletics program.

Since Perry never was a booster, season ticket holder, or contributor to the university, the NCAA hoped to tag UNLV on the third point—that he was "assisting in the recruitment of prospective student-athletes." But UNLV argued that Perry was directed by his pal from the horse tracks, Daniels's adviser Arnie Hershkowitz, not anyone at the university, to help Daniels.

"How can a guy be a booster if no one had ever met him before he brought a kid to you?" Tarkanian asked. "Don't you have to ask this guy to bring him down here to help before you've got to be responsible for him? If they can make Sam Perry a booster of UNLV, then he's a booster at a lot of schools where he's helped kids go. But the NCAA doesn't want to go after that."

Tarkanian complained that the NCAA's selective decision to ding UNLV for the Daniels guardianship and Perry's relationship—while similar cases go untried at other universities—is but one of many signs that the organization has improved only marginally since it set out on his trail in 1973. During the four years encompassing the Daniels investigation, Tarkanian again heard reports that the NCAA organization was engaged in investigative tactics reminiscent of some Third World governments.

In a sworn statement, Daniels claimed he was contacted by an unidentified NCAA investigator in May 1989, when he was at Mary Immaculate Hospital in Queens recovering from gunshot wounds he had received during a drug-related shooting. Daniels said the investigator offered him "an unspecified sum of cash to give evidence of possible recruiting violations by UNLV." Daniels claimed he refused the money and told the investigator he knew of no such violations.

Though Daniels's allegation seems far-fetched, an affidavit

provided to the magazine *HoopScoop* by Kevin Barry, a Columbia University graduate and founder of the Give a Kid a Chance Foundation, also raises concerns about the NCAA. Barry said that while he was allowing Daniels to live at his home, NCAA investigator Robert Stroup visited more than once. On one of those occasions, at 2:00 A.M. on August 15, 1989, Stroup told him that he and Daniels would be "great American heroes" if they provided the NCAA with information damaging to Tarkanian, Barry said.

The NCAA's David Berst said he was aware of the affidavits but declined requests to comment on them. "Isn't it interesting that if the allegation is against Tarkanian, they'll go after it like it is the end of the earth," said *HoopScoop* publisher Clark Francis. "But when it has to do with one of their own, Berst manages to sweep it away."

David Chesnoff, Daniels's Las Vegas attorney, said two NCAA investigators visited his office in 1990 looking for information. "They said, 'You would do a great service for college basketball if you would talk and Lloyd Daniels would talk,'" Chesnoff said. "I said I thought you were here to investigate the fact I stole my college soccer uniform when I graduated. I said I'm used to dealing with the FBI, the DEA and all kinds of alphabet-soup organizations. I don't trust them, why should I trust the NCAA?"

Tarkanian also heard another question about NCAA ethics when, during the winter of 1989, investigator Stroup went to a practice at Dixie College in St. George, Utah, to interview Karl "Boobie" James, a point guard who played at UNLV during the 1987–88 season before transferring to Dixie. Todd Street, a student manager for the Dixie basketball team at the time, later told Dixie coach Ken Wagner, who was not at the practice, that Stroup had said he was a newspaper reporter there to "do an article" on James. "The team was running drills and [Assistant Coach Dave] Rose looked up and there was someone sitting at the top of the gymnasium," said Street, who graduated from the junior college and went on to the University of Utah. "Coach Rose told me to run up and see if we could help him in some way. So I ran up there and asked him what he wanted, and he said he was going to write an article about Boobie. He said it at least twice, that he was there to do an article. He didn't say a particular newspaper, but he left no doubt that I was to think he was a reporter. I told Coach Rose it was a reporter and he sent Boobie up there." But when James came back from his face-to-face "interview" with the "reporter," he told Street the man was actually an NCAA investigator. Wagner wrote the NCAA's Dick Schultz to question the investigator's ethics.

The NCAA's own code of conduct makes it a violation for any investigator to misrepresent himself or attempt to mislead others into believing he is anything but an NCAA investigator. "After I found out [who he was], I was a little mad," Street said. "I always thought they had rules that required them to be straight with us. He should have let us know what his full purpose was."

When the *Los Angeles Times* asked Berst about Street's charge, he seemed unconcerned. "Putting the best light on it, there may have been some form of miscommunication," Berst said. "If what they say is the truth, it may be a matter of somebody [Street] jumping to the conclusion that this guy [Stroup] was there to interview the player for a newspaper instead of interview him for another purpose."

James also told reporters that Stroup had threatened to take away his eligibility if he didn't cooperate in the investigation. Shades of Moscow—and the NCAA's 1977 investigation of UNLV—hung all over this case.

Also during the university's investigation, UNLV was told by two former players that NCAA investigators had used a microcassette recorder to tape their interviews. Though many who have been investigated by the NCAA have requested that their statements be taped, the NCAA's policy at the time was to deny such requests. Tape recording of interviews, by the NCAA's own rules, was forbidden.

"When you look at all the things in this investigation and you look at all the incredible things in the 1977 investigation, one thing is clear," Tarkanian said. "Things don't change with the NCAA. If they want you, you better look out because they'll ignore their own rules, they'll change the rules if that will help them."

Ironically, the NCAA's slipshod handling of Tarkanian's 1977 case makes it almost impossible for them to get their gloves on him in the Lloyd Daniels case. As a result of the U.S. Supreme Court ruling declaring that the NCAA was not a state actor and therefore not subject to provisions of the U.S. Constitution, several state legislatures, including Nevada, enacted laws requiring that the NCAA recognize certain due process rights when it came to those states for investigations.

Nevada's law, which includes provisions allowing thirty-day advance notice of hearings, copies of all evidence upon demand, a hearing before "impartial fact finders," and a requirement that all statements used by the organization be sworn affidavits, twice caused the NCAA to put off hearing UNLV's case. The NCAA delayed the case because it refused to provide the university with copies of its evidence.

"They don't have, after four years of investigating, one piece of evidence that complies with the Nevada statute," said attorney Roy Smith, who represents Assistant Coach Tim Grgurich. "Every bit of what they've got is a summary of a statement taken by one of their investigators. By having summaries, they have the ability to tweak little things, change words here and there, to their advantage. We had one interview with Tim where there were seven of us sitting around a table all taking notes because they wouldn't let us tape, as you know. Well, after the interview was over, they told us we would be allowed to review their summary of the interview and make any corrections. We were called back to make changes and were appalled at how grossly they had misinterpreted the interview. Their summary, well, it was just off the wall. We said Tim would sign it, but only if they would allow us to attach our transcript to it. They told us it didn't work that way. I mean, there were names mentioned in the summary that neither Tim nor I had ever heard of. They said those names came up in conjunction with other information they had gathered. We argued that nothing that wasn't said by Tim should be included in his summary. Again, they said it didn't work that way. After two hours [NCAA investigator Dan] Calandro finally said, 'We don't care whether you agree with what is in the summary. We're not here to negotiate. You can sign it or don't sign it.' I asked him if the purpose of all this wasn't to get to the truth. I didn't get an answer. It sure seems pretty obvious this isn't about truth, it's about revenge. Once you've read an NCAA investigator's summary, you understand why coaches are scared to death and why everyone facing them needs a good lawyer."

Nevada is just one of four states—Illinois, Florida, and Nebraska are the others—to have enacted due process laws as a result of the Tarkanian decision. Several other states, including the NCAA's home state of Kansas, have passed the bill through either the House or the Senate or are scheduled to hear the bill in 1992. The Kansas bill, sponsored by Senator Wint Winter, includes a provision revoking the NCAA's tax-exempt status in the state if the organization attempts retribution on any school in any state that has passed the bill.

The NCAA's legal counsel, John J. Kitchin, said the due process bills really won't affect the NCAA because the organization already has built due process into its proceedings. "Institutions are given all kinds of written notices about alleged violations and given all kinds of opportunities to present their side of the facts," Kitchin said. "They can have hearings and can have counsel present, if they elect. The NCAA believes in fair enforcement."

"If that's true, why are they fighting so hard to kill these bills?" Tarkanian asked. "They're spending hundreds of thousands of dollars to hire lobbyists to kill these. Remember, they earned that money off the backs of these athletes, and now they're spending that money to keep those athletes from getting due process. Is this an incredible organization, or what? If David Berst's job was at stake, I bet he wouldn't want to sit on the other side of the table and face this system."

"You noticed, didn't you, that the NCAA changed its rules on tape recording right after Executive Director Dick Schultz got caught up in their investigation of Virginia, where he was athletic director," Chuck Thompson said. "But even with their new rules, it is pretty obvious the NCAA's attitude didn't change. The only difference between this investigation and the 1977 case is that the NCAA didn't have to play the heavy this time. They had a willing president and a willing university to do it for them. The NCAA used the UNLV administration, and the UNLV administration used the NCAA. They both had the same goal—getting rid of Jerry Tarkanian—only for different reasons. Working together was beneficial for both. It's not hard for me to imagine, from what I know of Berst and Maxson, their activities and desires, that they were in bed together. I mean that figuratively, of course."

9

An Athletic Director on a Mission

Although Tarkanian swore he and his staff had committed no major NCAA violations, he knew the NCAA well enough to assume the forthcoming sanctions in the Daniels case would be more than a slap on the wrist. He knew that, given half a chance, the NCAA definitely would do damage to his program.

But Brad Rothermel was looking at it from a different perspective. He saw the investigation killing his cash cow. In an athletic budget of slightly more than $9 million, the men's basketball team generated more than $6 million. It was the only athletic program at UNLV that made money. Nothing else was even close. The football program lost $2.5 million, more than any other school in the country.

It also became apparent during the summer of 1990 that much of the blame for the NCAA violations would fall at Rothermel's feet. Some Regents, major boosters, and others determined that the ship he was running was too loose. They said he lacked "institutional control," to use the NCAA's favorite phrase.

Coupled with the pressure he had felt since that day in 1984 when Maxson made it clear he wanted to fire Jerry Tarkanian,

Rothermel knew the political winds at UNLV slowly had shifted. Finally, he decided, he'd had enough. He announced that he would resign, packing up as soon as a replacement was named. Maxson said it was too late in the year to conduct a full-fledged search for a replacement.

His resignation cleared the last major hurdle the president had between himself and Tarkanian.

"I think the minute that Brad Rothermel was gone was when everybody got crazy, things started to change," said Maxson's ally, Elaine Wynn. "That's when the groups started to really polarize, when the basketball program finally knew that they were being persecuted … and they were being targeted now finally. Because their buffer was Brad. You know, Brad was their guy, and when Brad wasn't there no one would take the heat."

Rothermel knew the day he resigned that his departure meant it would soon be over for Tarkanian as well. "I came home that night and told my wife that Jerry wouldn't last a year," Rothermel said. "I actually gave him two months more than I should have. It was pretty obvious what was going to happen once I left. But he [Maxson] wasn't going to let up until he got what he wanted."

Earlier that spring, as the Rebels were on their way to the national championship, the UNLV ticket office committed a series of errors, including promising tickets to several hundred ticket boosters who traveled across the country only to discover they had no seat at the game. Rothermel appointed a committee to deal with the ticket controversy, but offended several university supporters in the process.

The ticket problems highlighted what Maxson and some others had said was Rothermel's greatest weakness. He was a nice guy, very personable. But he wasn't a businessman, they said. He wasn't hard-nosed when it came to such things as setting a policy on how tickets would be distributed. He had let too many things go.

Rothermel's philosophy, admittedly, was to give coaches what it takes to win and then step out of the way. That was precisely the type of athletic director Maxson no longer wanted. Rothermel's greatest clue came when, after winning the national basketball championship and watching nine of his fourteen teams qualify for NCAA postseason play in their respective sports, Rothermel paid a visit to the president to discuss his pay raise. "You've done an adequate job," the president told him, placing an emphasis on adequate.

"I didn't know for sure what excellence meant if winning the national championship was simply adequate," Rothermel said. "You get your messages, you know. I'd gone to the president consistently every year with requests, ways the administration could assist with the emergence of the athletic program, not just the basketball program. He was deaf, dumb, and blind to any of it. He wouldn't respond affirmatively to any of the ways he could have been helpful."

After Rothermel resigned and took a low-profile job on the UNLV teaching faculty, university administrators made him the scapegoat for nearly everything that was "wrong" in UNLV athletics—including the ticket questions, NCAA violations, and Tarkanian.

His replacement, Maxson said in a backhanded criticism of Rothermel, had to be "a leader," a strong-handed administrator.

As Maxson looked for an interim replacement, he briefly flirted with the idea of appointing general counsel Brad Booke. But Booke was tied up trying to answer the NCAA's allegations. And, for Maxson's purposes, there was a better man.

Dennis Finfrock, a well-known political climber in the athletic department and a longtime Tarkanian adversary, fit the bill perfectly. Originally from Yuma, Arizona, Finfrock had played college football at Brigham Young University during the 1960s, earning honorable-mention All-Western Athletic Conference honors as a defensive end. He graduated with an A average as a zoology major and, as a senior in 1970, went on a weekend road trip with BYU teammate Horace Smith, who was from Las Vegas. Smith had arranged a job interview with the Clark County School District, so Finfrock decided to apply, too. Both were offered jobs as teachers.

Finfrock spent three years at Jim Bridger Junior High School before moving to the county's newest high school as a science teacher and wrestling coach. His timing and political savvy, though, were generally considered to be much better than his coaching. In 1976, the wrestling coaching job opened up at UNLV. It wasn't much of a job at the time, but Finfrock thought he saw its potential. It looked like UNLV had made a good decision as well when Finfrock hired two of the best assistant coaches in the country, then stepped out of the way. His first team was 19–2 in dual matches, and his four-year record was 65–22. Finfrock's decision to seek out great assistants, while allowing him to compile a healthy won-loss record, also allowed him to focus his efforts in another direction.

"There was no incentive besides your own personal drive to do anything because he was a businessman, not a coach," said Mike Couch, who wrestled for Finfrock during the 1978–79 school year. "I had a good coach at Cerritos College, where I came from. He looked out for the kid's best interest all the time. Finfrock never did. He looked out for himself."

Jeff Gianni, another of Finfrock's wrestlers who came to UNLV from junior college, echoed Couch's comment: "He's a sneaky guy. I never had a coach like him. I came from a class junior college program. All of a sudden we're dumped into Division I, which is the highest form of wrestling, except Olympics, and we've got a coach like him, who's more like a businessman. He wasn't a coach. He wouldn't even be in the workout room half the time. He'd come in there and he'd say a couple words, then his assistants would take over and they'd do all the coaching."

The business Finfrock chose to build also allowed him to slip a little extra cash into the pockets of his wrestlers. In a city known for fights and marriages, Finfrock didn't have to drive far down the chapel-lined Las Vegas Boulevard to figure that the wedding market had long ago been sewed up. Finfrock focused on the fights.

About once a week in Las Vegas, some hotel sponsors a fight card. The sometimes raucous crowds occasionally need help with more than finding their seats. Sometimes they need to be controlled. So Finfrock established an usher/security company called Finco, which according to state records was incorporated in 1978, two years after he took the job at UNLV. The only officers of the company were Finfrock, his son, Jason, and wife, Kay. Finfrock apparently realized the conflict that existed between his day job and his moonlighting effort because, according to a source who dealt with him during the early days of Finco, he continually referred to it as "my wife's company."

Four years later, Kay Finfrock opened K's Clean House, Inc., a service which could sweep up after the events. Dennis was listed as president and his wife as secretary/treasurer, but the dayto-day operation of the business was left to her. The promoters of these fights found a full-service family in the Finfrocks.

And Finfrock found in the student-athletes of UNLV a cheap labor pool. Though NCAA rules prohibited student-athletes working during the academic year, Finfrock apparently paid no mind. He said he never actually paid the athletes—a point contested by several of those who worked for him—but sent the money they earned to their sport's offices for use in paying travel expenses or other expenses incurred by the university on behalf of the student. By making that argument, Finfrock chose to ignore the reality that many of the athletes earned many times more in tips at the fights than the $25 check Finfrock offered. NCAA officials said if the athletes earned tips that were not turned over to the athletic department, Finfrock and the athletes would be violating bylaw C 3-4-(d)-(1) of the organization's 1978 rules manual.

Finfrock reached beyond his wrestling team, asking football players and members of the basketball team to provide him the low-cost, high-quality beef his company needed.

"All I did was act as a security guard and show people to their seats during fights while I was going to school," said Danny Budak, a former strong safety on the Rebel football team. "My roommate at the time was a wrestler, Bob Northridge, and he was friends with Dennis Finfrock. He basically got me the job, and from the first time out, we were pretty much steady workers there. This was ten years ago, but I remember receiving twenty-five-dollar checks. But mostly, it was the tips that we made. Good tips. That's why we did it. It was easy money."

One former scholarship wrestler said Finfrock knew that the athletes did the work for the cash tips and rewarded certain of his "favorites." "He gave the priority seating jobs, where the most expensive seats and the best tips were available, to the athletes he liked the most," said the wrestler, who asked that his name not be used because he still lives in Las Vegas, where he said Finfrock "has developed a powerful group of friends." He added, "You could make a hundred to two hundred dollars a night in tips if they knew you were a UNLV athlete."

Couch, another scholarship wrestler, also made money during the school year working for his coach's side business. "The security company was his real scam," said Couch. "I worked for him for a long time. I worked the fights for his company. You would stand around the ring between rounds or at the end of the fight, usher people in. You'd seat everybody and wipe the chairs off. I got the job through him. He had most of the wrestlers, most of the athletes do that."

Budak, who played football in 1977 and 1978 for Coach Tony Knapp, was a junior college all-American before coming to UNLV. He said the Finco work, which also included events other than fights, gave him the spending money that doesn't come with an athletic scholarship.

"I worked one time an off-road race out past Nellis Air Force Base," said Budak, now an operations manager at Sony Corporation in San Diego. "I sold tickets at the front gate. He paid me for that. When you're broke, you've got to survive. He paid me. I'm just telling the truth. He did pay us. I have nothing against Finfrock. He was basically my employer."

Rich Abajian, a former assistant football coach who also worked the fights, said he remembered Finfrock using classrooms in the physical education building at UNLV—a state facility—to hold his prefight meetings with the student-athletes. "That's where he gave everyone their assignments," Abajian said.

Former wrestler Gianni said he found it ironic that Finfrock complained of what he perceived to be cheating in the men's basketball program. "It was really peculiar, I remember him telling me how the school was trying to get rid of Tarkanian," said Gianni, who now works as an electrician just outside Palm Springs, California. "That was in 1980. He said their interests were not to keep Tarkanian, that deep down, they'd like to get rid of him because he was such a headache and he'd created such problems with the NCAA. It was just causing too much distraction to the school. He wouldn't be vocal because Tarkanian had a lot of power. But Finfrock was against Tarkanian. He acted like Tarkanian was doing all these things wrong."

At the same time, Finfrock was getting more than wins out of his wrestlers. He also used the players to do manual labor at his home. "I helped over at his house a few times, landscaping, building walls and stuff, something to do with his backyard. I remember moving something major, too," Gianni said. "We couldn't say no. If you knew Finfrock, you'd understand how he is. He's sort of that kind of guy. He puts you in, it's not like a pressure situation, but he doesn't give you a choice about doing it, you just do it. He'd put it in a certain manner like, men, this is what we're going to do. He didn't give us an alternative. He had quite a lot of power over us in his position and he knew how to use his power quite well."

Mike Couch said, "He'd always try and get the team to come and build a wall or a barbecue or some shit at his house. At the end, he'd have a barbecue and the whole team would eat, then go home, and he'd have a barbecue built. It was always a good deal for him."

Finfrock, according to friends, looked at his company as a means of compensating both himself and his players for the small budget he was given by the university. He also "compensated" by asking Las Vegas businessmen to give him money—cash only—to aid his athletes, longtime booster and prominent Las Vegas insurance salesman Jay Hodapp said.

Hodapp said in a sworn statement that in 1980 he was asked by Bill Scoble, a UNLV staff member at the time, to provide Finfrock cash "so that he could take care of his wrestlers at UNLV." Hodapp said he agreed to do so, coming up with cash three different times. He said Finfrock "personally came to me for cash. The first occasion was in late fall, and the last occasion was in the spring of Finfrock's last year as wrestling coach. I gave him a total of $1,500." He said Finfrock "told me that the money was to be used to support his wrestlers. I always gave Finfrock cash, and I was never provided a receipt." Hodapp said Scoble told him ten to fifteen other boosters had agreed to give Finfrock cash "so that the UNLV wrestlers would be taken care of financially."

Scoble, who has received premium complimentary tickets to UNLV events through Finfrock, denied that he ever collected cash for Finfrock. He acknowledged that Finfrock asked him to get business leaders to contribute to a booster club, but said all transactions were by check. "Dennis Finfrock is a guy who wears a white hat. I've never seen Dennis do an illegal thing—ever. Nobody ever gave Dennis cash that I'm aware of. I know Dennis too well."

Finfrock refused requests to discuss these and other allegations, claiming he was doing so "on the advice of legal counsel."

Though Finfrock was making good money, the athletic department was not. When Rothermel arrived in 1980, he inherited an athletic budget that was $500,000 in the red. He was forced to cut ten of the twenty-two sports UNLV had competed in and looked for every way possible to consolidate positions. Finfrock had applied for an open assistant athletic directors job before Rothermel had arrived and had been asked to work at both the administrative and coaching positions. Finfrock's chief assignment in the athletic department was handling team travel, a job which occasionally put him at odds with Tarkanian, who didn't like some of Finfrock's arrangements.

Two years later, UNLV opened the magnificent Thomas & Mack Center. It would replace the Las Vegas Convention Center not just as home to the Rebels but also as the site of many conventions in this burgeoning convention market. The arena needed a director, someone with good business sense. Finfrock had approached Regents chairman Jack McBride about the job. At the same time, he told McBride that the arena, then under construction, could be used for many more events if certain structural changes were made. Finfrock's idea was to strengthen the ceiling, allowing it to safely handle up to 60,000 pounds of added sound and lighting equipment for concerts and other events. McBride ran Finfrock's idea by others involved in the project, and the change was made.

So was Finfrock's next move up the ladder. The Regents rewarded Finfrock, making him manager of both the new arena and the 30,000-seat Sam Boyd Silver Bowl, where the football team played its home games.

The move was a real bonanza for Finfrock. He now not only had a side business that was earning him cash, hand over fist, but he had a job that allowed him access to each of the hotels that would be hosting conventions in his arena. Some of those hotels also sponsored the fights, special events, and concerts that he wanted Finco to work. He also had the ability to combine and train his private employees with those who were working at the Thomas & Mack. As his influence in those circles increased, so did his cash flow. As his business increased, so did the attention given the very obvious conflict of interest. One former regent saw the conflict and suggested something be done about it.

"I know others had concerns about it," Rothermel said. "Someone, I can't remember who, had mentioned it to me, and I spoke to

Dennis about it and asked Dennis what the situation was and he said, 'Don't worry about it, I'll handle it.'"

According to Brad Booke, Finfrock got out of the business in 1983, though records at the secretary of state's office show he held the license on the company through December 1984. Once he agreed with the university's request that he sell the business, nothing was ever done about the apparent NCAA violations.

Finfrock arranged to sell Finco to Nick and Annette Lexis in 1984. The Lexises had called a realtor friend of theirs asking about a piece of property they were interested in buying. Instead, the realtor turned them on to Finco, a business that "was making good money, but had to be sold quickly," Annette Lexis remembers.

"He told us it was a conflict of interest with his job at the university, that they told him he either had to do one or the other," Nick Lexis said.

"Neither one of us knew anything about the business," Annette said. "But after meeting with Finfrock, I bought the business the next day."

The Lexises agreed to pay Finfrock $70,000—$30,000 up front and $40,000 over the next two to four years as a "consultant." During that four years, Finfrock agreed not to compete with his former company, a clause that didn't seem necessary since he was selling the business because of his conflict of interest at the university. "At least that's what we thought at the time," Annette said.

They thought wrong. In the first four years after buying Finco, the Lexises turned the company into a $250,000-a-year business. "We had the town locked up," she stated. Then, in February of 1989, just four months after the noncompetition clause expired, Finfrock called the Lexises and asked them to meet him for lunch at the Macayo's Restaurant.

"He told us either we would give him seventy-five percent of our business or he would run us out of town," said Annette, who tape-recorded the conversation. "My words to him were 'That's extortion.' He said, 'That's too bad you think that. No, it's not extortion, it's business.' He saw that he could start making the money again and the Mirage Hotel was just opening and was going to be having a lot of fights so there was going to be a whole new big business. He figured he would just go for it. When I said no, we had one more meeting and then he said, 'You better get back with me real soon because I'm going to bring in another company if you guys don't decide.' Then we didn't hear from him and I tried to talk Nick into going with it because from what I knew about him [Finfrock] I knew we'd be blown away. Nick said, 'Absolutely not, I'm not going to do all the work while he makes all the money.'"

"I asked Dennis why when he wanted to sell the business it used to be a conflict but it's not a conflict now," Nick said. "He said they [the university administrators] feel that Tarkanian has bars and stuff so they feel like he can do stuff, too. My wife went to Maxson about it and told him what Dennis was doing, and he said the same thing. He gave the same excuse about Tarkanian having a bar."

Tarkanian laughed at Finfrock's excuse. "The Shark Club I never owned," the coach said, talking about a popular local nightclub. "And Tarkanian's bar, I was approached by people who wanted to use my name. They said they'd pay me two thousand dollars a month. That probably doesn't even cover one night's profits for Dennis's business. They sent me the first check. But every month after that, they told me they were in the hole and never paid. I let them keep using the name because I felt sorry for them."

The Lexises' refusal led Finfrock to do as he promised. He started looking for a new way of getting back into his old business. He found it eight months after his meeting with the Lexises, when, in October 1989, he became a member of the company's board of directors and the registered agent for StaffPro, Inc., a Los Alamitos, California, company that also provides security and ushering services. According to Nevada state records and the Clark County Business License Department, Finfrock was appointed by the company to negotiate its contracts in Nevada. As of late 1991, StaffPro had contracts with a number of Las Vegas's largest hotels, including the Mirage, the Las Vegas Hilton, and Bally's. Many of the hotels StaffPro now works with once were under contract to Finco. The Lexises, in fact, have letters of recommendation from many of those hotels. But when Finfrock reentered the security business with his new company and his even greater influence, the Lexises' once loyal customers flocked to Finfrock. One by one, those hotels called and said they were making a change in their security companies— without offering an explanation.

As Finfrock promised, his work with StaffPro caused a quick tumble for the Lexises and Finco. "The business that was worth $250,000 went to shit in a matter of days," Annette said. "That's what I made the last year before he came after us. It's not worth anything close to what it was."

According to one former Thomas & Mack employee, it was not uncommon for there to be confusion among staff about the separation of work for the arena and Finfrock's private interests. "We used to have people coming in [the arena] asking for applications to work the fights," she said. "One time, when a person came in for an application, one of Dennis's friends on the staff took the guy down the hall to give him one."

All while Finfrock remained director of UNLV's athletic complexes.

Finfrock was appointed interim athletic director by Maxson— who referred to Finfrock as "one hundred percent honest, I don't think I have met a more honest man"—in the summer of 1990.

Finfrock's appointment to the interim job caused an immediate split in the athletic department. His undisguised disdain for Tarkanian "forced everyone in the department to choose sides," said John Peterson, an assistant in the athletic development office who later was fired by Finfrock. "You had to determine who your loyalties were with. There's a place where the tile meets the carpet at the men's basketball office. One time I was down there talking to Annette [Tarkanian's secretary] and Laura Clontz, who worked down in my office, came down and said someone up front was waiting for me. They made a joke that I'd stayed down in the basketball office too long and a buzzer had gone off. We used to call the basketball department 'the DMZ.' You couldn't cross into the zone and keep your job. It was like a civil war."

"As soon as he came in, he started firing people who had devoted their lives to the university," Tarkanian said. "That's not something you expect from an interim AD. Usually, an interim tries to keep things afloat until the full-time guy comes along. His reason for firing everyone was a 'difference in philosophy.' If there's a difference, you call people in and tell them what the new philosophy is and give them a chance to adjust. He was a hatchet man."

As the baseball and soccer coaches talked openly about how

morale was dropping like a rock, Finfrock instituted a policy that allowed staffers to open and inspect mail that came into the atheltic department. Letters were then resealed and passed on to the addressee. "It was like working for the Gestapo," said one former employee. Then Finfrock instructed the ticket manager to require Tarkanian to personally walk down to the ticket office before each home contest and sign for his tickets. Previously, Tarkanian's secretary would pick the tickets up for him. "It was just an attempt to screw with Tark," Peterson said. "Everybody knew it."

Finfrock and Sheila Strike-Bolla, his assistant, then decided that the athletic department needed to sell the sideline tickets that traditionally had been given to the families of the assistant basketball coaches and given them seats in the end zone instead. Tim Grgurich's wife found out about the move when a friend showed her the season tickets she had just purchased. Grgurich's wife recognized the seat numbers as hers and called the ticket office. "They didn't even have the decency to tell us," Cathy Grgurich said.

Finfrock also consolidated some positions that he claimed were "duplicated" by having separate business operations at both the arena and the athletic department. And he surrounded himself with those Peterson described as "his loyalists."

While Finfrock definitely was a political climber, Sheila Strike could build ladders around him. A former Canadian women's basketball player, the 6'2" burly blonde was hired in 1980 as UNLV's women's basketball coach. She had come from the University of Oregon, where she had been assistant coach. Strike was hired at UNLV midway through the summer, a late move given the terrific needs the team had at the time.

"When I accepted the job, I was told that twelve scholarship athletes would be returning, and when I arrived in late July or early August, there were five," Strike remembers. "And so, actually the first year, we had to post notices on campus and we were comprised of five scholarship players and seven walk-ons. And by walk-ons I mean literally people who were walking by the office and called in and asked to join up. They were nonscholarship walk-ons. And that year we went twelve and twelve and it was a long year. We had five scholarship players, and we were in trouble if anyone got tired or in foul trouble."

The excitement of being a head coach wore off quickly, as her team was repeatedly embarrassed on the floor. A year later, men's assistant coach Tim Grgurich suggested she hire Jim Bolla, a 6'8" former center on the University of Pittsburgh team that Grgurich had coached before coming to UNLV. Strike and Bolla later would marry and become co-head coaches of the team.

That same year, Strike and other members of the UNLV athletic staff made a tactical decision which helped her build the foundation of a winning program almost overnight. To the chagrin of many in the women's athletic movement nationally, UNLV became one of several schools to abandon the Association for Intercollegiate Athletics for Women (AIAW) and join the NCAA. In an effort to eliminate his competition, NCAA executive director Walter Byers had expanded his organization to encompass women's sports. While most women's athletic advocates looked at the power play as a negative for women, Strike and Bolla saw it as their great opportunity to make it big in the world of women's coaching. The women's athletic programs that joined the NCAA were able to offer much more than their counterparts who stayed in the AIAW. Not only could they offer full-ride scholarships, but they were allowed to pay for and entertain prospects who made weekend recruiting visits, just like the men's programs.

"That gave us a jump start on recruiting, and we had probably the best and biggest recruiting class that we've ever had that year," Strike remembers.

Although the NCAA and Byers had fought Title IX, Congress's effort to equalize university funding for women's athletics, it now was giving them the opportunity to take over the potentially lucrative world of women's sports. And, like an attempt to break a union, Byers knew he only needed a few scabs to jump and do well before the others would bail out en masse. UNLV was one of his first successes.

That first year in the NCAA, Strike and Bolla combed the country—combed two countries—and came up with one of the best recruiting classes ever in women's college basketball. The decision to forsake the women's movement already had paid dividends. When, a year later, that team went 24–4, the payoff was evident.

Strike also started using her forceful personality to demand more and more support for women's sports at UNLV, in general, and her basketball program, more specifically. Those demands offended Tarkanian, who knew, for example, that Strike's women's team was flying for extended tours to Hawaii while the men's baseball team—which produced players like San Francisco's Matt Williams and Detroit's slugger Cecil Fielder—was forced to bus all night for many contests.

"I think the friction that people see, or that they interpret as friction is more personality conflicts than it is actual basketball," said Jim Bolla. "I can go down there and talk basketball with any of the coaches, and Jerry Tarkanian helps us recruit. I mean, when we have recruits in, if Tark is in town, we'll knock on the door and say, 'Hey, we have a recruit in,' and he talks to the kid and says, 'Hey, this is the place where you need to come,' takes out a picture, signs an autographed picture for the kid, and you know, it's not that big a deal. I think it's more personalities."

While Tarkanian admits to having problems with money spent by women's basketball, he said he never intended for his views to be taken personally. But that's how it ended up. Strike, who said she built a program "that was run by our standards," became a vocal critic of Tarkanian's, often referring to him as a sexist, a chauvinist—and a cheater.

"She was always using words like 'cheating slime' and 'fucking men's basketball' when she was walking around the office," said Peterson.

"Sheila liked to ask questions that made you think she knew something that she probably didn't," said one person who still works in the athletic department. "She'd ask questions about how Tark was doing this or that. Then just say something like 'Cheaters never prosper.'"

"She felt that they cheated, and she said so," former director of athletic development Doug Sanderson said. "She would say they must have brought someone in through some illegal way, and she'd say things about players' grades. Sheila made no bones about the fact that she thought the men's program was bad. She wouldn't be the one to light the match, but she wouldn't mind fanning the flame. Since we knew what was going on [in the women's program] we'd let it blow over. She would say these things and it's like her shit don't stink. We knew better."

Strike-Bolla denies having made those statements—sort of. "I think that it's really unfair for someone to say that or put those words into my mouth because I don't think that I said those things to people I work with and I think that it's grossly unfair," said Strike-Bolla, who declined several opportunities to flat-out deny having called Tarkanian a cheat. "I'm searching, trying to think of who would have said that I said that and how, when would I have said that and in what context."

Strike-Bolla blames her differences with Tarkanian on her aggressive pursuit of additional funding of her basketball program. She said the men didn't like the fact that she played the game a different way—their way—and didn't gush with thanks for all the money men's basketball made at UNLV.

"I philosophically am from a different sporting background by virtue of my Canadian upbringing, and I am really, really academically oriented," Strike-Bolla said. "I earned my doctorate here at UNLV, my master's at Oregon, I was educated in Canada, and—while I wouldn't label myself as a feminist—I have a real passion for women's sports and for equal opportunity. I think people see a six-foot-two, blond Canadian with a Ph.D. that is a real advocate for women and I think some people don't like that. I think there's been a lot of resentment because the women's program grew from a tiny weeny budget with five kids on scholarship into a really fully well-funded, broad-based program very quickly. And there's no question that I had to fight for that. No one gave that to us. My perspective is a little different from theirs, and one of the things that I think is really important is to look at the money that is being provided by the state and the money that comes under student fees that supports the athletic program. Just as an example of that, this year [1991–92], if you took the entire funding for the women's programs and you took half of the state budget appropriation from the legislature and half of the student fees, which if you took half for the men and half for the women, that is a total of three hundred thousand dollars shy of the entire women's program budget, including salaries, scholarship, operating expenses, recruiting expenses, the whole shebang. So, I guess from my perspective, I just don't see that we need to be thanking anybody for what we've fought for."

"She's such a hypocrite," Tarkanian said. "Because of men's

basketball, she has one of the best budgets in the country for any women's team. She used to call everyone else cheaters. But when Tates Locke was our assistant coach, she approached Tates and Grg and asked them to work with her players in the summer. They both thought the women's program was just getting started, and so they did it. It was a violation of the NCAA no-practice rule. And someone who would do all that she did would turn around and bad-mouth us. She just said whatever the person she was trying to impress wanted to hear."

If Tarkanian was in need of a few political lessons, Sheila Strike was the one who could give them to him. Shortly after Maxson arrived in Las Vegas, Strike made a concerted effort to enlist the president as a supporter of her basketball team.

"He's been really supportive of our program," Strike-Bolla said of Maxson. "Almost since the beginning of his tenure here, we made a real attempt to include them [Maxson and his wife, Sylvia] in things that we did with our program. Absolutely, we planned that. As great as he is, have you met Sylvia? She's a pretty inspiring woman. And she's really bright, and she just is a really well-balanced woman, and I felt like she had a lot to lend, not just to the people on the team but our staff as well. What we did in women's basketball was try to create a program that we were really proud of that was run by our standards, given our resources. They helped us do that."

Maxson was so taken by Strike that athletic department staffers remember her being invited on several occasions to share her thoughts about the athletic department with the president. "She was never very shy about letting us know he [Maxson] had called her for a visit," one former employee said.

Strike also established an "honorary coach" for each home game, giving the Maxsons and several of the city's influential business leaders the worthless title and a game souvenir before each contest. It was a simple move, but one that helped the women's basketball team become a fixture among the establishment in Las Vegas.

By convincing the president and business elite that she had built her program honestly and was graduating her players, she gave Maxson what he thought was the flip side to the Tarkanian coin. The women's program side of that coin, though, might best be described as tails—make that tales.

While building this program "run by our standards," she received a little help, first in manipulating statistics and second in keeping her athletes happy.

The Bollas have been fond of saying that they've graduated all but one of the women's basketball players who were part of their program during the eighties. But a little probing shows there's a huge asterisk attached to that claim.

"Our graduation rate's not 100 percent, it's 96.667," said Jim Bolla, who quickly explained why that number differed from a *USA Today* chart that listed his team's graduation rate at 14 percent. "Basically what we do, is we feel, I mean, and statistics can be manipulated any way you want them to, we feel that any kid that we've brought into our program and has stayed in our program for the number of years required, finished their eligibility, we take credit for those people. We don't feel it's our responsibility if someone comes in for a year or two or quits, gets married, or has a baby or whatever, and they leave our program, that we're responsible for those people in our graduation rate. So, what we do, we say that every kid that's in our program in the last ten years who has finished their eligibility, has graduated with the exception of one. This is my biggest complaint, according to the NCAA statistics, if you have a freshman that enters your program and that freshman does not stay in your program and leaves, they still count in your incoming number of students. If we would do that for every institution in the country, can you imagine what the graduation rates at every institution in the country would be for every freshman that started classes and did not finish?"

But in order to calculate a graduation rate they could brag about, they had to use their own version of the new math—one that ignores the fact that only eight of thirty-two players in Strike's first five years finished their degrees. The others left early, allowing Jim Bolla to eliminate them from his count.

Ironically, the men's program graduated all but one of its players during the 1980s who met Bolla's criteria and completed four years of eligibility at UNLV. But because he has been branded a renegade coach directing renegade athletes, Tarkanian has never been known for his graduation rate so much as his winning percentage.

"That's probably because I didn't brag and twist numbers like the Bollas did," Tarkanian said. "Maybe I should have."

Strike's effort to drag Maxson into her corner was successful. Not only did the president brag about the women's program and its doctored graduation rate, but he lined the walls of his office at the president's mansion with promotional posters from the program. And during a tour of Hawaii, the women's coaches took up a collection from the players to buy a ring for Mrs. Maxson. Some of those players had little money to chip in, but felt the squeeze from their coaches and anted up.

One women's player who found money was not a problem during her days at UNLV was Misty Thomas. A 5'10" blond, blue-eyed guard, Thomas became the most famous athlete in Strike's first recruiting haul and an Academic all-American who so embodied everything the coaches bragged about that they retired her jersey.

Like Strike-Bolla, Thomas was a Canadian women's star, taking the Canadian Olympic team to a fourth-place finish in the Los Angeles Olympics and a third place finish in the 1989 World Championship Games in São Paulo, Brazil. She came to UNLV in 1982 and led the Lady Rebels in assists in each of her four years and in scoring her last two seasons and still holds the Lady Rebels career scoring and assist records and is the program's sixth all-time leading rebounder.

Not long after she moved to Las Vegas, Thomas was introduced to a man who spent hours hanging around the women's basketball program, attending practices and games and talking to coaches. The man, H. Jordan Rabstein, or "Junior" as he was known around the women's basketball program, was a wealthy sort—and a three-time convicted gambler—who befriended several of the players and then showered them with meals and other small gifts.

Some of Rabstein's gifts, though, were not so small.

According to records from the Nevada Department of Motor Vehicles, the Fiat X19 sports car that Thomas tooled around Las Vegas in during her junior year had been purchased by Rabstein and "lent" to the star player.

Rabstein originally denied being the owner of the car, but when told that state records clearly showed he was not telling the truth, he said he only provided the car to her "as a friend." Both he and the coaches, though, have admitted efforts were made to enroll him as a donating booster at UNLV.

"When I had that car, I lived about two minutes' walk to campus," said Thomas, now head women's coach at the University of British Columbia. "So the most I would use it was to run errands, something like that. I didn't often use it to get to campus."

"Wow," Sheila Strike-Bolla said when told the records showed her star was driving a car owned by an unofficial booster. "Junior was very close with Misty. Very close. Does that surprise me? Yeah, it does."

Strike's claim that she was surprised Thomas was driving Rabstein's car caused former Lady Rebel Lori Arent to chuckle. "Everyone on that team knew that little green car was from Junior. Junior would brag to us that he'd done that for Misty."

Arent, who played for the Rebels from 1982 to 1984, said she, too, was a recipient of Rabstein's "kindness." "The car that [teammate] Penny [Welsh] and I drove the first year I was there belonged to Junior. He gave us a white convertible sports car to use when he didn't need it. He'd let Penny drive it because it was a stick, and I didn't know how to drive a stick. We'd go to practice in it. They [the Bollas] knew whose car it was. If they say they didn't know, I can't believe that. When I came [to UNLV], I got the impression Junior was a booster/assistant. He was always around. I met him in the Bollas' office. He was in the office all the time."

Doug Sanderson, who rented a room to Misty Thomas at one time, said Rabstein's open-wallet approach in dealing with the women's team was well known. "JR became more or less a godfather to a couple of the women, particularly Misty," Sanderson said. "He primarily was a source of money for at least Misty. It always seemed to me that an act is either legal or illegal. The way I perceived Sheila to visualize things is that her acts were just little things and men's basketball's were big things. There is no distinction, in my view. I mean you're either operating aboveboard or you're not."

Rabstein's involvement with Thomas and other players should raise eyebrows for more than just his largess. Asked what the women's coaches knew about Rabstein, Jim Bolla said: "When he was here, he basically was a gambler. He was, you know, he was at the horse races, stuff like that."

Actually, he was into much more. H. Jordan Rabstein was born and raised in New Jersey but began making regular trips to Las Vegas in his late twenties, according to police records. By the mid-seventies, Rabstein was a well-known gambler, and, in 1974, he was indicted on two different occasions for federal gaming violations in Las Vegas. The first case simply alleged that he and another man had defrauded the telephone company by rigging their lines to avoid paying long-distance charges while they were wagering on games and races around the country.

The second charge stemmed from a full-fledged FBI sting operation aimed at Rabstein and several other men who allegedly were phoning betting information to sources around the country and taking bets by phone, both violations of the law. Rabstein pled guilty to the first charge and to one of the counts in the second case. He received five years' probation.

On November 4, 1975, Rabstein was convicted by a Birmingham, Alabama, jury in another case, this one involving "gambling conspiracy." The judge ordered Rabstein to serve eighteen months in prison. He appealed the verdict and remained out on bail. Almost a year later, FBI investigators obtained search warrants for Rabstein's cars and homes in another sting operation that was looking for evidence of illegal gambling. At the same time, FBI agents in Shelby County, Alabama, executed search warrants in the same investigation. According to FBI records, both searches turned up ample evidence that Rabstein was again engaged in the business of illegal gambling, a violation of his parole.

Using the information gathered by the FBI, Rabstein's parole officer, John H. Robinson, filed probation violation charges alleging that his involvement in the illegal transmitting of gambling information—including college basketball and football games—between Las Vegas, Buffalo, New York, and Pelham, Alabama, made an order of prison time prudent. According to FBI wiretaps and surveillance reports, Rabstein was working with an illegal gambling joint in Alabama.

His appeal on the 1976 conviction was turned down by the U.S.

Court of Appeals in June 1977, and he was ordered to report to the United States marshal in Birmingham on October 11, 1977, to serve eighteen months in federal prison.

But before he got to the marshal's office, he was convicted again, this time by a federal court in the Northern District of Alabama, for several additional federal gambling violations.

Federal Bureau of Prison records show Rabstein stayed in prison on the growing list of gambling convictions until October of 1979. Shortly thereafter, he moved back to Las Vegas, where he met Sheila Strike a year later.

"Wow," said Strike-Bolla when told of Rabstein's extensive criminal history. "I knew that his background was, he did some things. But he was one of those guys who'd never, he made a real effort to keep himself separate from our athletic program, he would not donate money, he would come to games but he would not, he didn't want to be like totally involved. He would never join the booster club, but he was at every contest. I think that yeah [there were attempts to get Rabstein] to donate money to the program, yeah. God, he was a total sports junkie, and he was around all the time. He'd come by every day with his little dog."

"I think basically ... that because he didn't have any real involvement with our program, it's ... like, we have kids on our team that have boyfriends," Bolla said. "We can't control who they date, who their friends are."

For that reason, Bolla said, the coaches never advised the women players to stay away from Rabstein.

"This is a weird, gray area," Strike-Bolla said of her responsibility to control relationships between women players and older men like Rabstein.

The one area that has never been gray is the red ink that the women's program produces at the end of each budget year. Building a women's program, especially one that receives almost no gate receipts from the several hundred fans who attend games, can be expensive, especially in Nevada, where many school systems dropped their junior high school girl's basketball programs years ago. According to the Bollas, only three Division I women's basketball prospects have been groomed by Nevada high schools in their twelve years at UNLV.

That makes recruiting a national challenge. It also means the women's program is forced to pay the higher out-of-state tuition for its scholarship athletes. That's not always been the case, though. From 1987 to 1990, eleven of the twenty-one out-of-state women's basketball players were "reclassified" as in-state students. On at least one occasion, the women's basketball staff creatively declared one of the team's players an in-state student, falsifying financial aid documents in the process.

Recruit Tasha Bradley of Los Angeles was admitted as an in-state student in January 1989, even though she had lived at home in California during the summer of 1988. The UNLV financial aid book states that to be declared an in-state student—and therefore be eligible for a lower tuition rate—one must be able to prove he or she has lived in Nevada for an entire year and have a Nevada driver's license or be registered to vote in the state. Because Bradley had gone home to California, declaring her an in-state student looked impossible.

But Jaina Preston, who was then the academic adviser to the women's program, found a way to make it look like Bradley had been in Las Vegas during the summer.

"Jaina said, 'Hey, do you know a guy who would give us payroll stubs?'" said John Peterson, a former UNLV athletic department staff member. "And I knew immediately what that meant, but I said, you know, 'What is it for?' And she said, 'Well, we're trying to get Tasha Bradley eligible and we're also trying to save by trying to get her in-state residency.' You know if you can get in-state residency, you save your budget thousands of dollars. So, I told her I'd check."

Peterson went to David Chapman, a young dentist who was just getting involved in UNLV athletics. "I called him up, and he had the type of payroll stubs that didn't have the carbon or any traceable leftovers," Peterson said.

"He asked me if I could get him any paycheck stubs, and I said sure, I throw them away all the time," Chapman recalls. "If it's a salary check, I give the stub to my employees. But if it's for supplies, you know, office expenses, I just throw them away. He [Peterson] didn't tell me what they were used for, but I understand now that they were used for women's basketball players. I was told one was Tasha Bradley. I've never met her so she couldn't have worked for me."

"I got her [Preston] a ton of them [pay stubs]," Peterson said. "I got her like a year's worth and then she filled them in. I can't remember how many months she needed, but I remember she typed them in. She made up the hours and the dollar amounts."

Preston said she can't remember "anything unusual" about her work with Bradley: "She was from California. I can't say that she did become a [in-state] resident, but it was possible."

Asked if she would have helped Bradley make such an application, Preston said, "Probably I did. I don't have any clear memory of it. I worked with Tasha when she was a freshman and a sophomore. When she was a sophomore, she probably was eligible to become a resident and I probably did help her. I don't even remember if she went to summer school. I remember a lot of things about Tasha, but nothing in particular about that [residency application] stands out. It was a pretty standard procedure. There wasn't a lot of gray area in that whole procedure."

This was not the first time the ethics of the women's program had been called into question. Former player Stacy Green, who was recruited from Detroit, delivered a letter to Strike and to Rothermel detailing several allegations of wrongdoing that had occurred during her two years at UNLV. Green said she had been informed by Strike that her scholarship was being revoked during the middle of her second year. The coach's decision came right after Green had severely injured her ankle.

In the letter, Green pointed out, among other things, that she and several other players had been asked by Strike to join middle-aged male boosters for dinner. "I let them know I would go to the NCAA regarding these matters if I did not receive my scholarship," Green said. After delivering her letter to Rothermel, who then met with Strike, Green's scholarship was renewed.

Rick Sias, a Las Vegas businessman who had become Green's friend and mentor, helped her draft the letter about Strike and instructed her on how to handle the meeting.

"I told her not to let Sheila intimidate her," Sias said. "Sheila can do that. I told her it was time to shine the light on the cockroaches. You know, they've been scurrying under the counter long enough. There are people over there [in the UNLV athletic department] that are doing things, that really are doing things in deliberate violation of NCAA rules and regulations, not just the spirit of them."

In a sworn statement taken in 1991, Green said the dinner arrangements were only a small part of the "unethical" conduct she watched her coaches practice. She claimed Jim Bolla purchased and sent her an airline ticket so she could make a second visit to UNLV during Easter break, 1982, a violation of NCAA rules. She said that during the second visit, Sheila and Jim Bolla took her to lunch and that Burt DeArmand, a women's booster, took her to dinner and "gave me money to gamble." She said she was sent another airline ticket in the fall of 1982 for her trip to enroll at UNLV and that Jim Bolla provided her and two other players with furniture from a local hotel for their apartment. Sanderson confirmed that women's coaches supplied furniture to their players from hotels.

Green also said the Bollas introduced her to Rabstein and that he gave her cash, once in the presence of Sheila Strike. And she said Sheila once wrote her English paper for her.

Despite the questions Green raised in her letter, Strike continued her political climbing, being rewarded in 1988 with a job as assistant athletic director, another step up on the UNLV ladder.

When, during the summer of 1990, it became common knowledge that Maxson was going to appoint an interim athletic director, Strike organized a petition and asked most of the major sport coaches and athletic department senior administrators to endorse Finfrock. The only coach who didn't sign was Tarkanian. Once Maxson gave him the job, Finfrock rewarded Strike by making her his chief deputy.

Together they were going to clean up the athletic department. Not long after being appointed, Finfrock met with the department's senior staff. "He walked in and told us, 'Our job is to clean it up, clean up men's basketball,'" Sanderson said. "As soon as Dennis got in control, there was like a line drawn. It was Dennis against Tark. Whether it was little things or big things, Dennis was going to do all he could to make Tark uncomfortable. It would be things like, in the NCAA Tournament, you get a healthier meal allowance for the team. The money comes from the NCAA. But Dennis wouldn't let the team have the NCAA money. He said they had to live on the university stipend. When Tark found out, he went down and blew Dennis away. Dennis caved in, but it was an attempt to prove he was in control."

Based upon the poor handling of the ticket situation during the 1990 postseason tournament, Finfrock's first effort to clean house, he decided, would involve an examination of the complimentary tickets traded by the athletic department for goods and services at local businesses. This plan seemed perfect, too, because some of the ticket trade-outs were with Tarkanian's friends. Finfrock announced that each and every ticket being traded out would be reviewed by his office.

Then he called reporters from the *Review-Journal* and slyly put them on the trail of what he believed would be a story damaging to Tarkanian—an agreement made by Rothermel on his last official day as athletic director to extend the trading time period of eighteen season tickets to Tarkanian's friend, restaurateur Freddie Glusman. In exchange, the athletic director and the football and basketball coaches would split $18,000 in free meals at Glusman's five-star Italian restaurant, Piero's.

"I'll tell you exactly, Greg Bortolin, a member of our staff, and I sat down with Finfrock [within a week of his getting the job] and he did indeed direct us toward certain things that we should be checking on to show some problem areas, like the tickets and the trade-out agreements," said Bob Sands. "He helped us get copies of that [Glusman] agreement and suggested it was a good story. He made it clear, he said, 'What we've got to do is clean up the university.' He said that you've got to get Tark out to do the things they need to do [at the university]. The stories and things started to happen, I think directly when Finfrock took over."

Glusman also was criticized by Strike-Bolla and Finfrock for having access to several other tickets which he received, ironically, when he owned the Sporting House gym in Las Vegas. Glusman said the additional tickets were given to him when he agreed to let the women's basketball staff and the team's players work out at his club at no cost. Glusman produced affidavits from three former employees of the Sporting House supporting his claim of a trade-out agreement.

Years later, when it became apparent that Sheila Strike-Bolla and her husband were reveling in—and even encouraging—Tarkanian's troubles, Glusman made the facts surrounding the trade-out public, questioning whether that wouldn't be an NCAA violation. The charges were too old, though, to gather much interest, and the Bollas explained that this, too, was really the fault of the men's program.

"When I came here at UNLV, I was taken to the Sporting House by the men's program," Jim Bolla said. "Tim Grgurich took me to the Sporting House and they say, 'Hey, we have this deal here' because our facilities at school as far as weight training and things like that weren't adequate. I mean we had an archaic weight room situation when I first came to UNLV. So they take me over to the Sporting House and they introduce me to [manager] Bobby Nichols and he says, 'Here, this is Freddie Glusman' and all this, and 'Here's our facility, and we have this agreement where you can come over here and use the facility in lieu of you working.' I would referee league games, we would do clinics, and our other assistant did that, too. And I had no knowlege of any kind of agreement as far as tickets were concerned."

When Finfrock saw how Pastagate (as the Glusman trade-out jokingly became known) was damaging Tarkanian in the minds of local fans who wondered why those tickets weren't available to all, he began stepping up his whisper campaign. He would tell reporters about the "outrageous" number of complimentary tickets Tarkanian was given by the university, forgetting to mention that the 223 tickets were part of the coach's compensation package that was put together when he came to UNLV. And at that time UNLV basketball tickets weren't worth the flimsy cardboard they were printed on.

Finfrock even suggested to one reporter that Tarkanian should return some of those tickets—for the good of the university, of course. That one prompted the generally nonconfrontational coach to dash off a letter to Finfrock. "I am deeply concerned about the incomplete and inaccurate information being given to the media by yourself and members of your department," Tarkanian wrote in a memo dated October 10, 1990. "Your latest comments on Channel 8 television regarding the tickets given to me as part of my contract were uncalled for. You could have stated that the tickets were mine by contractual agreement and that the contract should be honored. I think it would have been appreciated for you to state that we built the program to a national championship level and certainly I deserved the tickets that I received. Instead, you made statements that indicated some of the tickets should be returned, which has put me in a bad light with many members of the community."

Tarkanian's request in the letter that Finfrock "please stop leaking information" fell on very deaf ears.

"He used to call my house at all hours of the night," Greg Bortolin said of Finfrock. "My wife told me she thought that was weird. She called him a snake."

Finfrock's constant haranguing about Tarkanian's contractually guaranteed tickets bothered some in the community who had known Finfrock for several years. They saw in that criticism, as one businessman said, "the height of hypocrisy."

As director of the Thomas & Mack, Finfrock has a luxury box and scores of tickets at his disposal for every event that comes to the arena, not just basketball games. And the hottest ticket in Las Vegas in recent years has not been for Rebel basketball. It's been for the National Finals Rodeo championships which come to town every December.

Finfrock, one businessman said, used the lure of seats in his box to trade with some of the world's most expensive hunting outfitters. In exchange for a prime ticket to the rodeo, Finfrock would receive hunting vacations from the guides to exotic regions all over North America. For example, for $10,000, the outfitter takes a hunter from Las Vegas to British Columbia and guarantees that he'll come back having killed a brown bear, a moose, and a caribou. The outfitter supplies everything for the hunt.

"Dennis receives $100,000 running the Thomas and Mack," the businessman said. "There's no way he could afford to go on the hunting trips he's been on. He got those by trading out. Dennis invites all those outfitters down, sits them in the box, gets them comp hotel rooms, gives them cars to drive, and then they take him on a $15,000 hunt. If that's not exactly what he's accusing Jerry of, I've got to be the blindest man alive. The difference is those seats don't belong to Dennis for his personal use. It's supposed to be used for business development at the arena. Jerry got his tickets as part of his contract."

Within weeks of being appointed interim athletic director, Finfrock began firing some of Tarkanian's closest supporters in the athletic department, starting with Doug Sanderson. When Sanderson left, he told reporters that Finfrock's "assignment" from Maxson was to get Tarkanian to resign. That was in September, nine months before it ultimately would happen.

Sanderson wasn't the first to determine Finfrock had been given a "mission" by Maxson. Rothermel told close friends that Finfrock was being sent in "to do what I wouldn't."

"I'm sure Maxson let him know that he wanted Jerry's demise," Rothermel said. "He may have started the same way he started with me, which was to ask him if he knew whether or not there was anything Dennis might do. If he'd had a conversation with me [in 1984] about getting rid of Jerry, why wouldn't he have the conversation with Dennis. If he approaches me in relationship to it, why wouldn't he approach Dennis? He probably learned somewhere along the line that Dennis and Jerry did not relate very well and Dennis would be willing to do it. And I'm sure Dennis felt if he got it done, he'd get the [permanent athletic director's] job."

"To say that he [Finfrock] wasn't Maxson's hit man is just absolutely asinine," said Bob Sands. "I mean, that's totally ridiculous. You didn't have to be a rocket scientist to figure it out. All things point to the fact that they [Maxson and Finfrock] met and said, 'Hey, look, one of your first duties is to get Tarkanian out of there.' I don't understand why a man would say that [he's not been assigned that job] when all of his actions and performances show that indeed he was the point man. Being around them and seeing what they were doing, hell, yes, they wanted Tarkanian out. Did they succeed, yes, they did."

If discrediting Tarkanian and the past handling of athletic department administrative activities was part of Finfrock's assignment, the ticket "scandal," as the newspapers were calling it, looked promising. When his inquiry showed that several thousand dollars in tickets had gone unaccounted for or were missing, Finfrock asked his friend, campus security director David Hollenbeck, to take over the investigation. But it was decided that the irregularities Finfrock believed had occurred in the ticketing process might require legal action, so the charge of investigating these questions was given to the attorney general's office. The investigator for that office just happened to be Dorinda Hollenbeck, wife of the campus security director.

Finfrock used the ticket controversy as reason to reassign ticket manager Le Riggle, another Tarkanian supporter who routinely helped the coach when he needed tickets for special guests or friends. Finfrock locked Riggle out of her office and assigned security officers to watch as she cleared it out. Chuck Thompson, who represented Riggle as well as Tarkanian, said Finfrock handled her case with "all the dignity of a firing squad."

Glusman, whose criticism of Finfrock and Maxson had by this time become more heated, rented a billboard just off The Strip to raise his objections. The billboard had slashes through the names Riggle and Sanderson, then asked "Who's next, Dr. Maxson?"

With Sanderson gone, Finfrock moved Sheila Strike-Bolla into the job of athletic development, allowing the vocal Tarkanian critic to spend time with the athletic department's chief donors. With Riggle gone, Finfrock now had control over the ticketing process as well.

With the money and the tickets now under his thumb, it was only a matter of time, it seemed, before either the attorney general or the NCAA helped him put Tarkanian in checkmate. The only question was which agency would get there first.

Finfrock would later find out that it wasn't going to be the attorney general's office, which completed what Attorney General Frankie Sue Del Pappa termed "the most exhaustive investigation ever done by this office," issuing a sternly written report but no indictments. The report blasted the ticket office for improper record keeping—no record keeping in some cases—and irregularities in dealing with the nearly 2,000 tickets per game that were traded out or given away by the athletic department. Investigators found that in some cases tickets were given out under fictitious names and that in other cases those whose names were listed on ticket envelopes never received the tickets. But after all the frothing at the mouth Finfrock did about Tarkanian and his tickets, the report didn't even mention him.

It would have to be left to the NCAA, then, to provide UNLV with a reason to fire the winningest coach in college basketball history. In December, Finfrock and Maxson found the NCAA's allegations might not be able to do the job either. The list of charges against UNLV included only two minor potential infractions naming Tarkanian—a player's unauthorized use of a telephone credit card and making a public statement about a potential recruit's athletic ability—and no charge of unethical conduct on Tarkanian's part.

"That put the president and Dennis in a bad spot," Rothermel said. "I think the president really felt, I think the reason it happened the way it happened, the way it unraveled, was because the president hoped, based on the NCAA, that he could move Jerry out. When the charges came from the NCAA and Jerry wasn't prominently mentioned, suddenly the president doesn't have anything. He doesn't have a way to move on Jerry at that point. So now he's got to start putting something else together."

Lois Tarkanian went to Brad Booke and pled for honesty. "I told him, 'If you don't want Jerry, just tell him,'" Lois said. "And I said to him, 'Please, don't have them come with the phony stuff, don't come and say, "Hey, this is terrible, your kids are terrible.'" Our kids weren't terrible, our kids were good kids. Don't have them come and say, 'Hey, the NCAA has all these serious allegations against you.' They didn't have them against us. And we know it. And they knew it. You understand what they were waiting for when that letter came from the NCAA? They thought the NCAA was going to get Jerry. They thought Jerry was going to be charged with stuff. They were literally hoping for it. They were waiting for someone to do the job for them, and then it comes out, 'Hey, there's nothing really on Jerry.'"

For all its effort, the NCAA failed to find anything more on the Daniels situation than had been reported by *Newsday* nearly four years earlier. In fact, the organization found little evidence to support the allegations the newspaper made.

There was, however, the Richard/Sam Perry factor. If, as the NCAA alleged, Perry was connected to Tarkanian or his basketball program, it seemed almost certain that would be one change the coach could not survive.

So Finfrock started looking at pictures, lots of pictures.

10

In a Fix:
Richard Perry

The face Finfrock would spend hours looking for was that of a slender, dark-complected, bespectacled man named Richard Mark Perry.

After reviewing the NCAA's allegations against the university, it became apparent that Tarkanian's decision to pursue Lloyd Daniels, as ill advised as it was, likely wouldn't topple the coach. There was enough doubt about what the president knew and approved and what the NCAA knew and approved that this one couldn't be laid entirely at Tarkanian's feet. And Tarkanian's long-standing reputation of squeezing tough academic cases through the front door of UNLV, while repugnant to some, was not a sore spot to many of his fans. Some even found it refreshing that he was more honest about it than others in college sports.

But there was one possibility that even the most loyal fan had trouble justifying—a relationship between Tarkanian's Rebels and a man known to specialize in "fixing" the outcome of athletic events.

Richard Perry was that man. And he was baggage that came with the Lloyd Daniels recruitment that even Tarkanian couldn't handle.

Tarkanian said neither he nor his team knew the true story behind Richard Perry until he read a short sidebar in the April 3, 1989, edition of *Time* magazine detailing a lunch at Caesars Palace where Perry joined Bernie Glannon, owner of the Continental Basketball Association's Topeka Sizzlers, and Bill Bertka, assistant coach of the Los Angeles Lakers. The Sizzlers, Daniels's next stop after being booted from UNLV, were then affiliated with the Lakers, who were playing an exhibition game in Las Vegas that night. Glannon invited Perry to join Sizzlers coaches and front office staff for lunch with Bertka to "just talk basketball." But during the meal, *Time* reported, Perry received a call on his cellular phone from UNLV players Moses Scurry and David Butler. He told them where he was having lunch and suggested they come by. While the two players ate at a different table, *Time* quoted "sources" saying Perry allegedly handed Scurry and Butler $100 each to pay for their meal. "I gave them a hundred bucks, so what?" *Time* quoted Perry as telling former Sizzlers coach Art Ross, who was fired by Glannon. "Everybody does it. It keeps them out of trouble." Glannon said Ross's account wasn't true. So did the two players. Though Scurry said later that he received $20 to pay for lunch and Butler denied the claim altogether, there was one portion of the story that was undeniable—an accounting of Richard Perry's life with the law.

Perry gained fame and a small fortune as a gambler extraordinaire, a wizard with numbers and odds. He put those skills to work as the brains behind two sports-fixing setups that shook college basketball in Boston and horse racing in New York.

His talent for fixing sports events was featured in the 1985 tell-all book *Wise Guy*, written by former Lucchese family mobster Henry Hill. Hill, who is now in the Federal Witness Protection Program, said Perry was one of the first big-time bettors to develop a network of sources from coast to coast who could provide him with the little extras that gave him an edge as he placed bets. "He knew what kind of shape the field was in, the injuries to key players, whether the quarterback had been drunk, all kinds of things that gave his handicapping an edge. He used to find things in small-town college newspapers that never made the wires, and he had people calling him right up to the minute he was ready to bet."

Perry's connections with the Lucchese family run deep. They

also provided him his first run-in with the law. In 1974, Perry was one of twenty-eight people indicted in a major New York betting scandal involving fixed harness races in Roosevelt and Yonkers. The indictments—which included charges against Peter Vario, son of the late head of the Lucchese family, Paul Vario—alleged that Perry masterminded a plan to reduce the odds on races by arranging to have certain drivers keep their rides out of contention.

In his book, Hill explained the arrangement this way: "In the Superfecta races ... a bettor had to pick the first four winners in a race in their exact order. Perry figured that by getting two or three of the drivers to pull back or get their horses boxed in, we could eliminate two or three of the eight horses from the race. Then we could bet multiples of the remaining combinations at minimum cost."

To buy all the combinations in a standard superfecta bet costs $5,040. Winning the bet would bring $3,000. But by only betting on the horses that had not been eliminated in advance, Perry and his troops would only have to lay out $1,089 per race, assuring them of nearly a $2,000 profit with each set of tickets. Perry arranged to pay off the drivers that had pulled back by giving each a set of tickets, worth the $2,000.

"For a while we were doing so well that, rather than alert the track that we were winning all the time, we had to hire ten-percenters just to cash our winning tickets," Hill wrote.

Published reports on the scandal estimated Perry and the Lucchese family earned more than $3 million in the thirty races that were bet over the four months before they were caught. Hill said that figure likely was high.

Lawyers for Perry and the other defendants argued that accomplished handicappers with good knowledge of the horse-racing business could win the superfecta honestly, but they sent none of the accused to the stand to explain that possibility. The eleven-week trial ended with the convictions of only Perry and horse broker Forrest Gerry, Jr.

Perry was fined $10,000 and sentenced to 2½ years in the Allenwood federal prison camp in Montgomery, Pennsylvania, where he coached the prison basketball team and served six months before being paroled.

Just three years after his release from prison, Perry was brought in as an "adviser" in the Lucchese family's plan to fix Boston College basketball games. Hill said that Tony Perla, a Pittsburgh bookie, told him that Boston College player Rick Kuhn was ready and willing to help the group shave points in exchange for $2,500 per game during the 1978–79 season. Kuhn, a barrel-chested occasional starter at center who averaged only 3.5 points per game, told Perla that he could get team captain and point guard Jim Sweeney to join in the plan as long as they weren't required to actually lose any games. They would be willing, though, to make sure the Eagles didn't cover the spread. Hill said he arranged to bet against the Eagles, who finished the year 21–9, nine times during the season.

Hill and Jimmy Burke were included in the plan as "muscle," making sure that bookies paid off. Burke reportedly took details of the plan to Paul Vario, who told him to run it past Richie "The Fixer" Perry. Perry told Burke they needed one more player, the team's leading scorer, Ernie Cobb.

"He [Perry] said you always got to have the center and the leading scorer," Hill told *Sports Illustrated's* Kristina Rebelo in 1991. "We had two already and he made us recruit the leading scorer. If he has to, he will use threats. He has a whole family behind him, you know. Anybody who agrees to do business with him better not cross him. He has the mob behind him."

Cobb was left out of the deal during the first five games that were fixed but joined in the effort during the last four. Of the nine fixed games, Boston College failed to beat the spread six times, allowing Hill to pocket between $75,000 and $100,000 in eleven weeks. The players earned about $10,000 apiece. But the real winners were Perry and Peter Vario, who cleared $250,000 on the scam, Hill said.

Hill told *Sports Illustrated* in a 1981 feature on the scheme — which also detailed Perry involvement — that the players were "near perfect" in shaving points, which is much more difficult to spot than actually tanking a game. "I felt great," Hill recalled when asked about watching Boston College play Harvard. "I watched the boys throw the ball out of bounds and it was gorgeous. Here are a few examples. Sweeney has a great night with eighteen points, if you just look at the box score, but three times I saw him throw the ball away. Kuhn seemed to be doing his part, too. On one play, he fumbled the ball out of bounds. On another play he fouled a guy but the basket counted. The Harvard player missed the free throw, but the ball bounced over Kuhn, and the same Harvard guy grabbed it, drove around Kuhn and scored. I liked what I saw. I mean Kuhn was pretty bad."

That was the first of the fixed games. Boston College, a twelve-point favorite, won by only three, 86–83. "Look, kids have made thousands of bad passes by mistake for nothing," Hill explained in the 1981 *Sports Illustrated* article. "So what was so bad about making just one more bad pass and getting paid for it?"

Kuhn was convicted and sent to prison for his part in the fix, Sweeney became a government witness, and testified against his teammates in exchange for not being charged, and Cobb was acquitted in 1984.

Perry was indicted in the Boston College scheme in November 1983 but wasn't caught until April 1984, when he was arrested crossing the border into Washington state from Canada. He was held for the next twenty-one days in several federal prisons— including Leavenworth—before deciding to plead guilty in U.S. District Court to the charges in exchange for one year's probation and a $5,000 fine.

In a statement Perry released in 1991, he vehemently denied that he was involved in the Boston College scandal—going so far as to claim he actually "advised against the proposal" when Hill brought it to him. He said he pled guilty only because he knew that the offer of a fine and one year's probation was a better risk, given his background, than facing a jury. "Unlike the other defendants in the case who received substantial prison time, the court recognized that I pled guilty because I was promised probation and a $5,000 fine," Perry wrote in the statement. "Obviously, because of my prior conviction, I was concerned that if I went to trial I would be convicted because of my prior conduct or my punishment might be enhanced if I was convicted."

A year after he pled guilty in the Boston College case, Perry was introduced to the reigning legend of New York playground basketball—Lloyd Daniels. The two had a mutual friend in Arnie Hershkowitz, who was one of several adoring adults who pampered Daniels and one of Perry's pals from the horse tracks.

Perry, who had coached several summer league and AAU

teams over the years, knew Daniels by reputation. Perry's years on the sidelines had taken him from the famous Rucker Tournament played in Harlem to the city leagues in Yonkers and Mount Vernon, New York. He had coached such Division I talent as Mark Jackson of the New York Knicks, Duane Causwell of St. John's, Gerald Green, a draft pick of the NBA's Miami Heat, Boo Harvey of St. John's, and Conrad McRae of Syracuse. He had also coached future Rebel Moses Scurry.

Like nearly everyone who came in contact with Lloyd Daniels, Perry immediately became one of those Daniels would call "my man." During that first meeting with Daniels, Hershkowitz told *Newsday,* Perry handed Daniels a little cash. "You want to show you have an affection for the great players," Hershkowitz told the newspaper in explaining Perry's instant generosity. "Why do you love your parents? Because they take care of you. If they didn't, you would find someone else. That is what the world is all about."

Based on that friendship, Perry said he was willing to help Daniels make the move to Las Vegas. By his own admission, Perry provided Daniels cash, clothes, cars, and living expenses during the player's early time there. They were seen palling around several Las Vegas sports books, reportedly placing bets together on horse races and other sporting events. But Perry said everything he did with and for Daniels was done as a "friend" because he had no relationship with the basketball program.

But was it really "friendship" that made Richard Perry dig into his pocket for Lloyd Daniels? Henry Hill told Rebelo he had doubts: "Richard does everything for a reason. He wouldn't even talk to a player unless he had something going." The thought of a convicted sports fixer attaching himself to the greatest recruit Tarkanian ever had is enough to run chills down the spine of rabid Rebel fans. If Perry's intentions weren't wholly pure, imagine what could have happened had Daniels been handed the point guard position at UNLV. "The worst case scenario is that he saw this as a very malleable person that maybe could be utilized down the road in some certain betting scam," one reporter said. "We all hope that was never his intention."

When Perry's relationship with several UNLV players became known, the Nevada Gaming Control Board announced that it was considering adding him to Nevada's List of Excluded Persons—the infamous "Black Book" of mobsters and cheats who are banned from Nevada casinos. Published reports suggested that although it was illegal to bet on UNLV basketball in Nevada, illegal bookmakers had begun doing millions of dollars of business taking wagers on the Rebels. If so much was at stake, legally or illegally, on UNLV games, the potential for Perry to embarrass the university and the gambling industry by sidling up to a few Rebels was tremendous.

In a perverted sort of way, then, the best thing that ever happened to UNLV basketball might have been Daniels's arrest at a Las Vegas crack house in early 1987, an event that kept him from ever having to make the choice of listening to a coach or one of many hangers-on.

The extent of Perry's friendship—and whether or not it could be construed as a relationship with the university—became a little hazy, though, when Daniels was arrested. Mark Warkentien called Perry and asked him to spring Daniels from jail by posting the $1,500 bail. Perry signed the bail slip "Sam R. Perry," the first public connection between the "commodities broker" from New York and the erstwhile UNLV recruit.

Perry exploded when Tarkanian announced that Daniels never again would play for the Rebels. "He got all ticked off at me after the Daniels thing," Tarkanian told reporters. "He said I made a grandstand play and was trying to improve my image at the expense of the kid. He said that, as far as he was concerned, I had killed myself [as a recruiter] in New York. He said, 'Don't even show up in New York again because you're dead there.' And that was the last time I talked to him."

But for nearly two years after Daniels was arrested and dropped from the basketball program, Warkentien kept in occasional contact with the man he knew as "Sam Perry." His connections to the playgrounds of New York made him a potential source of talent, Warkentien said, and he was comped like all other summer league and high school coaches who come to UNLV games.

That all ended, Tarkanian and his players said, when *Time* revealed the true identity of Richard Perry. Tarkanian said he called a team meeting and immediately warned all his players to stay away from the gambler.

"It was like a big deal when the coaches sat down to tell us about Perry," Greg Anthony said. "Coach didn't even know the guy, initially. Our guys, we heard the name, but see, he didn't use that name, Richard Perry. I had seen him before, I had been introduced to him. But when I was introduced, his name was Sam. I never put two and two together, I mean, plus I didn't really care. I wasn't thinking about it. I was just having fun going to school. Then when we found out, you know, Coach really got up and said, 'Hey, you guys need to stay away.' We could tell he was real serious."

By that stage, though, the damage already had been done. Perry's name had been included in the *Newsday* series, had been used on the bail slip, and had become a topic of hot conversation after the *Time* story.

Finfrock knew that a character with Perry's sordid past would be an instant draw for the press. And he knew it would be a turnoff to the public if he was linked to the program. For a town that looks at its basketball team as its one "legitimate" winner on a national scale, the possibility that any unsavory relationship could exist, even on the periphery, would be deeply disturbing.

After receiving the NCAA's allegations, only one thing stood in the way of Finfrock's using Richard Perry against Tarkanian — proof that Perry was anything more than a gadfly who had handed a couple of players a few bucks.

Just days later, it sounded like that proof might just fall into his lap. Television reporter Dan Burns told Finfrock he knew that Perry was attending UNLV games. Burns, who had been leaked a copy of UNLV's confidential response to the NCAA allegations, was compiling footage of all the central figures in the case. Just prior to UNLV's December 19, 1990, home game with Princeton, Burns asked David Chesnoff, Perry's lawyer, to relay a request for an interview.

"He [Chesnoff] told me he'd ask Perry as soon as he got to his seat," Burns said. "I couldn't be too obvious, but it was obvious I could then figure out what Richard Perry looked like."

Burns watched Chesnoff climb two dozen rows into the stands and sit next to a man he hoped was Perry. He took a mental snapshot of the face and, when he returned to his station, looked at the file video of Lloyd Daniels's arrest. Perry, unshaven and wearing a baseball cap, had come to bail Daniels out, and television crews had captured the moment. The man on the screen was the same man Chesnoff had joined in cheering for the Rebels.

Burns told Finfrock that Perry had attended the Princeton game, at which UNLV had unveiled its 1990 championship banner. An excited Finfrock asked for more information. Burns said he'd give him more information once he was ready to air the story.

Finfrock couldn't wait. He turned to his friends at the *Review-Journal,* telling them he had a hot one for them and asking for the newspaper's help in making his case. Bob Sands said Finfrock asked if the newspaper could send a photographer to a series of UNLV home games and shoot just the crowd.

"He [Finfrock] had mentioned that Perry had shown up at some games," Sands remembers. "So we at the paper, we took pictures of all the high rollers and the donors and so forth in each section. We got a map of where Tark's seats are from Dennis. We took pictures of the entire arena, all the way around, and then pieced them together. He became a willing colleague, if you will, in this."

Once the photographers had pictures of the entire arena, Sands took the photos to Finfrock, who distributed them to his staff. He wanted to know if anyone knew where Richard Perry was sitting.

"It was weird," said John Peterson, former assistant director of athletic development. "He had all these pictures of sections all over the arena. I realized most of them were of Tark's seats because he has tickets throughout the arena; there's a bunch upstairs, a bunch in the end zone. And I could recognize longtime donors, car dealers and stuff. But Dennis stood there, and, I didn't understand why the hell he wanted that information, but he'd point at someone and say, 'Who's that guy?' Then he'd point at someone else—'Who's that guy?' It made me wonder because the pictures were blown up, bordered, chrome-coated photographs that were professionally done. I remember seeing Bob Sands in the office earlier that morning, that's why I thought something must be up."

After hours of looking for Perry, the crew finally gave up. "We couldn't find him because, really, we didn't know who we were looking for," Peterson said.

But it was obvious Finfrock had taken the ball Burns had handed him and run with it. "A couple of weeks after I told him I'd seen Richard Perry, I remember him telling me that 'come the end of the season, when we find out who's sitting where and we've got photographic evidence to show where they're sitting, we've got them,'" Burns said. "That made me think at the time that they were photographing the whole arena. I couldn't believe it. That's when I thought I better get pictures of Perry or I'm going to get beat on the story."

At UNLV's January 9 game with Utah State, Burns spotted Perry and Chesnoff again. This time, he arranged to have a video shot. When he next saw Perry at a UNLV game, it was February 14 and the Rebels were playing UC Santa Barbara. Burns set his cameraman in the Thomas & Mack's rafters and got long aerial shots of Perry rooting for the Rebels.

The next week, Burns decided to do a story questioning whether a criminal with Perry's record should be in attendance at UNLV games and he asked Finfrock for comment. It looked as if it was all coming together—or falling apart, depending on your perspective.

Two days before Burns could get his story on the air, *Review-Journal* columnist John Smith said Perry had been seen at games and should stay away.

Burns's story aired February 21. "Finfrock called me within minutes of my coming off the set," Burns said. "He said he wanted a copy of that story."

"The day after the story was on, Dennis had their tape," Peterson said. "He brought us all in, our staff, the ticket manager, myself, another girl in our office, and Sheila, and he plays the videotape for us. He ran the tape over and over. He wants to know if any of us knew who Chesnoff was and we all deny it because, I mean, I know who he is but I'm not admitting to it. He wants to know where these seats are and how he got them. Here was the director of the arena asking us where we thought the ticket location was."

It's the kind of unholy alliance that occurs regularly in the field of journalism. But even some of the reporters who were accepting the information began to question why Finfrock was handing them stories that were damaging to Tarkanian without first confronting the coach. "If you're going to do it inside, then don't talk out of both sides of your mouth," Sands said. "Because Tarkanian is doing things wrong doesn't mean that you step in and do things wrong.

Maxson was very, very political on the thing and would not stand up and fight in a public manner. He chose to fight it his way, to send a point man out to do it. Maxson has played it very smart. Some of us asked ourselves why it was being done like that. But we never asked them [Maxson and Finfrock]. We didn't want to lose sources."

While Finfrock was looking for pictures of Perry, Maxson started meeting with community leaders seeking support for his impending decision. Steve Wynn was one of the first supporters Maxson visited to discuss Tarkanian's fate in light of the just-then-released NCAA allegations.

"We can overanalyze Jerry Tarkanian and what happened," Wynn said. "But what happened was he failed to be accountable once too often and the president of the university decided it was time. And when the president of the university decided it was time, he started opening conversations with people. The conversations were all started by Bob, you see. 'What would you think if …?' He was trying to hold together his constituency, like every other president of every university. So he went around sniffing. 'These charges were pretty stiff. They're pretty rough. I'm in a tough spot.' It started with that period. Maxson himself went looking around to see is this going to be the kind of thing that splits the community. 'The last thing I want to do is split the community over Tarkanian. But I think I'm trapped. What do you think?' I told him I thought he was trapped. He had to deal with it. Bob Maxson had no choice. When he asked me that question I thought that he had no choice. He had to decide what the hell he was going to do. My advice to him was, whatever you decide to do, say it. He decided to handle it in a different way than I would have handled it.

"I had a definite piece of advice. I thought when all the press started badgering Bob Maxson about what he was going to do, I thought Maxson should have said, 'Now look, the fact that somebody accuses this school and some of its key people of misconduct is unfortunate. But it is not final. It is an accusation. I intend to investigate, along with the NCAA, all the things in the charges. If I find out at the end of that period of time that someone woefully neglected their responsibilities, whoever it is, I will take corrective action. If I find out that they did not, I will not. In any case, I will wait until all the facts are in, and then I will decide. But if you want to know what I'm going to do once I find out, that's what I'm going to do. I'm not going to talk to you anymore. I'm not going to speculate on Jerry Tarkanian until we get all this crap sorted out. But being accused is not enough.' Bob decided to take a softer, more inside, approach. And in retrospect, it may very well have been right. He was trying not to fan the flames of controversy. My position was that silence on the matter was going to let the press run wild with speculation, which would damage Jerry and him."

Maxson denied having discussed Tarkanian's future with Wynn, saying Wynn must have "overread" their conversation. "I trust Steve and I trust his honesty and he would never be dishonest, he would have no reason to," Maxson said. "I've never used the word 'trapped' because frankly I've never felt that I've been trapped into anything. My discussions with any community leaders over the situation dealt with infractions and penalties and what that might do to the community. I did not discuss Coach Tarkanian, I didn't go around to community leaders and discuss Coach Tarkanian. I discussed the problems that we were facing and the possible results if we had probations, if we had penalties. But I did not discuss, I didn't go around to civic leaders and privately discuss Coach Tarkanian. I've always considered that a personnel matter, I still consider it a personnel matter, and as far as the word feeling 'trapped,' I've never felt trapped. I don't feel trapped now, I didn't feel trapped last year, I didn't feel trapped four years ago when the Lloyd Daniels thing broke. I'm very mindful that I'm the president and I'm also mindful that I have very strong support of the Board of Regents, so I would have no reason to feel that I was trapped in any way."

Wynn's recollection of his conversation was much stronger— and much different—from Maxson's. Wynn said Maxson went so far as to say he would be "dealing with" Tarkanian once the season ended, a prediction that proved accurate.

"Bob used to say, 'I'm going to sit down. I'm going to discuss this after the basketball season is over with Jerry,'" Wynn recalled. "'We're going to talk about all these things. About what's going on with accountability.' I think there were things in that report from the NCAA that were a little surprising to him. 'Cause I kept asking him, 'What do you think about this?' And he'd say, 'I'm not sure they're all correct, Steve. Some of this stuff is hearsay and very flimsy.' He said he wanted to separate reality from the near reality, then he was going to see Jerry. I think he would have loved to have had a third choice. His first option was to put pressure on Jerry to resign or fire him or negotiate a way out without costing the university a lot of money because he had a contract. That was number one. Then there was ignoring it. And saying we believe in Jerry. Doing what Freddie Glusman or Irwin Molasky would have done. The third choice would have been between those two things."

Maxson, again showing great deference to Wynn, said the casino owner must have misunderstood their conversations: "Steve would never intentionally tell you anything wrong, but I never said that he [Tarkanian] was coming up for review by the Regents because he wasn't," Maxson said. "Now, I do an evaluation every year of people. Maybe that was the confusion."

Asked how much weight he gave to the opinions—solicited or not—of Wynn and other major donors about Tarkanian's future, Maxson smiled and said simply: "They bought their right to be heard."

Maxson and Wynn's wife, Elaine, also paid visits to several of the city's other influence leaders, taking advantage of the basketball team's spate of bad publicity to reinforce their "academics first, sports second" pitch.

"Elaine Wynn and Dr. Maxson came to my office in January," said superbooster Bruce Becker, chief executive officer of Arizona Charlies Casino. "They asked me to join the corporate council and wanted six thousand dollars. I told them my family generally donates to the athletics side. Maxson said, 'We want this to be an academic school.' I told them that was fine, but I don't go to the university to see the ballet or to the opening of a book room. Elaine Wynn said, 'So does this mean you're not going to give a donation? You can't get employees for Arizona Charlies out of basketball recruits. You can't get the people we need to build Las Vegas out of the basketball team.' They sat there and told me I needed to give to the academics and bad-mouthed basketball."

It seemed everyone in Las Vegas had an opinion on how Maxson should handle Tarkanian, and several of Maxson's confidants at the university were joining him in keeping their thumbs on the pulse of his wealthy support group. Sheila Strike-Bolla, who was appointed by Finfrock to handle the athletic department's gift-giving campaign, was meeting regularly with John Goolsby, president of the Summa Corporation, Dick Etter, chairman of the board of Valley Bank, and Kenny Guinn, chairman of PriMerit Bank. These three, along with the Wynns, were Maxson's staunchest defenders in the business community.

"Are you asking me if I ever expressed personal opinions?" Strike-Bolla said, repeating a question asked her about those meetings. "I answered direct questions and I don't think I was out there advocating one side or the other, but yes, I would express my opinions. And just by the way, there's so much ongoing stuff in the newspaper, I mean, these people would be picking up the paper every day saying, 'God, one more problem, one more this, one more that.' And that was not always easy, and quite frankly, there were people who hesitated to become involved because of this thing called our image."

With the work of dealing with the corporate elite safely being done by Strike-Bolla, Maxson, and Elaine Wynn, Finfrock concentrated his efforts on pushing the media to remain as aggressive as he was in pursuit of news connecting Tarkanian with Perry.

"There was a considerable amount of interest in getting more stuff in the newspaper after Finfrock became AD," Sands said. "There was more interest in really pushing to come up with stuff on UNLV. And he was calling up and said he thought the paper should get it going, get stories and things in the paper quicker. He didn't think we were working fast enough. One time he called me up and said, 'How come you didn't run this Perry thing I told you about?' I don't remember what the circumstances were, but I think we were waiting to get some facts, to find out what the deal was. But he felt as if we were kind of dragging our feet. He did direct us to certain things that would get us started. Sometimes he would call when certain things weren't run faster than what they were being run and I would have to tell him we're working on it as fast as we can, we're trying to do this in a professional manner and we need verification and so forth. Interestingly, he called my bosses. Then my boss would come by and ask why we didn't have a certain story."

Through it all, none of the media exposed Finfrock, even though many, in retrospect, see the ethical questions that can be raised about taking so much information from someone without ever holding him accountable.

"I think the media was played with, " KNEWS Radio sports director Rich Martin said. "The whole thing, from start to finish, was too neat. It was a slick package. Too tidy. And never did one media outlet break the whole story. Each of us got a little piece. They got us all into it. It was like an orchestra."

The only question was whether the conductor was Finfrock or Maxson. To some reporters and others, the answer became obvious as the leaks kept coming. "His [Finfrock's] job was to get rid of Tark," said Channel 8 sports director Scott Higgins. "Maxson comes in and says you play hardball with Tark and get rid of him. It probably was that blunt. How's Finfrock going to do it? Put out a bunch of dirty stories about the program and just sit back with Maxson and watch it happen. He forced Tark to resign basically by giving all this stuff out in the media. They [Finfrock and Maxson] did it and didn't have to take the blame for it. So now everybody hates the media in Las Vegas. They think we're the bad guys. But it was Finfrock feeding us all stuff and he's sitting back saying 'Oh, well, you do what you have to do.'"

"He [Finfrock] said to me one day, 'You know, it's the best thing, he [Tarkanian] has got to go,'" Assistant Athletic Director Tina Kunzer said. "He said that to me a couple of times behind closed doors. We would talk occasionally on what was going on in basketball, and I told him I wouldn't be a part of bringing down Jerry and his basketball program. And he basically said to me a couple of times you're either on our side or you're not; you know he wanted me to commit to being on their team and I wouldn't. He told me at a later time that everything he does he clears through Maxson, everything. Everything that he does is cleared, and the president knows everything."

"This was orchestrated by Maxson," Sands said, not a hint of doubt in his voice. "You know, he would talk to other people and say, you know, 'We've got to get this cleaned up, I mean this is getting to be absolutely ridiculous. Every time I try to make a positive gesture, we have this supercomputer that comes in, we're getting these valedictorians and we've got to talk about the fact that we've got another NCAA investigation coming.' Could Finfrock have been doing all this without approval from Maxson? I don't think so. I think it would get back because there were enough stories in the newspaper that quoted sources that people knew were Finfrock that if you're the president and you cared to stop it, you would just call him in and say stop. I think you'd have to be extremely naive that this whole situation is not being done at Maxson's insistence. I don't know why President Maxson wouldn't be up front, it would have given a lot more credence to everything and we wouldn't have this cloak of secrecy at all and it would be a simple thing of 'Hey, we don't like what Jerry Tarkanian's doing, ergo we want to get rid of Jerry Tarkanian.' It would be much more simple to do."

One reporter said Finfrock was careful—make that paranoid—when he handed information to the media. "If we were in his office, he would close the door and turn on his TV before talking because he was sure he was being bugged by the Tarkanian people," the reporter said. "That's how bad he believed these people were."

Details of stories Finfrock had leaked to some reporters filtered back to Tarkanian, increasing the tension within the athletic department. "It was so thick, you had to cut it with a chain saw," one current employee said of the friction.

But damned if the team didn't keep on winning. And that was complicating things. Even with Lloyd Daniels, even with Richard Perry, even with the NCAA breathing down your neck again, how do you fire one of only four coaches ever to win back-to-back national championships, as it appeared Tarkanian would do by the season's end? The team, claiming it was oblivious to all the sideshows, was continuing to pound opponents. Sometimes they weren't doing it with as much intensity as Tarkanian liked, but the Ws kept piling up. All the way to Indianapolis.

It seemed Tarkanian had left his troubles in Las Vegas and could focus on making history. Then, at the Final Four, there was Perry again. This time, he was sitting in the stands in seats given to the National Association of Basketball Coaches, which holds its convention in conjunction with the tournament.

Sands was busy preparing to cover the semifinal game when an usher handed him a slip of paper. "It was a note from Sheila [Strike-Bolla]," Sands said. "It said that Richard Perry was sitting in the stands, and it gave me a seat number and everything. I sent a pho-tographer to shoot it."

While Strike-Bolla was working with Sands, Finfrock had grabbed Tina Kunzer and asked her to go find Greg Cava, a free-lance photographer who shot pictures for the athletic department. Finfrock gave Kunzer the same instructions as Strike-Bolla gave Sands—get us a picture of Perry, and get it quick.

Sands said his photographer snapped several shots of Perry at the game, as Strike-Bolla requested. But he said he recommended that his newspaper hold off on publishing the shot until it was determined who had provided Perry with the seat. Editor Sherman Frederick voted him down.

"We ran that on page one, even though I still think we were wrong," Sands said. "I was told to write some innocuous story about it, cutlines really. It should not have run until we got all the information. I said this is kind of silly to run this right now. We should probably do some checking. From what was said to me, I believe Finfrock indeed called Dave Osborne [publisher of the *Review-Journal*] or Sherm Frederick and said. 'Hey, what's the deal?' I don't know who said what, but we ran the picture."

That was one of several stories Finfrock provided to reporters around the time of the Final Four. He was working hard, several reporters said, to damage both Tarkanian and the previous athletic director's way of doing things. He kept reminding the reporters that he had arrived and would clean it all up.

The dead horse Finfrock was riding hardest during the postsea-son was his improved handling of tickets for the tournament games. "I'm just proud of the fact that nobody showed up at the [NCAA Tournament] regionals or Final Four without tickets that were paid for," Finfrock told the *Review-Journal*. "And nobody showed up selling groups of our tickets."

That's not exactly so, one of the nation's leading ticket scalpers said. Gill Eshom of Ticket Outlet in Los Angeles said he bought 120 of UNLV's best seats for resale at the Indianapolis Hoosierdome. Worse, the source of those tickets, Eshom said, was Debbie Barran-tine, Finfrock's hand-picked successor to Le Riggle, the ticket man-ager whose professionalism and ethics Finfrock had spent most of the previous year questioning.

Eshom said he had told friends in Las Vegas that if the Rebels made it to the Final Four, he'd be willing to pay a premium for good seats. One of Eshom's friends promised to ask Runnin' Rebel team manager Shawn Foster to keep his ears open.

Foster said he knew it was a long shot, but he decided to ask Barrantine to let him know if seats came open, promising that she would be paid handsomely for them. "I said, 'Is there any way you can get me extra tickets to the Final Four'" Foster remembers. "She said, 'How many?' I said, 'Maybe a hundred.' She said, 'No way, that's impossible.'"

Eshom encouraged Foster to keep pushing, giving him $3,000 to entice Barrantine to come up with tickets. By the Wednesday before the Final Four, Barrantine had begun dropping hints that she might be able to deliver some tickets to the scalpers, but probably not 100 and probably not good seats. As the team plane left Las Vegas Wednesday afternoon with Barrantine and Foster aboard, Foster showed Barrantine the wad of $100 bills he had available if she could deliver tickets.

When they checked into the hotel in Indianapolis, Foster told Barrantine he needed the tickets as soon as possible. UNLV's newly established ticket policy stated no tickets would be distributed until Friday morning, so Barrantine told Foster there was little chance he'd get them any sooner.

But Thursday night, Foster said, he noticed an envelope slipped under the door of his room. It had twenty-two tickets in it. Good tickets. Make that great tickets.

Friday morning, Foster was given even more tickets, he said. Barrantine handed him twenty tickets, and another twenty-two were slipped under his door. "I picked up a few from her room and a few were delivered under my door," he said. "I told her that most likely I'd be paying $120 per ticket, which is twice face value."

After receiving his third batch of tickets, Foster said Barrantine counted the money in his room, then went with him down to her room. "We went down to her room because she had to check them off the ticket chart," Foster said.

On Saturday, the day of the game, Foster said he picked up another fifty to sixty tickets, paying Barrantine at least $100 for each. He finished the week by collecting 120 tickets for Eshom, a portion of which were in the premium downstairs portion of the arena. He said he paid Barrantine $5,000 more than the face value of the tickets.

"We were surprised by the quality of the seats we were getting," Eshom said. "Selling tickets is my business. I knew this was too good a deal to pass up."

As a bonus, Foster said he gave Barrantine another $3,000 "out of appreciation" when she paid a final visit to his room. "The whole deal was done in cash," Foster said. "Hundred-dollar bills and fifties."

Barrantine denied Foster's claim, saying that any tickets she sold were "strictly for face value."

"Let me think back for a minute," she said when asked if she had sold any tickets for cash. "Yeah, we sold some there [Indianapolis]. Mostly, they were requests from people who were with the university and that was before the game started. Before we left to come back, we had lost that first night, we sold the balance of the Monday tickets so the school would not have to pay for them. The people that we sold the tickets to, what they did with them after that we have no idea and we have no control over."

"The rules of the 'honest' ticket program were violated," said Chuck Thompson. "There were fans in Indianapolis—I was one of them—who had to wait until Friday morning and stand in line to get tickets. Then they're sliding tickets under some guy's door the night before. This whole thing was a real mess."

UNLV's loss to Duke in the tournament semifinals was a blow to the team and to the Rebel faithful. But it assuaged the fears of those who worried that discarding the coach of a two-time defending national champion might be impossible.

"Now that Jerry didn't win a second straight national championship, it's going to make it easier for Maxson to do it," Denny Hovanec, a UNLV radio commentator, told the *National Sports Daily*. "Believe it or not, Jerry may have had to win two games this weekend to save his job."

"Maxson couldn't get Jerry out before because he knew people in Las Vegas wouldn't accept it and would be crying for his head," another source told the *National*. "But with the pressure from the NCAA, and with the team losing to Duke, he probably feels he can make his move."

Though Maxson denied the story, those who openly had said

Tarkanian needed to go picked up the pace when they returned from Indianapolis. A few days after the game, Strike-Bolla and Barrantine came to work in sweats, an unusual outfit given the generally professional attire the two were known for.

"We wondered what they were doing," said Peterson. "Then they said they were going down to the Silver Bowl to look in the storage areas for boxes with old ticket information in them. They were going down to see if they could find comps given to Richard Perry."

"I went to the Silver Bowl on several occasions because the attorney general's office had made records requests of us," Strike-Bolla said. "The AG's office took all of the development office records."

Strike-Bolla denied Peterson's assertion that she and Barrantine were looking specifically for ticket information involving Perry.

Finfrock got into the act, too. He paid a visit to Cava's photo studio and made a rather odd series of requests.

"Dennis called and wanted to meet with me here and go through some negatives and see if there were pictures of Richard Perry," Cava said. "I told him to come on by. When he came over he asked me if anyone else was in the studio and I said, 'Well, no. Everybody has the day off.' I was kind of joking because I don't have that many people working for me. So, he pulled out the program from the basketball awards banquet that had taken place after the Final Four. And he pointed to a picture of the Rebel starters sitting on the bench cheering for the reserves. In the background, you can see Richard Perry. He asked me if that was my picture, if I'd shot it. I told him no, I could tell it wasn't mine. So, he just said okay, and he put that away. Then he goes, 'Well, can we go through, you know, your negatives of the games. At first it was just 'games' that he asked to see. Then it was the Duel in the Desert, the game against Florida State. He said he wanted bench-only shots. Usually, I run over and try to get the two coaches shaking hands at the end of the game. I got Tark and the Florida State coach [Pat Kennedy]. And in the background of that picture there's Perry and another gentleman getting up, and it looks like they're waving to someone or laughing at someone there in the background. Now, he wanted that picture. He wanted it bad. After we found that one picture, he didn't care about anything else.

"He asked me to print that. As he was leaving I asked him what he was doing and he said he was 'trying to get rid of the bad stuff for the boss. My boss doesn't like what's going on in basketball and I don't like what's going on and we're going to get rid, you know, we are going to clean this up, we're going to get rid of this kind of stuff.' I figured they were trying to get rid of Perry, and that's good, you know. But the more I think back on it, it's really scary that he mentioned his boss in there like his boss wants to get rid of all this bad stuff. Obviously, he was talking about Maxson. He's the only guy it could be.

"Then, when he left he said, 'Don't put your sticker on the back of the picture and no one will know where we got it, and we'll keep you out of this. No one needs to know I was here.'"

Cava did as he was told, printing the photos and sending them unmarked over to the athletic director's office. Finfrock filed the pictures away. Timing, he knew, was everything, and it wasn't yet time for those shots to end up in the hands of the media.

Cava said Finfrock's visit took place about April 15, two weeks after UNLV's loss to Duke.

With the season wrapped up and most fans looking ahead to the 1991–92 season that would be soiled by sanctions from the 1977 investigation, KLAS-TV's Higgins decided to check and see whether the ban against live television at Rebel games would wipe out the showing of live-game video on the television monitors inside Thomas & Mack. The monitors were hung near most of the arena's concession stands, allowing fans to buy a hot dog without missing a high-priced minute of the game.

"It was a pretty simple story," Higgins said. "I sent a reporter over there and he wanted a couple of comments from Dennis. At the end of the interview, Dennis stood up and happened to look out his window and said, 'Look at those cars out there, isn't that ridiculous?' He was pointing to the cars owned by some of the basketball players. He said it made him sick, I don't know if that was exactly his word, that he had to look at those nice cars pull up every day. Dennis ended up giving my reporter license plate numbers for the cars and telling him to go check them out. In other words, Dennis wanted us to go do a story about the basketball team's cars and then he subsequently, a few days later, said he was going to do his own investigation."

When Finfrock and Brad Booke announced two days later that the athletic department was going to check the registrations of the players' cars, they said they were doing so because they "had several inquiries from the media." Booke said KLAS was the first to raise the questions, setting off the university's interest.

Tarkanian expressed disgust at Finfrock's latest effort. "We've been giving our car information to the university for years," he said. "And both the NCAA and university checked them out. It was a cheap shot, what he did."

About that same time, KNEWS Radio sent reporters to scour the neighborhood where Richard Perry lived. Rich Martin of KNEWS said his station's general manager, Doug Trenner, returned from the NCAA Tournament trip with an interesting tip. Though Trenner never told Martin who his source was, he said he'd heard that Rebel players were frequenting the $165,000 home legally owned by Perry's brother.

"He was told that in Richard Perry's neighborhood, several of the basketball players had been seen hanging out with Perry, shooting baskets and doing basic kid's stuff," Martin recalls. "I was able to corroborate that with a couple of university sources who said they heard the same thing. Some of the rumors got real wild. I mean one guy told us that Larry Johnson's autograph was on the bottom of Perry's pool. But when we got back from the Final Four, Trenner got a little itchy to try and get this story going. So he went out to the neighborhood and talked to some kids, just ten-, eleven-, or twelve-year-old kids. They said they'd seen Rebel basketball players in the backyard, and he was able to corroborate it with one parent. I told him that I wasn't going to do the story because I had a problem depending on kids as your source. He put the story together and we ran it. We got some calls from parents who were upset that we would use their kids as sources. But we got calls from other neighbors who said we were right on.

"If there was anything that surprised me, it was that the university was very cooperative in giving out information on Tarkanian, as far as the basketball players, as far as hearing stuff like that. It was more in leading us to a direction, so if you go out and get the story yourself, they could say they didn't leak it. You wouldn't expect the university officials to corroborate a story like players seen at Richard Perry's house. Normally, universities are pretty closed up entities and they don't like the media knowing that kind of stuff."

A day after the KNEWS story aired, Lois Tarkanian received a call from a reporter who asked what her husband was going to do about this "disturbing" report that his players were consorting with Richard Perry. She slipped and said Tarkanian was going to announce that he would suspend any players who "hung out" with Perry.

Her words were reported as fact. Tarkanian, the station announced, would suspend his players if they spent time with Perry. Incensed, Chesnoff called Chuck Thompson and said Perry, his client, "took great offense" to the slap from the coach. He threatened to sue.

Tarkanian backed off from any thought of formalizing the policy, instead promising that he "would warn next year's players" about Perry. He said such a policy wouldn't do any good because it was so difficult to monitor. "I'm not with them twenty-four hours a day," the coach said. "How am I supposed to know who they're hanging out with?"

In the end, it wouldn't have mattered if Tarkanian had agreed to sanction players caught socializing with Richard Perry. The damage already was done. Fueled by leads from university officials, Las Vegas reporters had contracted Perry-mania. And there was no letting up.

11

The Week That Was

Stories with a distinctly inside-the-athletic-department flavor kept popping up in the newspapers and on television. They were troublesome, but not fatal. Most of the allegations, like the question about the players' cars, already had been checked out and passed on by the NCAA. Tarkanian kept wondering at what point the people he worked for would stop. The answer became clear; they would stop at nothing.

Then came The Pictures. The words that ran with them, really, were meaningless. The image—a word that keeps coming back— was what looked the worst. When Tarkanian finally resigned, the period that followed The Pictures became known as The Week That Was. It really was twelve days from publication of those photos to the day Tarkanian resigned, but The Twelve Days That Was just didn't have the same ring.

It was the kind of period most easily tracked in a diary; the events were etched in everyone's memory forever. Though none of the principals kept a written summary of those days of tension, this is what a diary—one from everyone's point of view—would have said.

Sunday, May 26

It probably will long be remembered as the most famous edition of the *Review-Journal* ever published. Handed to the newspaper several days earlier by a source known only as "Lamont" were pictures of three players from UNLV's national championship basketball team drinking a beer, sitting in a hot tub, and engaging in a two-on-two basketball game with the man whose mere presence at UNLV basketball games was enough to generate negative headlines. Now there was undeniable proof that Richard "The Fixer" Perry had befriended several Rebel basketball players. No longer were they just radio reports that neighborhood children thought they had seen UNLV players in Perry's company. This was the link many had feared and some had hoped for.

"I walked out to pick up the newspaper and had no clue," Maxson said. "I was sitting there reading it. Sylvia was getting dressed for church. I saw it and knew this was something Jerry and I had to discuss, that this was not something that was going to, after four or five days, quiet down. All of my instincts told me that this one was more serious than the normal problem. There's a difference between somebody from one of your sports getting caught using a telephone or practicing when you shouldn't practice. That picture put us into another category that other universities aren't facing. I knew this was national news and we were going to get roughed up a little bit."

"That's it," Sylvia Maxson remembers her husband saying. "That's enough."

"I almost was too embarrassed," Maxson said, "to go to church that morning."

Not long after Maxson brought the paper inside, Tarkanian called the president at home. The call had nothing to do with the pictures. Tarkanian hadn't even seen them at the time. The coach and president had a miscommunication about a meeting date. Maxson believed they were to have met the previous Thursday to talk through the university's response to the NCAA. But Tarkanian had put the meeting on his schedule for the following Thursday. Maxson, upset when he heard Tarkanian was out of town when the meeting was to have occurred, sent the coach a scathing letter questioning his true concern over the NCAA's charges. Tarkanian, when he heard of the mixup, had tried to call from his vacation condominium in San Diego, where he was spending a long weekend. Twice he had left messages for the president. Finally, on Sunday morning, he was able to get through and offer his apology.

Maxson, though, was no longer worried about the missed meeting. He had greater concerns, and it didn't take him long to share the morning's news with Tarkanian. "He's the one who told me about the hot tub pictures," Tarkanian said. "He told me how mad he was at the paper for running them. He said he 'could identify the kids; it's real clear who they are.' He said, 'This is terrible for the university.' He talked about how bad it was for me. Well, I told him they [the players] shouldn't have been with a gambler and that I'd warned the players. I told him that I was on my way home later that day and would check into it."

Tarkanian called his son and confidant, Danny. "He asked if I had seen the paper yet," Danny said. "I said no. He said he had just called Maxson, and Maxson had told him about the thing in the paper and he was really upset. My dad said, 'He was really mad at me, but I don't think he is at the point where he'd fire me.' To me, that surprised me, that my dad would even think that was a possibility at that point, but that was obviously something that was on his mind. That might have been one thing that led to his irrational decisions throughout the week."

After Tarkanian arrived back in Las Vegas late that evening, his phone didn't stop ringing. Reporters from across the country were asking about the latest of his troubles. "The media people, from like the *New York Times* and others, kept saying they had it from sources close to the university that this was the last straw," Tarkanian said. "Another guy from Associated Press said the same thing. That was the first I had any inkling about that. I didn't think it was that bad. There was no way you could tell when that picture was taken, and the players said it was before they knew he was Richard Perry. Greg Anthony said later that you could tell it was before 1989 just by looking at the players' haircuts. So I told the reporters, 'He can't fire me. I didn't do anything.'"

The key figure in the pictures—other than Perry, of course—was Moses Scurry. Scurry had played on one of Perry's New York summer league teams while he was in high school and had been an occasional companion to the coach when he found out Perry was living in Las Vegas. It was Scurry who encouraged his close friends David Butler and Anderson Hunt to join him for the afternoon at Perry's home that resulted in the photo session.

Tarkanian really had not been interested in recruiting Scurry out of San Jacinto Junior College in 1987. The coach was working overtime, though, to sign Butler, Scurry's teammate and best friend. Butler was rated as the nation's best junior college prospect that year.

Ironically, it was Maxson's decision in 1987 to call in the NCAA that caused Tarkanian to lose so many recruits that he offered a scholarship to Scurry, whose relationship with Richard Perry was the cause of the mess this summer of 1991. After Maxson's 1987 press conference, Butler had told the UNLV staff he would only come if Scurry came with him.

If he had tried to set it up so Tarkanian's recruits would make such an error, the president couldn't have been so lucky.

Monday, May 27

It was Memorial Day and university offices were closed. One, however, was open. Tarkanian called his coaching staff and summoned Scurry and Butler to the basketball office to answer some questions. Scurry told his coaches that he was sure the pictures had been taken not long after he arrived in Las Vegas in 1988, several months before the April 1989 *Time* article that exposed Perry's sordid past to the coaches, players, and people of Las Vegas. The two players drafted handwritten releases to the media, explaining the pictures and their relationship with Perry as best they could. Butler said he thought it was the only time he'd visited Perry's home. And Scurry said that he had "scaled back" his visits with Perry after Tarkanian's warning, but admitted that he hadn't cut them out altogether.

"I understood that," Tarkanian said. "He's known Perry since their days in New York. It's tough to tell these kids they have to stay away from someone that they've known and who has taken care of them."

Tarkanian may have understood. Maxson did not. The president was quoted in the paper saying he was "obviously upset" by the pictures. "It makes me angry because I think stories like this not only damage the program itself, but also in some way the university," he said.

Brad Booke added: "The long-term problems of being associated with such a person far outweigh the problems of an NCAA violation. The name of Richard Perry probably has greater potential for serious and lasting damage to the institution than does the name Lloyd Daniels."

Tuesday, May 28

Early in the day, UNLV announced—and Tarkanian endorsed—a proposal that would suspend any athlete who fraternized with known gamblers. Everyone agreed it would be a tough rule to enforce in a town of gamblers, but in the spirit of knee-jerk reaction, it was agreed this was the best route.

"I think it's great," Tarkanian said of the new measures. "Obviously, we can't have, and we don't want, our kids associating with gamblers. We tell our kids that every year. We bring in the FBI and the district attorney to talk about gambling and drugs."

Later that night Tarkanian was having dinner with several friends when he received a call on his cellular phone at about 8:30 P.M. from Booke.

"He said, 'Jerry, on your way home, can you come by and identify some documents for my response to the official inquiry to the NCAA,' which was due that Friday," Tarkanian said. "I left dinner and went over to see him. When I got there, he said, 'By the way, Dr. Maxson is going to stop by.' Booke started in by telling me how bad the Sam Perry incident is. He said, 'You can't have Sam Perry tied to your neck. Even if you're going to move in the NBA or sit in a front office, nobody's going to touch you if you're tied to Sam Perry.' They sat down and Booke brings out these comp tickets to Perry during the 1986–87 season. He asked me to identify them. There were five or six different games that he was given comp tickets to. One of the requests said it was at the request of Jerry Tarkanian, two said, requested by Mark Warkentien, and two said it was at request of the basketball department. I said I didn't request any of them, but it wouldn't be unusual for one of the coaches to request them and say, 'This is on behalf of Coach Tarkanian.' It kind of blew my mind as to when these were. I couldn't remember ever doing that. But one of them said it was requested by me. I looked at it and said, 'First of all, this isn't my signature.'"

Tarkanian said Booke and Maxson were coming at him so hard and fast that he did not realize at the time these were tickets that had been left before anybody in the basketball program knew that Sam Perry was really Richard Perry.

Next Booke and Maxson brought out a handwritten list with boosters' names on it. Each of those on the list were supporters who had called and requested tickets to the 1987 Final Four in New Orleans. It was Tarkanian's handwriting, and on that list was the scribbled name "Sam Perry." Tarkanian thinks Warkentien asked him to get two tickets for the game.

Booke did not tell the coach that the list he had handed him wasn't the list of those who eventually received tickets. It was just a list of those who had asked Tarkanian—or who had asked some-body else to ask Tarkanian—for seats. Perry's name didn't appear on the list of those who did receive tickets. Booke didn't give Tarka-nian a copy of the documents for the coach to share with his lawyers.

"We didn't find out what those lists were until the next day when we called Le Riggle and other people to try and figure it out," Danny Tarkanian said. "But that was what they hit him with."

"Jerry, the media's going crazy," Booke said. "We've got the national media in here. They're never going to stop. I think they've got us tied to Perry. I think the string has been played out. We're going to probably get two, maybe three more years of probation. You're the winningest coach in the history of the game. If you coach any longer, your record is going to fall. Why would you want to give that up?"

"You know [*Los Angeles Times* investigative reporter] Danny Robbins will write another story on this, trying to hurt you," Max-son said.

"You ought to resign, Jerry," Booke said. "Be a hero. Go out on top. Go out with trumpets. It's the only way to get everyone off your back."

Booke told Tarkanian that the attorney general had seen the hot tub pictures that Sunday and then sent the ticket requests to Dennis Finfrock in the athletic department on Monday. Booke said the information had been part of documents subpoenaed in the ticket investigation.

"I was aghast when I saw them," Booke told Tarkanian. "Particularly the handwritten list. It was so damaging."

"If you don't resign," Maxson chimed in, "it could reach the point where I'll have to fire you."

The president then pulled out a picture of Perry sitting behind the team's bench at a basketball game and asked Tarkanian to explain. "That's bullshit," Tarkanian said, raising his voice. "I don't know anything about that."

Maxson quickly tucked the photo away.

"He didn't make a big thing out of it so I didn't pay much attention to it," Tarkanian said.

Tarkanian, his mind reeling, said he needed time to think. "They ambushed me," he said. "I didn't have time to think."

He left Booke's office and headed home. On his way home, Tarkanian called Danny on his cellular phone. "Danny," he said in a voice that left no doubt something was wrong, "I just left a meeting with Maxson and Booke and they told me they wanted me to resign or they were going to fire me."

Danny, who was at the house he and a friend had just purchased, was as shaken as his father. "I was shaking and almost hyperventilated," the younger Tarkanian said. "I couldn't breathe. I couldn't believe it. It's hard to describe. It's something you have to experience because it was such a shock, such a complete shock. No one thought we were anywhere close to that point. I had known for some time that Maxson wanted to get rid of my dad, but I didn't think Maxson would."

Danny and Chuck Thompson rushed over to the Tarkanians' house. While Tarkanian waited, he started asking himself why he'd want to stay and put up with the pressure he was feeling at the time.

"Maybe this wasn't worth coaching anymore," Tarkanian remembers thinking. "At that point I thought I never really wanted to coach again, I really didn't. I thought about maybe buying the Sporting House and having a place to hang out. One of my dreams when I quit coaching was to go to the Oklahoma-Texas football game and a Notre Dame football game. I started thinking, 'Hell, I've got enough money. I could do something else.' I had it all figured out before they [Danny and Thompson] even got there. I was thinking about things I could do. Maybe this was the best thing."

When Thompson heard the story, he exploded. Booke knew that his meeting was intended to lead Tarkanian to make a decision on his future. He also knew that Tarkanian had lawyers who were advising him.

"Mr. Booke's ethics—or lack thereof—had concerned me for a long time," Thompson said. "But to call a man in with the intent of asking him to resign and knowing full well that he has counsel, even that surprised me coming from him."

One of Tarkanian's lawyers, Alan Jones, said he even warned Booke weeks earlier not to meet with his client without either himself or Thompson present. "We did not trust the situation or some of the people with whom Jerry was working," said Jones.

Though it wasn't the first time the ethics of Booke's actions in the Tarkanian case had been questioned—nor would it be the last—Booke offered no apologies for his call to Tarkanian on that Tuesday. He said he couldn't understand how Thompson or anyone might see his actions as "malicious or unethical."

"I do business all day every day, virtually every day talking to the employees of the university," Booke said in defense of his actions. "Keep in mind, my client is the university as an institution. It would paralyze the operation of the university to have people represented by counsel when we sit down to conduct the business of the university. Jerry has been fully represented throughout. And I'm sure that all of Jerry's actions have been taken after ample advice from counsel."

"Booke's real intent was to paralyze Jerry Tarkanian that night," Thompson said.

Lois Tarkanian, an elected member of the Clark County School Board, was attending a school board meeting while her husband, son, and Chuck Thompson met. When her meeting ended, she headed home, oblivious to the evening's events.

"I drove up, it was almost eleven P.M., and there were three cars in the driveway," she remembers. "My heart sank. I thought something was up when I saw Chuck's car there. I walked in and the three of them were in the bedroom. I thought I'd make a joke."

"What happened, did they fire you?" she said half jokingly.

"Sort of," Tarkanian responded. "They think it would be best if I resigned.

"I don't want to be here if this is the way it's going to be," Tarkanian told the others as they sat there trying to figure out their next move. "If they don't want me, screw 'em. I'm going to ask for one more year. I want to stay one more year, then get out."

Thompson tried to calm Tarkanian and began quizzing the coach on exactly what it was Booke had presented to him. Tarkanian couldn't remember too much. "I've never seen those comp documents before," he said.

As the quartet worried about the future, Tarkanian was struck by a bad thought from his past. He remembered when Maxson had forced his friend, football coach Harvey Hyde, to resign in 1985. He remembered how Hyde told him Maxson had visited with members of the Board of Regents in advance, giving his explanation for the coach's dismissal and soliciting each regent's support. He wondered out loud if the president weren't doing the same thing right then.

"You know, if I don't resign right away, Maxson will start going to the Board of Regents and giving them one side of the story," Tarkanian said several times.

Tarkanian mentioned his concern about the Regents, but everyone else in the room seemed more concerned about Maxson and Booke. "Stay calm," Thompson kept saying to Tarkanian. "Don't do anything rash." Tarkanian ignored both pieces of advice.

Wednesday, May 29

The next morning, Thompson and Danny Tarkanian called Booke and asked for a meeting to review the information. They had the documents faxed to Thompson's office.

On the way in that morning, Danny talked to his father again. "I'm worried that Maxson will be going to the Regents and undermining me. I want to tell them my story."

"I didn't think anything of it," Danny said. "I had no idea he was going to do anything."

Do something he did. Tarkanian went to visit regent Joe Foley in his downtown office. Tarkanian had chosen Foley because the Las Vegas lawyer had, at the Final Four in Indianapolis, told Tarkanian how good he had been for the university. "He told me he was in my corner and to call him if I ever needed anything, which I did," Tarkanian said. Tarkanian also knew Foley to be an ardent Maxson supporter.

During the meeting, Tarkanian repeatedly denied that he or his players had any connection with Perry. He acknowledged that the players had known "Sam" Perry, but said it was nothing more than a friendship.

Then, Tarkanian, a tactician extraordinaire on the basketball court, made an extraordinary tactical error. "I don't deserve this, Joe, not after all I've done for the university," Tarkanian said. "I want to meet with the Board of Regents and tell them my side of the story."

"I'll set it up," Foley said.

Then Tarkanian blurted out, "I just want to coach one more year."

Once Thompson and Danny Tarkanian had Booke's fax in hand, they started calling around, trying to determine exactly what the information really meant. Yes, there were copies of ticket envelopes left for Perry, and yes, one of the envelopes listed Tarkanian as the requestor. But this certainly wasn't the kind of information used to fire a coach, especially one that had endured so much for so long.

The two attorneys talked to others on the Final Four ticket list and discovered that fewer than one third of those whose names appeared there in Tarkanian's chicken-scratch handwriting had actually gotten tickets through the coach. "Sam" Perry was in the other two-thirds.

"We felt pretty good going over there," Danny Tarkanian said. "We didn't think it was that big of a deal."

At Booke's office, the university lawyer continued with the theme of the night before. "You know, Jerry should go out on top. He shouldn't go out in disgrace. The media's never going to let up.

"If Sam Perry is considered a rep [representative of the university] it will destroy the university and the basketball program," Booke said. "It will destroy Jerry, too."

Booke presented them with a list of events that had involved

Perry and the university. A number of the items on the list were, as Thompson said, "stretching it a bit." Booke pointed out that the coach had once dined at Richie's Place, an Italian restaurant that Perry frequented, but apparently does not own.

Danny asked Booke to show how any of those contacts would allow the NCAA to declare Perry a booster. Booke said: "The NCAA can come to that conclusion if it wants to. It doesn't have to be within the letter of its bylaws."

"If they do that," Danny Tarkanian said, "we'll have them in court quick. We're not going to let them screw us this time. He wanted an answer right then as to what my father was going to do."

Thompson said his assessment of Booke's "evidence" was that it was weak: "The tickets were left before he was known as Richard Perry, the number of occasions was minimal, and the list of requests for tickets to New Orleans was meaningless. I told him it seemed awful strong for him to try and get Tarkanian to resign based on that evidence. Booke told us he was just thinking about Jerry, that he wanted Jerry to retire as the winningest coach of all time. I told him he didn't understand Jerry. Because if he did, he would know Jerry didn't care about that stuff. If that's what Jerry was about, he would have left the year before when he had Stacey [Augmon] and Larry [Johnson]. Booke told me he figured that because he was vain, Tarkanian should be. I walked out thinking I'd made it clear their ploy didn't work."

When they met together for lunch later that day, Tarkanian told his son that he had met with Foley and "he had been perfect."

"Joe was great," Tarkanian said. "He said he was behind me one hundred percent. He said I should stay at least one more year while we fight the NCAA. He said I may even want to stay longer after the NCAA thing was done. He was all excited."

What Tarkanian didn't know was that Foley was on the phone to Maxson before the coach had reached his car. Foley told Maxson that Tarkanian wanted only one more year. Maxson and his staff started working on Tarkanian's letter of resignation.

Lois Tarkanian later said she could not believe her husband had gone to see Joe Foley. "How many times had we told him that both Foley and Carolyn Sparks were so enamored with Maxson that they would never believe the truth," she said. "But of all people, who did he choose to talk to?"

Thursday, May 30

Review-Journal reporters Greg Bortolin and Bruce Pascoe paid a visit to Finfrock seeking new leads on the story that was dominating each day's front page. Finfrock delivered. For more than six weeks, he had held on to the pictures he'd had Greg Cava print showing Perry sitting behind the team bench at the Florida State game. It wasn't time then to offer those up to the media. Now, it was.

Although Finfrock denied he provided the pictures to the reporters, both Bortolin and Pascoe indicated the athletic director was their source. "We weren't shown them in his office," Bortolin said later. "But you wouldn't be wrong to say we got them nearby."

That morning, Tarkanian went to Finfrock's office to present the athletic director with the disturbing rumors that Finfrock had been the source of the media blitz: "Right after I came in to work, Grgurich comes in and says a radio reporter at KNEWS said that Dennis Finfrock had been the leak. He's called KNEWS and given them all this stuff about us. I'm really upset. Grgurich is really upset. He said, 'Well, let's just go to war.' And I said, 'I'm going to confront Dennis with it; I'm not going to get upset behind his back.' So I go in to see Dennis, eleven-thirty in the morning. I went in and I told Dennis about this and Dennis denied it, got upset that anybody thought he would be doing it. He said, 'Well, who's your source?' and I said, 'A friend of somebody called Grg and told him that.' And he said, 'Well, who did that, I want to know who it is.' And I said, 'I don't know,' and then I started feeling bad. Here I was accusing Dennis of something that's come secondhand. People have done that to me and I get upset. So I apologized. I said, 'Yeah, you're probably right, I probably shouldn't have done that.' I said that to Dennis.

"Then Dennis gets into Richard Perry. He said, 'If you're involved with Richard Perry, I'm going to come after you. I won't protect you. I hope this is the end of the Perry thing. I hope there's no more that's going to come out on him.' I said, 'This is the end,

Dennis, there's no more. I had nothing whatsoever to do with him.' He said, 'I hope so. We can't have any more on Sam Perry.' So I go to lunch at twelve-thirty. And I'll never forget, I'm eating lunch with Mike Toney at the Sands and I'm feeling so bad that I accused Dennis of this all out of hearsay. I called him on the phone and I apologized to him at twelve-thirty. I apologized to him for accusing him of that. I said, 'Dennis, it was all hearsay, I apologize, but I wanted to confront you instead of talking behind your back,' and he thanked me for that.

"That was absolutely amazing and it's all been proven to be true. That Dennis did send those pictures over there. You know, he's telling me at twelve, 'I hope that's the end of Sam Perry, we can't have any more of that.' He said that knowing he had already given additional pictures to reporters. That is absolutely the height of hypocrisy."

Tarkanian also placed a call to Maxson that morning stating similar concerns about the repeated rumors that Finfrock was leaking information: "I called him about the leaks, told him they were coming from Dennis, how upset I was, and he told me that Dennis had assured him they aren't coming from him, he would be very upset if they were, that he was just as upset as I am at the leaks, so forth. So I called him; he said, he pointed out that those leaks were hurting him and the university as much as they were hurting me. I said, 'No, they're hurting me first and then the university.'"

While Tarkanian was being led astray by Finfrock, Bortolin and Pascoe reviewed a video of the game, looking to see if it might be possible to make Perry out for a still picture that could be used in the newspaper. They also checked with Sonny Vaccaro, the Nike representative who had staged the Duel in the Desert Tournament that had produced the shot. Vaccaro told them he believed the seats behind the basket had been provided to Tarkanian or his close friend Mike Toney.

At about five-thirty that evening, Tarkanian received a visit from Pascoe. He wanted to ask a few questions about the Florida State game. He wanted to know how Richard Perry ended up watching the game from Tarkanian's seats. He showed the coach a picture—one that looked a lot like the picture Maxson had pulled out briefly on Tuesday night—and said it would be running in the next day's newspaper. Tarkanian didn't have an answer. Again, he called his son.

"The *R-J* told me they have a picture of Perry at the Florida State game sitting behind me in seats that were mine," he said to Danny.

Father and son met for dinner at Piero's. "How could he be in those seats?" an agitated Danny Tarkanian asked his father. "I don't know. They're not mine," Tarkanian responded.

Danny decided to call the *Review-Journal* and ask if, in the spirit of fairness, the newspaper would let him figure out who had given the tickets to Perry. "I asked them if they had talked to Perry's attorneys yet to ask how he got his seats," Danny remembers. "I told them they at least owed us that." Bortolin put editor Sherman Frederick on the line. Frederick said that if Danny got ahold of Perry's lawyer, the newspaper would love to talk to them.

"I told them I was having difficulty reaching him because it was late at night," Danny said. "I asked him to wait until tomorrow. He said he couldn't promise that. I asked if they wanted the truth and he said that was all they were interested in. Then I asked why they wouldn't hold off until they got it. He didn't respond."

Danny made several attempts to call David Chesnoff in hopes that he might have an explanation. But Chesnoff was in Montana handling a case.

The Tarkanians also called Vaccaro from the restaurant. "I told them [the reporters] they could have been Mike Toney's tickets, I just don't know," Vaccaro said. Then they called Toney, who confirmed that he'd gotten tickets from Vaccaro. He said he'd given them out to casino friends along The Strip who were comping coaches in town for the Nike-sponsored two-game tournament.

Lois Tarkanian called Cava, trying to figure out if he was the source of the photo. After talking to Lois, Cava, who had been out on a shoot all day, checked his voicemail and found a message from the *Review-Journal*'s photo editor.

"She [Lois] was real upset and she asked, 'Is it true that you have pictures of Perry that are going to run in the *R-J* tomorrow?'" Cava said. "This call was out of the blue. So I said, 'Lois, the only picture I have of Perry is one that Dennis Finfrock got from me.' And then it was real silent for a minute. And she goes, 'Dennis?' I said, 'Yeah, the only picture that I ever gave them was one that Dennis came and got from me after the Final Four.' I said Dennis had told me not to mention it to anyone. I wouldn't have said nothing to anybody except that the *R-J* called and said they saw my pictures in Dennis's office. The *R-J*'s chief photographer said, 'Our writer was at the school today talking to Dennis and he saw some pictures you took with Tark and Perry in the background and we want to get ahold of it.' And so now I hear that message on the machine. Lois tells me before I know the *R-J* has called. I call the *R-J* and now it's ten o'clock and I kind of played dumb, I said, 'What's going on? What do you need?' And he goes, 'Well, we were looking for some picture you did of Perry and Tark but that's okay because we already have it, we already have something.' He was in a hurry because, of course, there is a deadline or something and I'm wondering what else he had. That's when I told my wife I think I'm going to go down to the studio and get that picture and bring it to Lois just so she can tell me if they were using my photo. I come down here and, luckily, when I made Dennis's picture up I made an extra copy. It was too dark or light or something and I had thrown it in the file. I brought that over to Lois. And she called Jerry up and tried to describe it to him over the phone, and he said that doesn't sound like the same picture."

A tremendous storm had battered Las Vegas that evening, knocking out power for much of the city, including the Tarkanians' home. When Cava delivered the extra picture to Lois, they stood there in the dark holding candles, attempting to identify someone who was sitting nearby, someone that might explain how Perry got that ticket.

Lois noticed that Billy Lastra, a former volunteer assistant coach and now a radio talk-show producer, was sitting four seats down from Perry. Lastra's was the only face she recognized. It just so happened that Tarkanian was slated to do Lastra's show that night, so when Lastra called at 11:30 P.M. to confirm the midnight telephone hookup, Tarkanian asked if he knew how Richard Perry had ended up with his seats to the Duel in the Desert.

Lastra explained that Toney had given him six tickets for running certain errands in preparation for the tournament. Lastra kept two and sold four to David Chesnoff. The coach hung up and quickly called the newspaper. He said he got no answer, though reporters at the paper said they were there at the time.

"What makes me so mad," Tarkanian said later, "is that I know Dennis had that picture for weeks before he gave it to the newspaper. The president obviously knew about it, too. If we had seen the picture earlier, we could have checked to see who was sitting around him and identified and showed whose seats those were, but he never even showed it to us. That was so unprofessional."

Friday, May 31

The pictures of a smiling Perry standing behind a coaching Jerry were powerful when displayed on the front page of the *Review-Journal*. Tarkanian was on his way to the airport when Billy Lastra, whose radio show he had done the night before, called on his cellular phone.

"Coach, like I told you last night, I'm the one that's responsible for the seats Perry had," Lastra told Tarkanian.

Tarkanian, on his way to Sedona, Arizona, to speak at a golf tournament, begged Lastra to call and explain the ticket situation to the newspaper. He hoped that Lastra's revelation might calm things down a bit before he returned the next day.

During a break in the golf tournament, Tarkanian took a call from his friend Irwin Molasky. Molasky told him Sig Rogich, adviser to President George Bush and a longtime Tarkanian supporter, wanted to help him get out of this bind.

"Sig was telling me how upset he was about everything," Tarkanian remembered. "He said he was in Las Vegas and would help if I needed him. I told him all I wanted to do was go through this last year, one more year so Grg and the players could all be taken care of."

This also is the day that the university's 300-page response to the NCAA's allegations in the four-year-old Daniels case was due. More than one onlooker was struck by the incredible coincidence—if that's what it was—that found The Pictures in the paper during the week Tarkanian would be weakest, when his popularity in the community might be lowest.

The university's response to the NCAA, prepared by Booke,

took a hard line in arguing that Perry was not connected to the athletic program.

Saturday, June 1

Speculation around town was that the pending Regents meeting Foley had set up at Tarkanian's request might spell trouble for the coach. No one knew it had been called at Tarkanian's behest.

The speculation only grew when Las Vegans woke up that morning to read the latest news in the soap opera "As the Rebels Turn." The coach, nervous that the newest pictures that had run in the *Review-Journal* had caused irreparable harm, told reporters he "was concerned I'm going to lose my job for something I didn't do. When you stop to analyze everything, what is the worst thing I've done? The worst thing is I've got a New York City kid like Moses who didn't obey my orders [to stay away from Perry]. I may be out of a job on Monday over this."

"I think this was his biggest mistake," Danny Tarkanian said. "When the newspaper quoted him as saying he felt his job was in jeapordy, people started to say it all over town."

Also on Saturday, Rogich, who was in town to attend his daughter's graduation from a Las Vegas high school, began an attempt to build bridges between the rapidly eroding sides of this dispute.

Tarkanian told Rogich what he'd told Foley: I want to coach just one more year. Rogich, a former regent, started calling Maxson and his former colleagues to test the waters. Everyone, it seemed, was willing to give Tarkanian that year, as long as he didn't attempt to stick the university for a buy-out of his last two years. Tarkanian said he never wanted the money. He had maintained that position from the very beginning. He said he was even willing to give up the tenured faculty position that he'd negotiated when he moved to Las Vegas.

"I knew the inevitable was around the corner," Rogich recalled. "I was afraid they were going to do something with him. I could step into the town and feel the feeding frenzy that was evident. I felt that something could happen that could embarrass him or they could force him to resign later under duress and I didn't want that to happen. I mean, I tried to resolve it. I just wanted everyone to save face, the university and Jerry Tarkanian. I thought it would be bad for the university if he went out under the worst circumstances and bad for Jerry Tarkanian. I thought it was a lose, lose across the board if they didn't resolve things reasonably, so I just injected myself into that whole episode just because I cared about Jerry and I cared about the university. Maxson kept talking about the overall scheme of things was bad, perception ... just the ongoing battle and it was time to make the move and he would go for a deal like this."

Sunday, June 2

In preparation for Monday's meeting with the Regents, Tarkanian met with his lawyers and others to plan strategy. An increasing number of reporters were calling, trying to get the coach to tip his hand on the real meaning behind his appearance before the Regents. Maxson said he is convinced Tarkanian's request that the Regents hear him out fueled national speculation that it was over.

Perry also chose to issue a statement through his lawyers, echoing those written by Scurry and Butler a few days earlier.

"I have known Moses Scurry for many, many years and also coached and advised him," Perry wrote. "I would like to believe I was a positive influence on Moses in drawing him towards college, college basketball and his subsequent professional career. At the time that I met Moses, he could have turned in an opposite direction considering the incredible disadvantaged background from which he comes. I have a great deal of personal affection for Moses Scurry and communicated with him regularly while he was in junior college and when we met up in Las Vegas. After the publication of the article in *Time* Magazine, I told Moses and his friend, David Butler, whom I met through Moses, that it would be in their best interest to tone down their relationship with me, not because of anything that was wrong, but because public perception was so misguided and nasty."

Perry went on to say that he had "paid my debt to society" and apologized for any damage he might have done to the UNLV program.

Monday, June 3

Along with the expected story setting up the day's Regents meeting, Tarkanian was greeted with another bit of news he just didn't need. Redshirt Rebel Barry Young had chosen this weekend to be arrested on charges of marijuana possession.

That morning, several of Tarkanian's former players decided to come to his aid, calling a press conference to ask the Regents and the city to stick with the coach through this tough time. The players, some of whom were bearing written statements from past teammates, shared memories of how Tarkanian had helped them grow through college basketball; he'd taken chances with them and succeeded and shouldn't be chastised for chances that failed.

Afterward, former Rebel stars Sidney Green and Armon Gilliam—who flew cross country on a moment's notice to stand up for Tarkanian—decided to pay a visit to Steve Wynn, who they had heard had turned against the coach. They asked him to help Tarkanian out. He refused.

"They were lamenting that Jerry was getting railroaded," Wynn remembers. "And I said, 'Armon, Jerry's not getting railroaded. He's much too well liked in this town to get railroaded. There's no anti-Jerry here. There is a moment of truth here because there's been a total lack of accountability. And the program and the reputation of kids like you and Sidney are suffering. What good is it if we do all these things and we're always known as cheaters? And we are! Let's talk about Lloyd Daniels.' Armon said, 'Oh, come on, he was trying to give a kid who had all kinds of problems a break. Is that bad?' I said, 'No, that's good. But that's only half the paragraph. The other half is that this is a university. It's not your private home or your private business. This is a university. We're subject to rules and regulations. Jerry is the coach. He's supposed to protect the team and the other players, their careers, their futures from probation and other bad things. He's supposed to, by his behavior, see to it that the program comports to the proper high standards of conduct. This is a college sport. Winning ain't enough. You've got to play by the rules. In the NBA, it may be different. But here, he's part of an institution. So when he wanted to give Lloyd a chance he had to realize it wasn't just his judgment, he had to follow protocol, a routine. It was an unusual routine to become a guardian of a boy and take care of him, which means give him things that might otherwise be prohibited. Then that scheme should have been passed by the people to whom we have accountability—the university, number one, and the NCAA, number two. Permission should have been gotten in writing. He owed that to the school before he owed a good chance to Lloyd Daniels. He owes it. That's the terms of his deal. At least in my opinion he does.'"

While the former players, including Danny Tarkanian, were meeting with the press to tell stories about how good Tarkanian had been to them, the university and the city and the coach and his lawyers were meeting at the renovated stucco house that Chuck Thompson had turned into his law office. Alton Burkhalter, a Los Angeles attorney whom the Tarkanians had just recently added to the team, and Alan Jones, a booster who had helped in the battle to get UNLV back into the 1991 NCAA Tournament, joined Tarkanian, his wife, and Thompson in the conference room for a strategy session.

Just minutes after they sat down, Danny Tarkanian called to give the crew the news that the players' press conference, in his opinion, had been a success. He said he was on his way over.

The strategy, all agreed, was to be informative and upbeat. "We felt we were going in from a position of strength," Thompson said. "Jerry had done nothing wrong."

Then Thompson's receptionist buzzed in with a phone call from Foley. "There was hate in his voice," Lois Tarkanian said. "He was demanding that Jerry sign a three-sentence letter of resignation and agree to stay one more year when the Regents met that afternoon. He was almost yelling when our lawyers said there was no way Jerry would sign that."

Foley told Tarkanian that he had shared Tarkanian's one-year deal with his fellow Regents. Now, Foley said, it sounded like the coach was reneging.

"I said all I wanted to do was finish this year and have a one-year contract," Tarkanian said. "He said I better not screw the deal up. He told me there was a good chance I could be fired if I didn't sign it."

Concerned that Foley's fire could lead the Regents to make a decision to dump Tarkanian, the attorneys told Foley the coach would not resign that day, but would do so within a week. They didn't want it to appear as if there was a direct relationship between The Pictures and Tarkanian's resignation. A few more days wouldn't make a difference, they argued. Foley accepted it.

Danny Tarkanian didn't. He stormed out of the meeting at Thompson's office, furious that his father was being painted into a corner. "I told him to fight them," Danny said. "They had no grounds to fire him."

Tarkanian, though, said he'd rather make this agreement than risk being fired that afternoon. "My career just doesn't need that," he said.

Everyone packed up shortly after noon and headed for the hastily called Regents meeting.

Tarkanian's two NBA stars, Green and Gilliam, joined reporters and dozens of Tarkanian supporters—including construction workers from a project nearby—standing in the hot summer heat outside of Brad Booke's office, where the Regents would gather to hear the coach out.

It was even hotter inside.

When the Regents meeting began, chairwoman Dorothy Gallagher turned the microphone over to Tarkanian. "You asked for this meeting," she said, quickly trying to break the ice. "What's on your mind?"

No one laughed.

"I hit them with three things," Tarkanian remembers. "First, I wanted to address the Sam Perry thing, and I got into step by step how we had no relationship with Perry whatsoever and how we met him, how the first couple of years we knew him as a coach and how when we knew him as a coach, we treated him as a coach. You know, at times, we left him some tickets at games and at times I think he may have even come to some practices possibly. I couldn't remember. Well, once we knew who he was, we had no relationship whatsoever. And I went step by step.

"Secondly, I got into the university, the image of the university. I got into everything that the Runnin' Rebels did, how we built all the positive things we could through basketball. I said I didn't like the negative things, they bothered me as much as they did anybody. I thought it was only fair for me to point out right there that Finfrock incident of how the *R-J* brought the picture in that Thursday night. I said this was the type of thing that created the negative image. I said some of this stuff that causes negative publicity could be avoided. I said if Dennis Finfrock brought that picture to us, we could have avoided this whole thing. Foley jumped up and started pointing his finger at me. 'Dennis Finfrock's credibility isn't at stake here, yours is,' he said. I just went on. I said we had a team that won with dignity and class, never abused people we beat. I pointed out how we lost with dignity, how we lost without making excuses.

"Then the third thing, I talked about what my future plans were and I told them at that time that my family had gone through so much hurt and I'd gone through so much hurt that I thought it would be in the best interest of the university that I resign after one year, but I would do whatever the university thought was best. I said I didn't want any contract negotiations because I didn't want to get paid if I wasn't coaching. I wasn't trying to get a settlement. I said if I wasn't coaching, I didn't want to get paid."

After Tarkanian completed his points, the Regents took a short break. Maxson walked up, threw his arm around him, and congratulated him on "a great presentation." Then the president walked over to one of Tarkanian's lawyers and said, "Remember, we have a deal. He's not going to back out, is he?" Another Tarkanian lawyer said that the coach was doing so well in his presentation that he remembered seeing Maxson's hands start shaking.

Finfrock then was asked to explain the situation with the pictures, and his response, according to Tarkanian and his lawyers, was "ludicrous." The athletic director said he had gone to Cava's studio on behalf of the attorney general's office, which was investigating the UNLV ticket office. He said investigators from the attorney general's office asked for information regarding Perry.

"That just couldn't be true," Alan Jones said. "The attorney general herself had said, on several occasions, that she had no interest in Richard Perry or anyone else that was not a state employee. He pulled that out of thin air. Why would the attorney general's office not send one of its own investigators down to Cava's studio? And why would they care about the Florida State game? That game was not part of the season ticket package. Nor was it considered a

UNLV home game. It was not available to be traded out. He said the reason he told Cava not to say anything was because he was sworn to secrecy by the attorney general. But he showed them [the pictures] to the *R-J*. Nothing that he said made sense."

Reporters who contacted Attorney General Frankie Sue Del Pappa after the meeting were originally told that no such request was made of Finfrock. Then Del Pappa, who had actively recruited Maxson when she was a regent, said her office might, in fact, have made the call.

"I don't believe her," sportscaster Ron Futrell said after talking to Del Pappa for the second time.

"It was all bullshit," Tarkanian said of Finfrock's explanation. "And it was all originated by the leader of bullshit, Brad Booke. When I look back on it it was a phony deal. I'll never forgive Joe Foley in the Regents meeting for getting upset because we were challenging Dennis's integrity."

Once Finfrock had made his excuses, Maxson said he had asked Donald Klasic, general counsel to the Board of Regents, to lay out the president's options. Klasic said that in his opinion, Maxson could do any one of three things at the time:

1) Fire Tarkanian and buy out the remaining two years on the coach's contract
2) Assign Tarkanian to another department within the university
3) Accept the one-year deal Foley had negotiated.

"If we don't work things out, I'm prepared to make the decision that's in the best interest of the university," Maxson said.

The words were ominous. No further explanation was required.

Booke was then asked by the Regents to share his impressions of the potential problems facing the university in the NCAA investigation.

"Booke's speech just turned my stomach inside out," Tarkanian said. "He started off by saying we were probably going to get three years', maybe two years', probation. He took some of the most minor things, things he knew there was no basis for a finding, and said this will probably be a violation. He painted everything as dark as he could. Like he said two of our former kids, Freddie Banks and Mark Wade, had talked to a high school senior at a basketball game in San Jose. He said that would probably be a violation. I said that can't be a violation. He had talked to the kids and must have known it wasn't a violation. Everything he did at that Regents meeting was to discredit me. It hurt so much because I had defended Booke, said what a great guy he was. I had told the newspapers that I'd trust him with my life. I supported him when he wanted the athletic director's job. Now he was knifing me. Then he got into Long Beach, saying, 'In light of the problems Coach had at Long Beach and had in '77, the NCAA certainly will weigh those in their decisions.' I was getting mad and I was yelling at him. I was so upset at him, I couldn't look at him anymore."

Then Booke handed out a 1½-page memo detailing contacts Perry had with the basketball program. He pointed out that while Jerry had claimed the contact ceased once *Time* identified Perry as a sports fixer, there were comp tickets left for an "Allen Perry" for an NCAA Tournament game. Booke said that was one of Perry's aliases.

"I looked at that and thought we were in trouble," Thompson remembered.

It wasn't until after the meeting that Tarkanian's lawyers realized Booke was mistaken in making his comment. Thompson requested a list of Perry's aliases from Booke and was sent a copy of a police rap sheet. On it, Perry is reported to have used three names in addition to his own: Richard Daniels, Richard Alan Cohen, and Ronald Coleman. Nowhere is it suggested he ever used the alias Allen Perry, although Perry's brother's name is Alan.

Booke also presented the Regents with notes from a statement he took from ticket manager Debbie Barrantine. He said that Barrantine told him that previous ticket manager Le Riggle had come into the ticket office crying one day after the NCAA requested copies of postseason ticket lists from the Final Four in 1987. Barrantine said Riggle told her Tarkanian was "livid" that Richard Perry's name had shown up on the list and that the coach wanted another list drawn up without Perry's name on it. Booke told the Regents he was still looking for that list.

Riggle and Tarkanian later denied the conversation took place, and Booke refused to share his notes with Tarkanian's lawyers. Barrantine's assertion was one of only two statements Booke took without notifying the attorneys of those accused in the NCAA case.

When Booke finished, even Tarkanian's lawyers were a little shellshocked by the revelations and the attitudes of Booke and Joe Foley.

"I was just glad to get out of there," Thompson said.

"He [Booke] set me up as well as a man could be set up," Tarkanian said. "I had just watched a professional do a professional job on me."

As the meeting drew to a close, Tarkanian said his lawyers would immediately begin work with Booke to draft a final-year contract. He said he would write a letter of resignation and schedule a press conference for the next week.

Everyone was in agreement that Tarkanian had one more year at UNLV. And they promised that all sides would follow the party line. No decisions were made. Tarkanian was still weighing his options. Peace would be waged, and neither side would speak ill of the other.

After six hours, Maxson and Tarkanian emerged arm in arm. "Jerry's future is up to him," Maxson said without a hint of insincerity.

Tuesday, June 4

Hard as it was to believe, there finally came one day when nothing of significance happened. The lawyers started their work. The pundits continued their speculation that Tarkanian was on his deathbed. But true to their agreement, neither Tarkanian nor Maxson said anything.

"It felt great to have a day like that," Tarkanian said.

Wednesday, June 5

Maxson asked Tarkanian for a meeting to plan the coach's final exit. Tarkanian thought it was a good idea. But when he heard that the press had been alerted and was lined up outside the president's office, Tarkanian asked if Maxson would meet him at Booke's office, six blocks away.

The meeting with Maxson, Tarkanian said, was cordial. Though rumors persisted that Maxson kept up the pressure during the meeting by suggesting other damaging information might be forthcoming if Tarkanian didn't resign, the coach denied that.

"That's totally false," Tarkanian said. "All we met about in that meeting was how we were going to make our presentation. How we were going to announce it. I said I wanted to have the press conference on Monday.

"At the end of the meeting, he asked if I'd go back to his office with him," Tarkanian recalled. "Maxson said, 'I think we probably should go over there. The media's there. They ought to see us walk in together, see us come out of the room together, be united together. We need a united front.'"

Tarkanian agreed. When they walked out of the elevators into the president's suite, reporters asked where they had been.

"We had coffee, then we played one-on-one," Tarkanian said. "I beat him, 18–16. I posted him up and slam-dunked on him a couple of times."

The coach went on to say: "I've said it many times that I don't have a problem with Dr. Maxson. He's a good man. All of our problems have been from the outside, from people speculating we don't like each other. That's the furthest thing from the truth."

In an interview with the *Las Vegas Sun*'s Steve Carp, Tarkanian also made light of the latest story linking Perry to his program. That morning's *Review-Journal* included two stories showing that Perry and Tarkanian's assistant coach Ron Ganulin played on the same junior varsity basketball team in New York City twenty years earlier

"Is that incredible?" Tarkanian said of the story. "I hear there were seven thousand kids at that school, but they made it sound like they were best buddies. You want to know the truth? I was the admissions director at Erasmus [High School] and I arranged for Ronnie and Perry to be in school together. I also got Bernie Fine [a Syracuse assistant coach], Al Davis, Barbra Streisand, and Billy Cunningham in."

Tarkanian was losing his job. He hadn't lost his sense of humor.

Thursday, June 6

Maxson called Tarkanian for another meeting. This was getting a little weird, Lois Tarkanian told her husband. "I felt he was trying to get his picture taken with Jerry like they were buddy-buddy so that no one would know what he was really doing," she said.

Lois asked her husband to take a lawyer along to the president's office. "I can't do that," he said. "This is the president of the university who told me he wants to meet. I have to go. I don't need a lawyer for this. All we're doing is being friends."

"He said we should do it [the press conference] on Friday so there wouldn't be speculation all weekend," Tarkanian said. "He said Sunday papers didn't need to be filled with this stuff. I agreed. It made sense. He said he was going to make this the most glorious year for me, how he was going to come down before every home game and shake hands and after every game, he said he'd tell the media, 'You just witnessed the greatest coach in the history of the game.'"

Later that afternoon, Tarkanian sat in his office surrounded by reporters from the *New York Times, Philadelphia Inquirer,* and *USA Today.* As Tarkanian said over and over that he "can't figure out how this happened," the three reporters looked at him in disbelief. Their short stints in Las Vegas had left them all with the same conclusion: Tarkanian was being undercut by a president who no longer wanted him.

They told him so, then told him that they had been given some of their best quotes from Maxson's top assistant, John Irsfeld.

"It was kind of obvious the way Maxson was operating," *USA Today*'s Steve Wieberg said later. "You would talk to him and he would say sternly things like 'We will do right here. We won't leave any room for mistakes.' But he didn't take an antagonistic stance toward Tarkanian himself. Then he would say, 'Now, before you leave, there's somebody here I want you to talk to.' And it was Irsfeld. Irsfeld would unload."

Tim Dwyer of the *Philadelphia Inquirer* told Tarkanian a similar story. "It's pretty obvious Irsfeld is sticking it to you," he said.

At dinner that night, Tarkanian heard from one reporter that Irsfeld had laid out the parameters of his resignation, which was going to be announced just twelve hours later. Feeling betrayed, Tarkanian called Maxson from Piero's and said the deal could be off if Irsfeld didn't shut up.

"Three times that night, he [Maxson] called me," Tarkanian said. "He said he put a muzzle on Irsfeld, Irsfeld won't talk to anybody anymore. He said he didn't think it was true, that Irsfeld had assured him he wasn't leaking anything. I told him about one reporter and then he told me how disappointed he would be in Irsfeld if it were true."

Either Maxson didn't check with Irsfeld, Irsfeld misled the president, or Maxson was covering for his assistant. There is little doubt Irsfeld was doing precisely what Maxson said he was not.

Maybe Maxson wasn't bothered by Irsfeld's actions because three reporters, each of whom said they liked Maxson and personally believed in his handling of the Tarkanian situation, claimed Maxson developed a mastery of making off-the-record comments that were derogatory to the coach.

"He'd be willing to give information about Tarkanian on very general terms and he would say, 'That's off the record now,'" said Rich Martin. "Usually, the type of information he would give, you could stand on and branch off into other sources. Sometimes, he even suggested who the other sources might be. He was a master at manipulating the press. You can rarely get him to say something strong on the record. But he knew what 'off the record' meant. One time I did an interview and he asked me how I thought he should approach the whole thing with Tarkanian, like he was asking my opinion. I told him that was his job, not mine, thank God."

John Henderson, a former *Review-Journal* writer now working in Denver, said he, too, was an occasional member of Maxson's off-the-record club. "I mean, he's really a two-faced politician," Henderson said. "He would come out publicly and try and support Tarkanian, but deep down inside, he has always wanted him out of there. He didn't try to hide it when he was talking to us. He would say that he was frustrated that every time the university did something good, every time it took one step forward, the basketball team and Tarkanian would take it two steps back. Then he'd say he was fed up, but we couldn't quote him. It worked because people would then write what he said without using his name."

"Bob Maxson's actions [with the media] were and performance shows that he indeed wanted Jerry Tarkanian out," said Bob Sands, a regular on Maxson's social circuit before being fired by the newspaper.

When asked if the president's "actions" included off-the-record criticism of his coach, Sands responded affirmatively. "I think more than specifics, he kind of dealt in planting the seeds that we were on the right track in trying to get Jerry out. I think if you talk to anybody [in the media], that was exactly their thoughts, too. He will not always deal in specifics. He'll say, 'Well, check that out with so-and-so,' you know, from that standpoint, but the seed certainly was planted. The thing that I want to make clear is the fact, though, that he did deal in some names, that he did deal in some things that I can't get more specific on because I promised to keep them off the record."

Sands, in fact, had one lengthy meeting in which Maxson fed him, among other things, a list of reasons why Tarkanian's departure was necessary for UNLV to progress. Sands returned to the newspaper and filed a column laying out those reasons, but never attributing them to Maxson—as the president had requested. He made little effort, though, to disguise for which side of the "Maxson-Tarkanian" battle he was rooting.

"I was talking to Maxson, and we're talking over some of the things Tark has done and that we've got to maintain a clean university and this, that, and the other," Sands said. "So he tells me this stuff, so I write a story. It said there was a struggle between Tarkanian and Maxson and one eventually would win and that would determine the future of UNLV. He would say there are certain things that are upsetting that Tark was doing and for us to really clean up the university, we've got to do something with the athletic department. He would name specifics, and I can't share those because I promised to keep them in confidence. He didn't want it on the record that they were looking into this and might get rid of Tarkanian. It's an example of how he [Maxson] dealt with us [the press]. Now, did the ends justify the means? I certainly think so. He got rid of Jerry Tarkanian."

The following day, Sands was called into his editor's office. It seems an influential couple from Henderson, Nevada, had read his column and called Maxson. The president said he had no clue where Sands had gotten his information and told them he disagreed with it wholeheartedly. Tarkanian was his coach, he told them, and no newspaper reporter was going to change that. The couple then called Sands's office to complain and followed it up with a tough letter to the editor.

Sands continued: "Maxson had told them he thought Tark was a legend. He told them he loved Tark. So I called him up and said, 'These people just wrote me a nasty letter, making me look like a dumb shit because they said they talked to you and you didn't have anything bad to say about Tark.' He said, 'Well, Bob, I can't say anything, he's an employee. You wouldn't say that about one of your sportswriters.' I said, 'No, but neither would I lie and tell them that, if it was true that one of my guys was a horseshit son of a bitch that he was a good guy. I would say it's none of their business.' He said he could see my point from that. I said, 'I sure hope so because here I am writing the story in a particular vein, that certainly is helping you in your cause; you'd have to be dumb not to see that this type of story is helping what you're doing.' I told him I agreed with what he was doing in cleaning up the athletic department, but I was madder than hell. I said, 'I talked to you and now you're telling this person one thing and telling me another. That means you're talking out of both sides of your mouth and that bothers me.'"

Maxson denied the words of the reporters, saying they must have misunderstood his comments.

"I never picked up the phone, called a reporter, leaked any information, suggested anything to them," Maxson said. "I don't believe that you will find any reporter that has heard me say something that would be considered damaging off the record."

Told that several reporters claimed he had done exactly what he just had said he did not, Maxson launched into a rambling defense of his media manipulation: "I don't know of a single case. There's not a reporter in town that can come up with a quote and I'll even, I won't even say they've got to have it taped, I'll trust their notes, that can come up with a quote that you can look at and say that I'd given them something off the record that in any way tarnished someone. Or specifically tarnished Jerry. I would absolutely be prepared to discuss with anyone from the press that said that I intentionally said something off the record that was intended to damage someone and tarnish someone. I'm just beyond that. I'll tell you what bothers me about the off-the-record thing, it's because, first place, there might be one school of thought that says, 'If you're telling the truth, then the truth is the truth is the truth.' But I don't think it's fair if you're telling the truth if you use a devious method to get the truth out. If it's the truth then there ought to be a proper process in which to tell it. And I have, I have absolutely prided myself, I have prided myself in not getting down in the gutter or in the mud or anything of this stuff. We're a city that has columnists that like to write on titillating things and they speculate on Maxson this and Maxson that. Never once have I said anything to anyone that they say that was an attempt on my part to intentionally tarnish or damage … I just haven't done it. I may be the only person … Now, let me quickly say because I won't answer something publicly doesn't necessarily reflect my opinion one way or the other, I'm just not going to, I'm not going to reduce, I'm not going to intentionally in any way lower the office of the president or diminish the office of the president in any way, and I think when you start telling young reporters things off the record and things that are really, can be damaging or tarnishing, I think you have diminished yourself, your credibility, and you've diminished the office of the president and I just steadfastly say that's not true. I just haven't done it. Not one single time. Please don't print that. It would damage the credibility of the office."

Friday, June 7

Tarkanian's announcement was big news, so big, in fact, that two television stations interrupted midday programming to carry it live.

The coach made his statement, then spent a few minutes answering questions.

Four months later, as the truth about the stories leaked to the media became known, he said the answers he gave that day no longer were valid.

"If I'd have known what was going on, I would not have resigned, absolutely not resigned," Tarkanian said. "I'd have fought them all. I'm a fighter. I'm not going to back away from a fight. And when you find out something like this is happening, it just makes you mad. What blows my mind, you get to the bottom of it you say, 'Why would anybody do this? We had the best program in the country, we had the greatest kids in the country. We support the entire athletic program financially, we united the entire community and the university. We've brought more pride to the university than anything else. We did all of these things. Yet why would people from inside do that to you? Why wouldn't they just be a part of it and enjoy it? This is what I have a hard time with, that's why I keep telling myself, 'What would be the reason for all of this? Could Maxson's ego really have been so big?'

"I think part of it was we won so much, that we were so good, that everything people knew about the university was Runnin' Rebels. Had we not been quite so good, maybe we wouldn't have gotten quite that much publicity and maybe it wouldn't have upset some of those people so much. Maybe we were better off had we won the league and wound up in the NCAA Tournament and got beat each year."

After the press conference, Tarkanian, his family, and lawyers went to lunch at the Sands.

"I hope I made the right decision," Tarkanian said.

"I believe we could have beat them in court if we'd have wanted to force them to fire you," Burkhalter said. "But what would you have won? And it would have been bloody for you and the university."

"There's been enough blood already," Tarkanian said.

12

Epilogue:
The Final Summer

And now, the head coach of your Runnin' Rebels, college basketball's all-time winningest coach by percentage ... Jerry
Tarkanian."

The words of announcer Dick Calvert, spoken just minutes
before UNLV's 1991–92 home opener against Louisiana State University, were greeted by a minute-long standing ovation from a
sold-out Thomas & Mack crowd. The reaction nearly reduced
Tarkanian to tears. He waved and tried to concentrate on the game
at hand, but emotions were high.

It had been a long summer—longer than the summer before,
when the NCAA announced UNLV couldn't defend its title. Even
by the standards set the previous two years, the events of the
months following Tarkanian's resignation were dizzying. Finfrock
showed no signs of letting up. Maxson showed no effort to slow
Finfrock down. And the NCAA kept coming hard, too.

Convinced that the circumstances leading to Tarkanian's ouster
were more than coincidence, a group of Tarkanian's friends offered
a reward of $10,000 for information linking the university adminis-
tration to the release of the hot tub pictures printed by the *Review-*

Journal. The hot tub pictures were printed the same week that UNLV had to respond to the NCAA charges in the Lloyd Daniels investigation and Tarkanian couldn't have been weaker, said Piero's owner Freddie Glusman, originator of the reward. "The university couldn't have been that lucky for this timing to have happened by chance," Glusman said. While Glusman's reward later climbed to $30,000, by January 1992 it still had not been claimed.

But even without documented proof, the conspiracy theory gained momentum—at least in the minds of Tarkanian friends—as the summer wore on.

It became apparent that Finfrock wasn't interested in putting a halt to the negative stories being aired about Tarkanian and the basketball team. First, Finfrock suggested (off the record, of course) to KLAS-TV that a reporter should do a story on cars being driven by Rebel players, promising to start an investigation of his own if the reporters queried him on the subject. And just days after the 1991 basketball team banquet, Finfrock called Bob Sands at the *Review-Journal* to point out that a picture in the banquet awards program showed Richard Perry standing several rows behind the Rebel bench. Women's basketball coach Jim Bolla called Collin Cowherd at KVBC-TV, alerting him to the picture in the program, forgetting to note that the program's production—and selection of pictures for the program—was supervised by Bolla's wife, Sheila.

Finfrock's continuing efforts to embarrass Tarkanian, even after Tarkanian had agreed to resign, led UNLV baseball coach Fred Dallimore to corner the athletic director and ask him to back off. "I asked Dennis why he was still trying to get something on the basketball program," Dallimore said later. "He said whatever it takes, he wanted to get rid of them. I told him that they'd already resigned and it was terrible that people would continue to be hurt and have their reputations damaged. He didn't agree. He kept saying 'whatever it takes.' The lengths he was willing to go to were unbelievable."

Review-Journal sportswriter Greg Bortolin said in a column that "it's time for the leaks to stop" and suggested that when the university finally hired a full-time athletic director, it shouldn't be Finfrock. "I basically believed that something that began as a noble act of clearing up the athletic department turned into a sick obsession,"

Bortolin said in a later interview. "For a long time, I thought Dennis was doing the right thing. When I wrote that he shouldn't be the athletic director he called me up and lit into me. He wanted to know why I hadn't told him what I thought, and not put it in the paper. I agreed to have breakfast with him. He told me that because of how bad Tark was, what he [Finfrock] did was justified. He thinks Tark is evil. In a lot of ways I agree with him. But you've got to show some discretion. You don't go to Tark's photographer [Greg Cava] asking about pictures about a game. That just looks sneaky."

As reporters with open ears flooded Las Vegas throughout the summer hoping to chronicle the end of the Tarkanian era, they found "sources" on all sides of the dispute willing to document information—from marital infidelity and financial troubles to long dated stories about why people had lost previous jobs—that would damage their opponents. After listening and taking notes, many reporters wisely realized that the information was too questionable, even for this story.

How bad did it get? Convinced his office might be bugged, Tarkanian authorized a friend to contact Al Kaplan, a Las Vegas surveillance expert, to make a sweep for listening devices. It turned out Kaplan couldn't take Tarkanian on as a client, because he was already on retainer to do similar work for the university administration.

When Runnin' Rebel assistant coach Tim Grgurich found a television news crew from KLAS-TV waiting for him and some former Rebels as they showed up at a local high school gym, he was convinced that he was being followed. Grgurich said he later was informed by the television reporters that they had been told by "administration officials" that he was conducting practices in violation of NCAA rules by working out with the team during the summer. Grgurich reported the incident to his lawyer, Roy Smith.

"After Tim told me he felt he was being followed, I called Brad Booke, whom I was still on speaking terms with at the time, and asked him point-blank if my client was being followed," Smith said. "Booke said he'd check it out. He called me back the next day and said, 'You can assume that Tim Grgurich is being followed by someone in the athletic department.'"

Suddenly, everyone in the athletic department became paranoid. Grgurich called Smith to say the coach's personal mail was being opened by the athletic department staff. When Smith complained, he was sent a university system legal opinion, written by Don Klasic, authorizing the opening of personal mail and suggesting that anyone receiving personal mail at their university office was misusing state resources and could be disciplined if they complained about his decision.

After being criticized in the local and national press, Finfrock suspended the opening of letters.

"The administration is kicking a dead horse," Smith said. "Everyone from the basketball office is gone, but they won't stop."

Smith went so far as to accuse the administration, in a letter to Maxson, of working in collusion with the NCAA in its effort to run Tarkanian and his staff out of coaching.

Despite the loss to Duke, the 1990–91 version of the Rebels was recognized (at least in the eyes of the NBA) as one of the greatest collections of talent of all time. Larry Johnson was selected first by Charlotte, Stacey Augmon was chosen ninth by Atlanta and Greg Anthony was taken twelfth by the New York Knicks. No college team ever has produced three of the first twelve players chosen. On the second pick of the second round, George Ackles was chosen by Miami. Anderson Hunt, who left school a year early to play in the NBA, wasn't selected—a fact some attributed to his poor showing at predraft camps and others blamed on the photograph of him with Perry. Hunt tried out with several teams, but didn't make an NBA roster by the season's start.

"That was the greatest day of my life," Tarkanian said later. "It was so exciting to see those guys fulfill their dreams. And there was so much love between them. When Greg got picked, Larry and Stacey and I walked down there to greet him. They were hugging each other and were so proud. That was great."

At the draft, Johnson, Augmon, and Anthony stood by their coach and were critical of Maxson, Finfrock, and the administration. "The worst thing about my career at UNLV was how they treated Coach Tark," Anthony told the press. "He's a winner and they didn't stick by him. UNLV is the loser in that."

Johnson made his feelings known when he decided to endow an academic adviser's position—but chose to send the money to his junior college, not UNLV. "They don't deserve it for how they treated the basketball program," Johnson said.

"Those guys had so many good things to offer UNLV in the future," Tarkanian said later. "But they don't feel like this was really their school. Was it worth that to the administration? I don't know."

Out of their loyalty to Tarkanian, Anthony, Johnson, and Augmon agreed to wear jersey number 2 during their NBA careers. That was the jersey Tarkanian wore as a little-used player at Fresno State.

"That's the greatest thing, isn't it?" Tarkanian asked rhetorically.

Among the players, both past and present, there continued to be a strong mistrust for the administration. At the first team meeting of Tarkanian's 1991–92 squad, the players gathered to discuss their feelings. They voted to wear two jerseys in this final season of the Tarkanian era—one saying Home and the other Away. "They didn't want UNLV on their jerseys," Tarkanian said with a smile. "I told them they couldn't do that."

Although Tarkanian required the team to wear UNLV jerseys, he decided that the university's letters wouldn't be placed on the shirts he ordered for the 1991–92 coaching staff. It was a mild form of protest that didn't go undetected.

While Tarkanian was hopeful that the people of Las Vegas would one day understand the role his own university had played in his downfall, he couldn't in his wildest dreams have predicted the events that unfolded in October and November.

Lawyers for Grgurich, Tarkanian, and others named in the NCAA allegations informed the organization that they wouldn't agree to participate in any NCAA hearing that didn't comply with Nevada's new due process law, which guaranteed the accused in NCAA cases certain rights.

At the same time, Booke and the university were trying desperately to find a way to expedite the NCAA hearings. Booke asked the lawyers if there was any way that their clients would waive their due process rights. When all refused, Booke and the NCAA said they were left with no way to proceed with the case and discipline the coaching staff.

On October 22, Booke called attorney Smith and asked him to

come over. Smith did so and "was absolutely shocked by what happened next."

Smith said that Booke "handed me a videotape and said the tape showed Tim in violation of the NCAA's early practice rule." They had filmed an October 8 conditioning class Tim teaches. They snuck into an air-conditioning duct overlooking the gym floor. Booke said the tape showed players who were taking the class practicing basketball in advance of October 15 [the NCAA's official opening day of practice]. Booke said he wanted Tim to look at the tape and plead guilty, agree to sit out one practice, and then the whole thing would go away."

Grgurich reacted in completely the opposite way. He decided to hold a press conference and tell the world just how far the university had gone in its effort to damage the reputation of the basketball program.

Two days later, Grgurich told reporters his story—showing the media that the man who taped the class had to pass through two boiler rooms, climb a narrow, forty-foot-high metal ladder, stand on a construction beam, and aim his camera through a hole.

The Las Vegas community reacted sharply. How, on a university campus, could the legal counsel authorize sending a campus security officer into the air duct over a class to secretly film students and teachers? How much did President Maxson know and why didn't he stop it? What role did Finfrock, then a finalist and the leading candidate for the full-time athletic director's job, know about the taping? Why would the director of campus security agree to send his officer on the assignment without a court order?

For the next two weeks, the story remained on the front page of the daily papers and was a lead story on each night's newscast. As the administration took a beating, Tarkanian was picking up community sympathy. *Review-Journal* editor Sherman Frederick, a close friend and supporter of Maxson, came to the president's defense, demanding an end to the critical columns his staff was writing about the videotaping. Frederick told the staff they could continue to cover the events in "objective" news stories, but could no longer take shots at the administration in columns.

The heavy fallout from this revelation forced Booke to issue a public apology to Grgurich and hastened Finfrock's withdrawal from consideration for the athletic director's job. Maxson congratulated Booke on "doing the manly thing" by apologizing, then admittedly tried to talk Finfrock into reconsidering his decision to back out.

The administration's story of who knew what and when changed daily. One day, Maxson said he had no problem with the videotaping, which he said was done only in the spirit of NCAA compliance. Three days later, after Booke apologized, Maxson said the taping "had no place on a university campus." The different stories became so confusing that the UNLV student newspaper, the *Yellin' Rebel,* devoted nearly an entire page to recounting the unfolding and ever changing versions of the event.

"We found out later that Booke had also made other tapes, including one on October 10, which proves he wasn't doing this for compliance purposes," Smith said. "If they were doing it for compliance purposes, they would have called Tim in on October 9, the day after the tape, and told him to cut it out. They kept taping because they wanted to embarrass my client."

After suffering through sixteen days of bad press, the university decided to release the videotapes, in hopes that the public would agree that Grgurich was breaking the rules. Some watched and saw what Booke did. Others, befitting the hazy nature of the rule, argued that the tape proved nothing, because the players had no basketball and spent most of the class time running and jumping.

The only thing that releasing the tapes guaranteed was that Grgurich would sue Booke and the university. He filed his lawsuit December 4. Two days later, G. Robert Blackey, one of America's leading legal scholars on the use of electronic surveillance, signed on as associate counsel to help Grgurich in his fight. After filing the suit, Grgurich and his lawyers learned UNLV had been using student employees of the athletic department to follow basketball coaches and players during the summer. The "spies," as Grgurich called them, reported back to Booke.

"We can't sit back and let them run over our rights like this," Grgurich said. "We've got to stand up. Could there have been any violation worth going to such extremes to prove? At most, this was a 'minor' NCAA violation."

It wasn't the only legal battle Grgurich and the basketball program had to worry about. The NCAA, claiming it was hamstrung by provisions of the Nevada due process law that it determined were too difficult to abide by, filed a lawsuit against the state seeking to declare the statute unconstitutional. The NCAA named Tarkanian, Grgurich, and others as defendants.

In response, Tarkanian's lawyers announced plans to file a countersuit against the NCAA, alleging that the organization's hard-driving and wrongful pursuit of the coach had damaged his reputation forever.

"We believe the NCAA came after Coach with a vengeance, using fraud to destroy his reputation and his career," Tarkanian lawyer Terry Giles said. "As a result, not only has he now lost his job, but he has lost many years of endorsement opportunities. They've worked, in our opinion, hand in hand with the university toward this end. We want to be clear that there needs to be an NCAA to police college sports, and that a university president is in charge and can fire anyone he or she likes. But what neither the NCAA or the president of a university can do—out of ego or revenge or spite—is ruin someone's career. That's the basis of the lawsuit."

All of these side shows—videotapes, lawsuits and press conferences—overshadowed Tarkanian's achievement of another coaching landmark. On November 23, he became only the second active Division I coach to achieve 600 wins when his Rebels won their season opener at BYU-Hawaii. But Tarkanian has grown accustomed to having his accomplishments overshadowed by controversy.

When the team returned to Las Vegas for its first home game against LSU, Tarkanian asked that Maxson present him with the game ball from his 600th win at a pregame ceremony. Maxson declined, saying he wouldn't be going to the game because of a wedding.

"I think he felt the crowd wouldn't have been too kind," Tarkanian said.

Governor Bob Miller presented Tarkanian with the ball instead. UNLV went on to pull a twenty-one-point upset of the ninth-ranked Tigers.

After the game, following a well-established custom, Tarkanian attended a booster club meeting at the San Remo Hotel. At these meetings, the coach generally gives a short synopsis of the game and answers a couple of questions. Those who have attended the meetings said that he has seldom ever stayed at the microphone for more than five minutes.

On this night, however, Tarkanian stayed at the podium for nearly thirty minutes, at times begging the crowd to ask him more questions. Those who know him best recognized what was going on at once.

Tarkanian knew that in a few months the stage he was standing on would no longer be his, and it hurt to let go. "Just one more question," he said for the fifth time.

Lois Tarkanian sat at a table after the meeting, tears welling in her eyes. She had seen her husband's pain and, though he seldom talked about how much he was hurting, it had become abundantly clear that night.

"As I watched Jerry standing there, I felt pain for him," she said. "These are the times when I hate what they've done to him, when I hate those who've done it. We'll get over it, but it obviously won't be easy. Is this what college sports is all about? I hope not."

A couple of weeks later, Tarkanian began the process of slowly taking down plaques and pictures from the walls of his office, packing two or three of the memories every few days. As the box began to fill and the walls began to empty, the shipping address on the box held one final irony. Tarkanian's home, where the box would be delivered, sits on Justice Lane in Las Vegas.